WILLIAM TROY: Selected Essays

WILLIAM TROY:
Selected Essays

Edited, and with an introduction by
STANLEY EDGAR HYMAN
With a memoir by ALLEN TATE

RUTGERS UNIVERSITY PRESS

Permission to reprint or quote has been kindly granted by
the following:

Mr. James Burnham—William Troy, "Proust's Last Will and Testament"
(a review of Proust's *Time Regained, The Symposium,* Vol. 2, No. 3);
"D. H. Lawrence as Hero" (William Troy, "Review of *The Letters of
D. H. Lawrence,*" *The Symposium,* Vol. 4, No. 1).

Dell Publishing Company—William Troy, "Antony and Cleopatra: The
Poetic Vision." (Reprinted from The Laurel Shakespeare *Antony and
Cleopatra.* Copyright © 1961 by Dell Publishing Co., Inc., and used
with permission of the publishers.) Though not published until after the
author's death, the article was submitted for publication in January 1960.

Editions Gallimard—Paul Valéry, "La Pythie" (from *Paul Valéry: Oeuvres,*
1957, © Editions Gallimard).

Miss Barbara Howes—William Troy, "Myth, Method, and the Future"
("Postlude: Myth, Method, and the Future," *Chimera,* Vol. 4, No. 3).

Kenyon Review—William Troy, "On Rereading Balzac: The Artist as
Scapegoat" (Vol. II, No. 3).

The Macmillan Company, N.Y., The Macmillan Company of Canada, and
Macmillan and Company, Ltd., and Mr. M. B. Yeats—From W. B.
Yeats, "Among School Children," "Leda and the Swan," and "The
Tower." (Reprinted with permission of The Macmillan Company from
The Variorum Edition of the Poems of W. B. Yeats. Copyright 1903,
1906, 1916, 1924, 1928, 1933, 1934 by The Macmillan Company, 1940
by Georgie Yeats. Copyright renewed 1931, 1934 by W. B. Yeats, 1944,
1952, 1956, 1961 by Bertha Georgie Yeats.)

The Nation—"A Note on Gertrude Stein" (Vol. 137, No. 3557), "Myth
as Progress" (Vol. 140, No. 3646); "Three Novels by André Malraux"
(three reviews entitled "Return to Tragedy," Vol. 138, No. 3599, "The
Canopy of Death," Vol. 140, No. 3634, and "Soliloquy in the Dark,"
Vol. 142, No. 3763); "F. Scott Fitzgerald, The Perfect Life (entitled
"The Perfect Life," Vol. 140, No. 3646); "Stephen Dedalus and James
Joyce" (Vol. 138, No. 3580); all by William Troy.

The New Republic—William Troy, "The Altar of Henry James," (Vol.
108, No. 7. Reprinted by permission of *The New Republic,* © 1943,
Harrison-Blaine of New Jersey, Inc.)

Oxford University Press, Inc.—From "On the Portrait of Two Beautiful
Young People," in *Poems of Gerard Manley Hopkins,* 1948.

Partisan Review—"A Note on Myth" ("A Further Note on Myth," Vol.
6, No. 1, © 1939 by *Partisan Review*); "Stendhal: In Quest of Henri

TO LEONIE ADAMS TROY

William Troy
A Memoir

I first met William Troy in the late twenties—1927 I believe—
and liked him at once. I did not know how long his family had
been in this country; he seemed at any rate to be very Irish, even
his accent was cultivated Dublin; and I thought then that his
aloofness from the in-fighting of the New York literary scene
came out of his sense of an Irish literary tradition which had
probably reached him through his early study of James Joyce.
Like other Irish-Americans and native Irishmen of his generation, he looked to France rather than to England for literary
standards; he knew nineteenth-century French criticism better
than he knew English criticism after Coleridge. This, also, was
in the high Irish intellectual tradition, which went back to seventeenth-century France. Young Irishmen, lay and clerical alike,
went to France for three hundred years to be educated.

As the years passed, and acquaintance became friendship, I
thought I saw in Bill Troy's uncompromising integrity traces of
the Jansenism which had survived in Ireland longer than it had
at Port-Royal. Bill Troy was a Catholic puritan who had left the
Church, but the Church had never quite succeeded in leaving
him. I am not sure that he ever saw Clongowes, but I could
imagine him there as Stephen Dedalus delivering to himself a
perpetual interior monologue on what I thought of as Pascalian

pyrrhonism. He had "lost" his faith, which was nevertheless crouching in the next room waiting to spring upon him.

One of his advantages as a critic in the late twenties and the thirties was his philosophical discipline, which in time became a part of his literary sensibility and lifted him above the political provincialism which narrowed the scope of some of his slightly older contemporaries like Edmund Wilson and John Dos Passos. His philosophy was eclectic: he was not a philosopher but a critic who brought Thomism and Bergsonism to bear upon his analysis of Joyce and Virginia Woolf. In other words, his philosophical tact was not limited by systematic lecture-room metaphysics, which he might have succumbed to had he had the bad luck to go through a graduate school. Like the best critics of his time he was self-educated. He had been a brilliant undergraduate at Yale, where he no doubt learned how to find the books that he would later need, but he did not linger at Yale to be told what to think about them; he found that out for himself in the crucible of immediate literary experience. He was as deeply "engaged" as anybody else; he had an extraordinary sense of the literary moment; but he was always himself, never a "party" man or an adherent to a clique; and above his intellectual gifts, and directing them, was a literary wisdom that no man can learn, but must be born with.

I do not know what success in literature means. Bill himself would have said that applied to a literary career it is an irrelevant category and a paralogism. He frequently complained to us—his old and close friends—that other critics were using his ideas without acknowledgement. Our one answer to the complaint was that he should get his essays out in book form so that acknowledgement would be obligatory. In the mid-nineteen-forties a publisher gave him a contract for a volume of essays. But Bill never got the material together to his satisfaction; he had to rewrite and improve, he had to write a few more pieces, the book had to be perfect. There was a deep compulsion in him that needed neglect and failure to complete the image of himself that he must have formed early in life and that he could wrestle with but not change.

For William Troy was a tragic character, not a passive sufferer of wrongs done him by others, but a man of great intelligence and moral dignity whose *hamartia* was within: like a classical tragic man he had to explore his self-image at cost; and nature, as in classical tragedy, collaborated by giving him a succession of diseases, the last of which, cancer, killed him.

I doubt that anybody knew the range and depth of William Troy's critical achievement until the manuscript of this book had been brought together by his widow, the poet Léonie Adams, and then edited with perfect tact and brilliantly introduced by Mr. Stanley Edgar Hyman. I at any rate saw the essays only as they appeared in various journals; but journals get misplaced or lost; and it was not possible in the thirty-odd years of his critical writing for even the most devoted friends to estimate the worth of his total performance. We have that privilege now. I for one rate William Troy among the handful of the best critics of this century.

ALLEN TATE

October 20, 1966

Contents

WILLIAM TROY: Selected Essays

Introduction

In 1948, in a book called *The Armed Vision: A Study in the Methods of Modern Literary Criticism*, I announced the birth of a great age of literary criticism, for which a handful of brilliant pioneers had prepared the way. In retrospect, that book turns out to be the tombstone erected over the grave of a great age of literary criticism. The distinguished generation of critics I celebrated—chief among them I. A. Richards and William Empson, Kenneth Burke and Richard Blackmur—has done little of significance since 1948, and their successors have done little more. R. W. B. Lewis is less than F. O. Matthiessen, Norman Podhoretz is less than Lionel Trilling, Hugh Kenner is less than Ezra Pound—I need hardly add that I am less than Kenneth Burke. We live in the Age of the Epigones, and we sing sad songs of the death of criticism. Our critics today inherit the methods of their great predecessors, but not their genius, their sensibility, or their full commitment to literature. It was the fault of *The Armed Vision* to underemphasize these qualities, as though method were sufficient in itself.

Of all that distinguished generation of critics, William Troy is the most neglected, since he alone did not publish a book. In his lifetime he published seventy-odd articles and reviews, many of great distinction. He could not bring himself to gather them into a book because of a mad Irish perfectionism: they were not good enough, his mind had changed on that matter, he could see more clearly now, he would rewrite them better. Troy never did. It was all that he could do to write them in the first place, since in his later years writing came hard for him—he was so purely a talker, an actor or performer—Troy was the finest lecturer on literature that I have ever heard. His essays were endlessly reprinted in anthologies, where they invariably stood out: it did not matter who had written on the subject, Troy's piece was always the best.

He anticipated so much that later critics became famous for discovering. The Joyce experts used to sit in on his lectures and have his insights in print over their names before the week was out. Troy opposed Jamesian form to the "large loose baggy monsters" of the novel many years before Richard Blackmur did, and he insisted on the influence of the senior Henry James on his son's work two decades before Quentin Anderson discovered it. Troy reviewed Malraux's *Man's Fate* when the English translation appeared in 1934, and pointed out what we have only painfully discovered in the 1950's, that it is not revolutionary or Marxist, but tragic. Leslie Fiedler wrote in *The New Leader* in 1951 (in a piece later reprinted in *An End to Innocence*): "And yet the *essential* appeal of Fitzgerald is elsewhere—astonishingly enough, in his *failure*." This was a brilliant observation when William Troy made it in 1945, more elegantly, and restraining his astonishment, in "Scott Fitzgerald: The Authority of Failure."

Troy's mind is always interesting, and most interesting, perhaps, as we watch him change his views about a writer. After taking Mann seriously in a long, brilliant essay published in 1938, we see him conclude sadly, in New School lecture notes written about 1956: "He is not perhaps, in the last analysis, *un homme sérieux*." After attacking Virginia Woolf, in essays published in 1932 and 1937, for "limiting herself to purely formal variations on the same old dirgelike tune," he apologizes in a 1952 afterword: "Since her tragic death Mrs. Woolf's work has found its own secure and appropriate place in the literature of our time.

That place has turned out to be neither so small nor so inconsequential as the prevailing tone here tends to predict."

William Troy was born in Chicago, Illinois, in 1903. He grew up in Oak Park, and attended Loyola Academy, where at fifteen he sold his first reviews to a newspaper. After his graduation from Yale in 1925, Troy taught for a year at the University of New Hampshire. He then joined the faculty of New York University, while doing graduate work at Columbia; and, on a Field Service fellowship from 1929 to 1930, he studied at the Sorbonne and the University of Grenoble, France. He married the poet Léonie Adams in 1933. Troy was on the faculty of New York University until 1935, and then taught at Bennington College until 1943, serving as chairman of the Department of Literature and the Humanities from 1938 on. From 1945 to 1960, except for a year as Fulbright Professor at the Universities of Bordeaux and Rennes in 1955 and 1956, Troy lectured at the New School for Social Research, specializing in Joyce and the modern novel, and in Shakespeare. In March, 1960, when a throat operation incapacitated him for lecturing, he retired from the New School. He died on May 26, 1961.

Troy was a regular reviewer for *The Nation* during the 1930's, and he published extensively in the literary quarterlies in the 1930's and 1940's. As a result of illness, he published almost nothing in the 1950's: a few afterwords to earlier essays being reprinted, and an introduction to a paperback edition of *Antony and Cleopatra*. Troy thus succeeded in outliving his earlier fame. Although his articles are still frequently anthologized, his name is unknown to today's college students and to many of their instructors as well. Meanwhile, those who sat in his classes and attended his lectures unanimously describe William Troy as the greatest of lecturers on literature, and Troy's peers—Kenneth Burke and Francis Fergusson, Allen Tate, and, in a later generation, R. W. B. Lewis and Joseph Frank—praise his published criticism comparably.

In its range and resourcefulness, as well as in the fineness of its discriminations and evaluations, Troy's criticism is a model of excellence for our time. There is hardly a method of literary criticism that he does not demonstrate on one occasion or another. "The problem," Troy writes in "The Lawrence Myth," "is always to discover the approach that will do least violence to the object before us, that will reconcile the greatest number of the innumerable aspects that every object presents to the understanding." He writes in "Stendhal: In Quest of Henri Beyle": "Like Beyle himself, nearly all the good critics in his own language have focussed his problem quite squarely, and rightly so, on the metaphysical problem of identity." Troy goes on to add: "But today we are so much impressed by the manner in which metaphysical considerations are bound up with psychological considerations and both with the general cultural situation, that the time is appropriate for the sort of comprehensive stocktaking that Beyle himself seems to have had in mind." The rest of the essay is nothing less than that metaphysical-psychological-cultural stocktaking of Stendhal.

Troy's term "metaphysical" may not be immediately clear. He means it literally, since, as he says in an unpublished lecture, "Man in the 19th Century," delivered at Bennington College in 1941, "it is impossible for the human animal to dispense with metaphysics." Troy writes in "The Lawrence Myth": "Both in his life and in his works Lawrence illustrates what Nietzsche, in his well-known analysis of the Dionysus myth, calls 'the agony of individuation.' This will have an unpleasantly metaphysical sound to modern ears; but it must be recalled that to the generation to which Lawrence belonged life still presented itself in terms of metaphysical problems. To these problems any serious discussion of Gide, Proust, Mann, and Joyce must likewise sooner or later be conducted. No matter into what unpopularity metaphysics has fallen, it is the only relevant approach to these writers." In another unpublished lecture, "Time and Space Conceptions in Modern Literature," delivered at Bennington College in 1936, Troy writes: "Of the various approaches to literature—the technical or esthetic, the historical, the socio-economic—the metaphysical alone has the advantage of throwing light at one and the same time on both the form and the content of a work." He goes on to give his fullest definition of the method: "When we speak of a metaphysical approach to literature, therefore, we do not mean that critical exercise which consists of summarizing a set of ideas and then showing how they have been applied or demonstrated in particular works. It is rather that approach which consists in showing the similarity of the problems consciously dealt with by metaphysics with those consciously or unconsciously expressed in literature. In brief, criticism, lacking a language of its own, turns to metaphysics as the only other realm of abstract thought having one at all useful for its purpose of definition and interpretation."

The approach with which Troy has been most identified, the mythic approach, is analogical in the same fashion. In "The Symbolism of Zola," a review of *Germinal*, Troy writes that the scene in the collapsed mine "brings us back to an atmosphere and a meaning at least as old as the story of Orpheus and Eurydice." In "Thomas Mann: Myth and Reason," he finds the sanitarium in *The Magic Mountain* to be "a kind of Mount Olympus," with Naphta and Settembrini as Apollonian figures, Clavdia "a modern avatar of Ishtar, Isis, or any other of those old fertility goddesses who combined in themselves the two roles of mother and mistress," and Peeperkorn a Dionysian figure. In "On Rereading Balzac," Troy treats the novels of *The Human Comedy* as mythic poems, and Balzac himself as a visionary poet in the situation of William Blake, "forced to invent his own mythology." In "Scott Fitzgerald: The Authority of Failure," Troy finds Gatsby to be "one of the few truly mythological creations in our recent literature," the novel itself taking on "the pattern and meaning of a Grail romance," and Stahr in *The Last Tycoon* as "the image of the modern Icarus soaring to disaster."

Sometimes this goes beyond myth to be a full ritual criticism. The Mann essay analyzes "Death in Venice" in terms of "the fundamental patterns of the ancient initiation rite." The Stendhal essay discusses *The Red and the Black* in terms of the ancient ritual stages underlying Greek tragedy, says of Julien's death, "Like Oedipus and Hippolytus, he will have a grotto erected in his honor and presumably become a local cult among the people," and concludes that the essential identity of Beyle himself is "the familiar and immemorial scapegoat hero." The Lawrence essay comes to a similar conclusion about Lawrence, that he succeeded in creating only one tragic scapegoat hero, himself.

The approach characterized in the Stendhal essay as dealing with "the general cultural situation" is historical and literary-historical placing. In essays on Henry James and Virginia Woolf, Troy does a sort of criticism-by-generation along the lines of T. S. Eliot's in "Baudelaire in Our Time." "The evidence is clear enough in her work," Troy writes of Mrs. Woolf, "that the fundamental view of reality on which it is based derives from what was the most popular ideology of her generation."

In the Mann essay, the placing is a wider cultural history. Troy writes of *The Magic Mountain:* "For the particular type of esthetic solution that he offers we must turn for a precedent to such works of the past as also belong to a transitional period between two cultural epochs, to such writers as Chaucer and Cervantes, for example, whose tone, style, and mixture of literary genres reflect the same precariously maintained equilibrium. These comparisons must never be pressed too far, of course, but they help us realize that final evaluation of a work of literature is inseparable from evaluation of the culture of which it is an expression." In the Balzac essay, Vautrin is identified with a literary archetype that arose as an "expression of the violent revenge that Feeling began to inflict upon Reason by the end of the eighteenth century."

For other works, Troy uses other methods. He writes in "The Altar of Henry James": "the great works of the last period, *The Ambassadors* and *The Golden Bowl*, are put together, if not like a vastly exfoliated lyric, like one of the final plays of Shakespeare. And to approach them in the manner of Caroline Spurgeon and G. Wilson Knight on Shakespeare is almost certainly to uncover conflicts of feeling that are more often than not belied by the overt urbanity of style." This "symbolic approach to James" leads him to study the symbol of the garden in James's fiction, with all its Edenic and other associations. At other times, Troy focusses not on symbolism but on literary archetypes: the Marked Man or type of the artist in Mann; the Noble Brigand or Fatal Man, and the Man of Sensibility or Artist, in Balzac; the Man of Feeling combined with the Satanic Hero in Stendhal.

When it seems warranted, Troy uses a biographical approach. In the Stendhal essay, he writes pages about the author's life and his curious relations with his parents, offering this justification: "For Stendhal must be classed with an important type of modern writer in whom the life and the work are so mutually indispensable that the latter does not yield up its real interest or significance when taken alone. Together they constitute what may be called a phenomenon—not only within literature but within their culture as a whole. Certainly Poe, Rimbaud, Nietzsche, and even Melville are more interesting when considered in this way rather than in relation solely to their incomplete and variously confused productions." Scott Fitzgerald, with whose "authority of failure" Troy became increasingly sympathetic over the years, was clearly another such for him. The Fitzgerald essay is heavily biographical and discusses two aspects of Fitzgerald with which Troy himself identified: "the large and positive influence of his Celtic inheritance, especially in his feeling for language," and "the permanent effects of his early exposure to Catholicism."

Sometimes Troy focusses on minute particulars. In "Paul Valéry and the Poetic Universe," he makes use of etymology, and in "The Worm i' the Bud," a review of *Tender Is the Night*, he studies the occurrence of the word "glamor" in Fitzgerald's fiction as "perhaps a key to Mr. Fitzgerald's sensibility." At other times his focus is the widest imaginable. Alone of the critics of our time, Troy attempted to revive the medieval fourfold approach. In "Thomas Mann; Myth and Reason," he reads "Death in Venice" and *The Magic Mountain* in literal, allegorical, moral, and anagogical terms. After giving the literal meaning of Hans Castorp's ascent of the mountain, Troy writes: "Allegorically, his ascent of the mountain corresponds to the arduous quest for certitude through the mind of a world conditioned to an absolute individualism in religion, politics, commerce, and all the other branches of life and thought. The particular nature and content of each of these categories are made amply explicit throughout the narrative. Morally, it provides an example of what Mann believes to be the proper mode of salvation—not surrender to one or another of the voices crying from the abyss but a still more vigorous application of the conscious mind to the problems of experience. (The arena of conflict is the brisk and sun-lit mountain-top of the mind as it had been the lush jungle of the sensibility in 'Death in Venice.') And, anagogically, it *leads* us back to the world of concrete living experience, to the world of men in action, where all the conclusions or resolutions of the mind must finally be brought to test."

Troy writes in "Myth, Method, and the Future": "What is possibly most in order at the moment is a thorough-going refurbishment of the medieval fourfold method of interpretation, which was first developed, it will be recalled, for just such a purpose—to make at least partially available to the reason that complex of human problems which are embedded, deep and imponderable, in the Myth." In his richest criticism, in his literal-metaphysical-psychological-social reading of Stendhal, or his literal-mythic-psychological-ethical reading of Mann, Troy achieved just such a refurbishment of the fourfold method.

The range of learning evinced in William Troy's work is impressive. In the Balzac essay, for example, he talks of "the promise of the harmonization of the most advanced biochemistry, like that of Dr. Carrel, with the most advanced modern physics," quotes Marx and Brunetière, compares Balzac with Meissonier and Delacroix, and contrasts him with Dante and Blake.

Troy was always something of a Freudian, although in his later work he tended to prefer Jung. It is hard to say how much of Freud's writings he had read, since he invariably paraphrases instead of quoting directly from Freud, and he never names specific

works. "Stendhal: In Quest of Henri Beyle" is Troy's most Freudian essay. In it he finds Stendhal's childhood "a Freudian classic
even for the *grand siècle* of the Oedipus-complex," on the evidence provided by *The Life of Henri Brulard*: "I wanted to cover
my mother with kisses, and for her to have no clothes on. She
loved me passionately and often kissed me; I returned her kisses
with such ardor that she was often obliged to go away. I abhorred
my father when he came and interrupted our kisses." A handful
of Stendhal's books are then read as expressions of this Oedipus
complex, and Troy hazards the guess that as a result of it
Stendhal was impotent. Troy even explains "the formal bankruptcy of the Stendhalian novel" in Freudian terms: "And, at
the end, as a Freudian critic would put it, the assertions of the
superego are successfully drowned out by the protests of the id."

The other essays are less thoroughly Freudian. In "Notes on
Finnegans Wake," Troy discusses the *idea* of the role of the artist
in Joyce's *Portrait* as "one of the projections of what Freud calls
the superego." In "Thomas Mann: Myth and Reason," Troy
finds Freudian symbols in *The Magic Mountain*, including a
hypodermic syringe which, "as scientifically described, proves to
be identical in mechanism with the phallus." In the Joseph series,
"the whole pattern of his adventures in the 'monkey-land' of
Egypt may be related to the Freudian description of the relations
of the individual ego to the world." Of Joseph's triumph in
Egypt: "In Freudian terms, this corresponds to the new equilibrium that has been set up in the individual psychology." Of
Potiphar: "For Joseph such a figure cannot stand as the center
of a new equilibrium of psychological forces, as the Freudian
analysis demands." Of Joseph's affair with Potiphar's wife: "As
happens when the individual cannot discover an adequate object
for self-identification in the outside world he makes the fruitless
attempt to lose himself in his own superego." Joseph's second
fall represents "the arrogance of the superego in playing with a
situation that is more dangerous than it is willing to admit." And
so on. In "The New Parnassianism and Recent Poetry," Troy

writes that the new poets make deliberate use of "what the Freudians call 'the traumatic experience' and 'the genetic history of the individual.'"

In 1939, Troy was still a Freudian, expressing serious reservations about Jung. He writes in an unpublished lecture: "Freud and his school in our time have devoted themselves to what we may call the myth of the individual. The description of Freud is so well known that it needs no elaboration. The individual is born with a shock into a world that turns out to be so hostile that, when he reaches adolescence, he has to make a great decision whether or not he wishes to accept its terms. In childhood the world of the individual is lonely, exclusive, and conservative; that is to say it tends to maintain the status quo of infantile security against the revolution of adolescence. The struggle at that period is an heroic one; it leaves many vanquished. Unless the individual transcends the self-centered childish world by finding a proper object of love and authority in the external world, he is lost. This object may not be a person, but a cause, an abstract belief, a vocation. If he discovers such an object, he achieves maturity, of which the token is some kind of creative social activity.

"The particular pattern of this whole experience is such that it has led Jung and others to the conviction that the great heroic stories of all races are simply the concrete and objective projection of this essential individual experience. It has led Jung also, however, into the undemonstrable hypothesis that every individual carries around with him the memory of these heroic stories in what he calls the 'collective unconscious,' a kind of second memory older and vaster than that of the individual. But this is turning us around in a vicious circle, for we cannot have it both that the stories are determined in their form by the psychology of the individual and the form of the individual by the psychology of the story. The importance of Jung's theory, however, is that it enables us to relate the myth of the individual to the myth of the tribe. We may say that a culture, too, has need of an object of love or authority by means of which it can transcend its merely selfish and practical interests and achieve an equilibrium between these interests and its obligations."

By 1941, however, Troy had turned sharply toward Jung and away from Freud, whom he sums up sadly in "Man in the 19th Century" as "a man of the imagination who lacked the courage of the imagination." He uses Jungian terminology in describing Fitzgerald in 1945: "The *imago* of the physical self had a way of eclipsing at times the more important *imago* of the artist." (As early as 1938 or 1939, in some unpublished lecture notes, Troy had written: "Freud failed sufficiently to realize that the symbolism of dreams was an attempt of the unconscious to return to a more integrated experience than is allowed the individual in the modern bourgeois world; Jung is right in enabling us to relate the myth of the individual to the myth of the tribe.") In New School lecture notes on Mann, dated 1956, Troy directs his hearer, not to psychoanalysis for aid with the Joseph series, but to analytic psychology, explaining: "For myths come out of the unconscious processes of mankind. The symbols on which they are based have more meanings or layers of meaning than the conscious mind can ever grasp."

Troy drew extensively on Frazer and *The Golden Bough*, sometimes peripherally, to make a point about awe of the sea in connection with Virginia Woolf, sometimes centrally, as in "The Lawrence Myth," which is a thorough and consistent Frazerian criticism, demonstrating that Lawrence finally came to take "the view of himself as a kind of contemporary reincarnation of the dying god." Other essays draw on "Pico, Bruno, and Vico," or "the excellent studies of Fernandez, Valéry, and Seillière." If Troy's learning was not encyclopedic, it was more extensive, both within literature and outside it, than that of most of the critics of our century.

Troy's range of method and his wealth of learning would have been nothing without his sensibility, scrupulousness, and respect and love for literature. He writes tartly in a review of C. Day Lewis' *Collected Poems*: "Mr. Lewis is so intent on being articulate at all costs that he does not permit himself to have any of the feelings which usually confuse and retard the poet. Among these rejected feelings must be included the distrust of rhetoric, the fear of repetition, and the sense of the difficulty of the craft in which he is working." In "A Further Note on Myth" Troy writes: "For it must be repeated that the real objection to the application of science to art and literature is not to science as such but to its fundamental inappropriateness in these realms. Unfortunately, it is much less difficult to say what literature is not than to say what it is: the anatomy of the imagination will probably remain the last challenge to the scientific mind." He concludes the essay with a tribute to "the moral imagination": "In that realm the potential is realized with a purity and vividness with which it can never unfortunately be realized in actuality." In his answer to a questionnaire in *Partisan Review and Anvil* in 1936, he rejects Marxism because "in the ultimate description of his role that it offers the individual, it leaves no place for the moral imagination."

Finally, Troy wrote with style and eloquence. He could be scathing, as in a 1949 review of French existentialist fiction that concludes: "Of all the members of the group Sartre is least endowed with the narrative gift, coldest in feeling, and most expert in sophistry." In a review of Hughes's *Imagism and the Imagists* in 1931 Troy says flatly: "About Miss Lowell the conviction becomes stronger that she will be remembered less for her poetry than for her berserk personality." At other times he is pungent and eloquent. In his review of Zola's *Germinal:* "Irony is an uncomfortable mode for the doctrinaire; having blundered into it, Zola retraces his steps as quickly as possible."

Troy writes in some 1939 unpublished lecture notes: "Pathos is to be applied to human life only when we are referring to that inherent suffering common to all nature; death in battle (when the aims of the battle are not integrated closely with the hero), death from starvation, the kitten crying in the wilderness. It is touching, because it is the touch of earth that makes the whole world kin. The modern world is pathetic because loud with the reverberations of innumerable kittens each crying in his private wilderness." He adds wryly, "Irony is the form that pathos takes to the detached mind."

Troy concludes "Man in the 19th Century" in 1941: "What we must ask is whether we can return to such a possibility of a unified and unifying symbol; whether the composite figure of man himself immanent in history—man magnificent in his suffering as in his triumph, man taken in his tragic reality, and not through any illusion as to his nature—may not yet provide such a symbol of love and piety." Troy writes eloquently to conclude "Myth, Method, and the Future" in 1945:

"Of these four levels of meaning, surely the most important for us today is the last, the *anagogical*, which teaches us 'whither we may turn ourselves.' For it should be implicit in this note that if we are to be saved, which also assumes that we wish to be saved, it can only be through some reintegration of the Myth in terms of the heartbreaking concerns of the times. 'The times are nightfall,' Hopkins said long ago, and they grow worse from hour to hour. Yet, when really everything has been said, are the most overwhelming problems of our age ultimately different from what have been the greatest problems of the race from its dark beginnings—love and justice? And it is exactly with these two problems above all else that the Myth is concerned. It is the cartograph of the perennial human situation, the more appealing for being concrete, the more persuasive for being not subject to final analysis. The Myth provides us not merely with illustrations of destiny but with a guide to its better control and mastery—the anagogical. 'We must love one another or die,' as Mr. Auden warns us. In a regenerated Myth alone we may hope to find a beckoning image of the successful alliance of the twin virtues of love and justice."

I do not mean to suggest that William Troy was a perfect critic. He had weaknesses and made mistakes of judgment—I think that the shift from Freud to Jung was one such, and I do not, for example, share Troy's low estimate of Hemingway's short stories or his high opinion of Yvor Winters' verse. But in a score of essays he produced a body of work that is timeless, permanent, a model of literary criticism, and a challenge to us all. He must assume his proper rank as one of the foremost critics of our age. "Great poetry," William Troy wrote in some unpublished notes, "impresses us with genuineness through its concreteness, its definiteness, and the exact correspondence between the object evoked and the full linguistic apparatus used to evoke it." Great criticism, too.

I PERSPECTIVES IN CRITICISM

Time and Space Conceptions
in Modern Literature*

[1936]

Of the various approaches to literature—the technical or esthetic, the historical, the socio-economic—the metaphysical alone has the advantage of throwing light at one and the same time on both the form and the content of a work. The technical endeavors, and usually with slight success, to detach the form from the content; the other approaches, especially the socio-economic, whatever may be their intention, end up by detaching the content from the form. The result is equally unsatisfactory whether a work is described in terms of its formal aspects, such as plot structure, metrics, syntax, or whether it is described in terms of its content, such as its geographical background, the nature of its action, the class status of its characters. In either case, we feel that something fragmentary, superficial, and facile has been offered in place of the complex, living whole which is the work. If literature is anything in itself it must possess a unity of form and content that the critical mind cannot ignore without running straight into a mischievous and essentially unreal dualism. Such a dualism was illustrated by those critics of the last century who pretended to an absolute indifference to the choice of subject matter in authors; such a dualism is illustrated for us today by

* Lecture at Bennington College. Previously unpublished.

those Marxist critics who are in the habit of praising certain writers of the past and the present for their "form" or "style" while rebuking them for their choice of subject matter. The only real difference between the esthete and the Marxist, from the standpoint of full literary understanding and appreciation, is one of degree: the first cares too little, the second too much for the nature of the content. Both are agreed that form enjoys a quite separate and autonomous existence. The unreality of this distinction, of course, lies in its denial of the fact that literature, or at least authentic literature, is an organism and therefore cannot suffer a dislocation of its body from its substance without severe discomfort or even death. And its mischievousness lies in the support it gives to those who, living in a scientific age, prefer to believe that literature, like everything else, is capable of being submitted to that drastic abstraction of the mind with which science is accustomed to deal with its objects.

Form and content, existence, reality—these terms remind us how difficult it is to take even the first steps in any discussion without having recourse to the formidable language of metaphysics. Now metaphysics is not literature; and it is a mistake to confuse the one with the other. Metaphysics is a field of human activity which exists parallel with other fields, such as art, literature, and science. It has its own structure, its own vocabulary and style. It has also its own history of defeats and triumphs, follies and revaluations. But, while it exists as something distinct from literature and should never be confused or identified with it, it deals ultimately with the same things. Like literature, it is concerned with reality and with the self that attempts to know and understand this reality. So close is metaphysics to literature in its fundamental motivations that the styles of certain of the philosophers (Plato, Pascal, Bergson), the form of the systems of others (St. Thomas Aquinas and Spinoza) possess just those qualities of beauty and order which we associate with the highest literature. Yet the difference between them is absolute: metaphysics is concerned with devising a picture of the world by means of the rational intellect, literature with re-creating this world in the fullness and immediacy with which it appears to an individual personality. It is the difference between explaining and rendering experience. For this reason, no philosophical system is ever the equivalent of any work of literature: Aquinas does not equal Dante, nor Bergson, Proust. The one is not reducible to the other. No statement about literature, therefore, is a greater heresy than the frequently expressed notion that a work of literature is a particular application or demonstration of an idea or a system of ideas, whether philosophical, political, or scientific. Even when an idea is found to have existed previously in the mind of a writer it does not exist for him as an artist until it has been assimilated through every pore of his personality. The most we can say about the ideas or philosophy of an artist is that they resemble some intellectual formulations with which we are acquainted. To refer to literary works as based on a philosophy is inaccurate; it is rather that such and such a philosophy happened to provide an intellectual correspondence for forms of experience and insight which were in the first place personal and spontaneous. It is true of course that artists tend to perceive things through the thought-forms of their time and culture; but it is difficult to establish the order of precedence. When we speak of a metaphysical approach to literature, therefore, we do not mean that critical exercise which consists of summarizing a set of ideas and then showing how they have been applied or demonstrated in particular works. It is rather that approach which consists in showing the similarity of the problems consciously dealt with by metaphysics to those consciously or unconsciously expressed in literature. In brief, criticism, lacking a language of its own, turns to metaphysics as the only other realm of abstract thought having a language at all useful for its purpose of definition and interpretation. Criticism itself erects a structure that is quite separate and independent from that of the realm with which it deals, so that criticism never equals the object which it attempts to translate for us into its own alien speech. But criticism has its value in forcing us to isolate, examine, and evaluate those aspects of a concrete literary creation which are intellectual and therefore capable of being dealt with by the mind. And the metaphysical method has the very great advantage of forcing us back to the most fundamental of those intellectual attitudes implicit in any work. It serves to render trivial and superficial a criticism of Shakespeare, for example, that his blank verse is metrically defective or that he expresses the ideals of the emergent bourgeoisie of the sixteenth century. So much by way of apology for a survey that will be centered pretty consistently on the purely metaphysical question of time. If this particular question rather than any other is selected, it is because more than any other it seems to have obsessed the literary sensibility of Europe in the centuries since the Renaissance. Our effort will be to see how this obsession throws a light on everything that was produced during this period—not only on the outlook of the world reflected in its works, but also on their form and even their style.

Now it will not be necessary to do more than remind ourselves of the two fundamentally different views of time that operate in our everyday experience. There is time considered as something outside us, something special, that is to say, and possessing all the properties of space. We speak of "a space of time" of a "length of time," and so on. Here we are ascribing to time that property of measurability on which most of our physics rests.

"Real" time, however, is the world of inner experience rather than outer physical experience. For example: "only an hour but it seemed eternity," as in a dentist's chair or in listening to a lecture. Here there is no system of objective measurement, no calendar, no division of the year into days, the day into hours, the hours into minutes, and minutes into seconds. There is only a sense of the passage of time, which runs at different speeds in different individuals and at different speeds in the same individual, now fast, now slow, depending upon the quality of the experience. If the first kind of time finds its appropriate symbol in the clock, the second finds its symbol in the stream or the river, rolling on in a straight direction from the past through the present and into the future.

Now Spengler and others have shown us that it is possible to write the whole history of mankind in terms of these two kinds of time, which correspond to two quite opposite orientations of the human mind, the one outward to a world of space perceived and then measured by the senses or by instruments contrived by the senses, the other inward to a world of infinite and unceasing time. We are all familiar with the distinctions that make the classical Greek world devoted primarily to space perception, so that its characteristic art is sculpture; the Western European world to time perception, so that its characteristic art is music. An even more sweeping generalization would have the East given over to real time and the West to physical or clock time.

The trouble with all these generalizations of course is that they make too sharp distinctions; and it is safer to say that individuals possessing both attitudes toward time will be found in every place and in every epoch, although certain epochs are more conducive to the one attitude than to the other. Spengler's *Decline of the West*, which is the most monumental application of time theories to the interpretation of history, appeared in Germany in July, 1918; and this date suggests that Spengler himself was possibly determined in his analysis by the dominating time attitude of his period. His work is better approached as a remarkable product of the modern imagination, in which whole cultures, peoples, arts, take the place of characters and the action is a personal vision of the unfolding of history.

In literature, as a matter of fact, we do find an astonishing parallel between the forms, techniques, and styles employed and the ruling orientations of the period in regard to time. During the Renaissance the expansion of space that resulted from the discoveries of Copernicus and Galileo brought with it a corresponding expansion of time; so that time in Elizabethan tragedy, for example, is limited only by the imagination of a Faustus or a Hamlet. All history is of one piece for an age that can put dukes in Athens, and even the concept of an anachronism was alien to the Elizabethan mind. Moreover, what with the multiplicity of scenes, their range in time and place, with the difficulty of establishing the exact time-intervals between the scenes of *Lear* and *Macbeth,* and with actual errors in time-sequence in Webster's *Dutchess of Malfi,* the form of tragedy had departed far from its Senecan model. The world of Elizabethan tragedy is a world in which spatial happenings are far less significant than the inner movements of the mind and the heart. It is only by a kind of courtesy that relations in the space world are still more or less observed by the dramatists. But only a few years later, in the seventeenth century, space was restored by a physics which contracted the world just as the new astronomy had seemed to expand it in the early Renaissance. For the universe that Newton created was enclosed by natural laws as completely as the medieval universe had been enclosed by the conceptions of Ptolemaic astronomy. Time indicated as an algebraic symbol becomes one of the terms of measurement in the description of Newton's universe. Time, that is to say, is subject to the limitations of space: it exists only as a function of observable phenomena in the space world. Literature, as we might expect, takes to the drawing room and the boudoir, with a clock on the mantelpiece to time the unfolding of the intrigue in a comedy by Wycherley or Congreve. It is the age of fly-by-night pamphlets, of the first magazines and newspapers—the beginning of journalism. We have the mechanical tickings of the heroic couplet in Congreve and Wycherley; the strict observance of the classical unities of time, place, and action in the drama; and the development of prose into a neat and well-balanced vehicle for logical thought. So restricted indeed in time and space was the world presented to the literary imagination by the seventeenth-century rationalists that it was only natural it should revolt after a very few generations. Romanticism as a reaction against the extreme limitations of the rational spirit is too familiar to need any extended treatment here. But while Romanticism has been often enough presented as a flight into space—the return to nature and exoticism—its time aspects have perhaps been less often stressed.

I am thinking here not only about the ransacking of the past for subjects to contain present sentiments and emotions, but also about the most superficial aspects of the form and style of characteristic works. It is no mere coincidence, for example, that most of the works of the romantics are of such considerable physical bulk. In the novels of Richardson and Sterne, in the *Confessions* of Rousseau, in Goethe's *Werther*, we have the feeling that these writers are actually engaged in filling space with words, with the materializations, that is to say, of their suddenly released sensibilities. Like a much later romantic, Walt Whitman, each of them seems to be saying, "I shall dilate you with time and space." Their books are based, not on the neatly organized intellectual patterns of the classical school, but on the vast, loose, and at times overwhelming rhythms of the sensibility. And the style and syntax of their sentences correspond, not so much to tidy space-like divisions and subdivisions of the mind, but to the diastole and the systole of the heart.

But the most important point to be made about the romantics for the purposes of our survey is the fact that here we have a reaction on the part of one section of the people of a period, the literary and artistic, against what is the dominating time-view of the period as a whole. We have, for the first time in European literature, a profound cleavage between the general culture of a period and its more serious art and literature. For the view of time as measurable space promulgated by science was *the* view of most people in our civilization from the eighteenth century right up to the present. There are from that time on two literatures running side by side, having little essentially to do with each other, either in their assumptions or in their audiences: the one objective, scientific, diagrammatic; the other subjective, intuitive, and finding its forms in the patterns of the individual consciousness of the writer. To understand this point is to understand most of the phenomena presented by recent and contemporary literature: its difficulty, its so-called obscurity or incomprehensibility, and its unpopularity. For a literature arising out of the private sensibility, finding its forms and its styles in that sensibility, observing neither the physics of Newton nor the movements of the clock at Greenwich Observatory, is hardly calculated to appeal to a society devoted to mechanical large-scale production in industry, to imperialistic expansion in politics, and to the ideal of progress in philosophy. The history of later European literature of the more serious kind, then, from the eighteenth century to the present moment, may be traced as the gradual but final and absolute disappearance of the clock from its pages.

Because we too are subject to the limitations of physical time and space, I shall limit myself for the rest of this essay to prose fiction and to a few important names. Everything that will be said is equally true for poetry, but for certain reasons the modification effected by the changing time-sense is more conspicuously illustrated in fiction.

I shall begin by referring to a curious episode in Dostoievski's *Crime and Punishment*. When Raskolnikov goes to the police office to confess, he is told that he is "rather early," although it is after sunset, and the last time he had visited the police office, at two in the afternoon, he was reproached for coming too late. Obviously what has happened is that Dostoievski himself has become so immersed in the thoughts and feelings of his character in this scene that he has ignored the obligations imposed on him by the conventions of physical time. Although such errors of calculation appear elsewhere, more often the relaxation of the usual time-sense is to be seen in the extreme length of certain scenes—take those endless conversations in *The Idiot* and *The Brothers Karamazov*—and also in the preponderance of subjective passages over straight narrative. The characteristic form of the new fiction is established: as in Elizabethan drama, it is the monologue.

It may seem an abrupt transition to the writings of Henry James; and in fact no more will be said of him than that, like his brother William, he was possessed above all else by what is known in philosophy as the problem of knowledge. All of his novels are exercises in cognition, what he himself somewhere calls processes of vision. Where other novelists had built on ideas or conceptions already crystalized in the mind, James makes the process of understanding the basis of interest and suspense in his work. He establishes what he calls a reverberator, a central character through whom we see everything put together and through whom we finally understand everything that belongs to a particular situation. Most of his novels are really in the form of long monologues, some of them groups of monologues. During the period that we are sharing in the central character's exciting pursuit of the truth, we have no consideration for the movements of the clock. We are in a realm of such concentrated mental activity that we cannot be bound by such conventions. James's novels are long, it may be said, and they are not popular.

Marcel Proust differs from James essentially in the area of his subject matter; James's selected terrain was the realm of the conscience, that of Proust the sensibility. Both were engaged in the precise transcriptions by a first-rate intelligence of these inner realms. Another difference will be found in the fact that the one bases his form on the solution of a problem of conduct, the other on what he calls the form of time itself. Proust says in the last volume of his work:

> In any case, if I had still the strength to accomplish my work, the circumstances which had today in the course of the Princesse de Guermantes' reception simultaneously given me the idea of it, and the fear of not being able to carry it out, would specifically indicate its form, of which I had a presentiment formerly in Combray church during a period which had so much influence on me, a form which normally is invisible, the form of time. I should endeavor to render that Time-dimension by transcribing life in a way very different from that conveyed by our lying senses.

Proust differs from most of his ancestors in the romantic and symbolist movements of the preceding century in that, as a highly skilled amateur metaphysician, he was consciously aware of the conceptions on which he operated in his book. He devotes much, perhaps too much of his work to the abstract expounding of these conceptions; so that he needs interpretation less than any great writer in literary history. Despite this fact, however, he has been subject to grave misinterpretations, the most popular of which in this country is the notion that the real center of his book is its criticism of certain social classes. It is true that the subject is the fusion of the moribund aristocracy of the Faubourg St. Germain with the successful bourgeoisie in France in the closing years of the nineteenth century. But this is only its *subject;* its theme is time and change, and this theme is presented most intensely and most tragically through the narrator's own personal loves, sorrows, ambitions, and the rest. Other characters and even whole social classes exist for him only as the outward and visible manifestation of the law of time. This use of the outside world as a symbol for an inner experience is expressed by Proust in a sentence toward the very last pages of his book. He has been at a reception at the home of the Princesse de Guermantes, whom he had known years ago as the vulgar and self-seeking Madame de Verdurin; there he meets many of the characters of the novel:

> In all these ways an afternoon party such as this, was something much more valuable than a vision of the past for it offered me something better than the successive pictures I had missed of the past separating itself from the present, namely, the relationship between the present and the past; it was like what used to be called a panopticon, but a panopticon of years, a view not of a monument but of a person situated in the modifying perspective of time. . . .
> A Punch and Judy show of puppets bathed in the immaterial colors of years, of puppets which exteriorized Time, Time usually invisible, which to attain visibility seeks and fastens on bodies to exhibit wherever it can, with its magic lantern . . .

It will be necessary to say a few words about a writer who, like Proust, was a brilliant student of metaphysics, a disciple of William James as Proust was of Henri Bergson, and whose work represents the absolute and logical culmination of the tendency I have been tracing in this lecture. It is not flippant to say that if she had not come to exist around the year 1913 it would be necessary to invent Miss Gertrude Stein. Miss Stein throws over conventional syntax altogether; for syntax, as we have hinted, is a product of the rational mind, and the rational mind works by putting things together as we put objects together in space. Now,

Miss Gertrude Stein is not concerned with space except to fill it with as many books as possible. She is concerned with rendering in analogical, unsyntactical language the precise movements of her own consciousness, in which physical time exists no more than it existed in the mind of a sixteenth-century mystic like St. Teresa or than it exists in a Hindu. Miss Stein wrote in "Melanctha," published in 1903:

> "I certainly don't rightly understand what you are doing now to me Jeff Campbell," wrote Melanctha Herbert. "I certainly don't rightly understand Jeff Campbell why you ain't all these days been near me, but I certainly do suppose it's just another one of the queer kind of ways you have to be good, and repenting of yourself all of a sudden. I certainly don't say to you Jeff Campbell I admire very much the way you take to be good Jeff Campbell. I am sorry Dr. Campbell, but I certainly am afraid I can't stand it no more from you the way you have been just acting. I certainly can't stand it any more the way you act when you have been as if you thought I was always good enough for anybody to have with them, and then you act as if I was a bad one and you always just despise me. I certainly am afraid Dr. Campbell I can't stand it any more like that. I certainly can't stand it any more the way you are always changing. I certainly am afraid Dr. Campbell you ain't man enough to deserve to have anybody care so much to be always with you. I certainly am awful afraid Dr. Campbell I don't ever any more want to really see you. Good-by Dr. Campbell I wish you always to be real happy."

Here Miss Stein is writing what she believes to be a letter such as might be written by a colored servant girl to one of her race who is too educated to appreciate her charms. And what Miss Stein emphasizes is the repetitiousness, the absence of causal development of statement, and the total effect of a section of the flux of consciousness. I quote from this early story to point out that in the beginning Miss Stein was copying living models and that her style is not entirely the product of the metaphysical systems of James, Bergson, and Whitehead. A further study of Miss Stein would show how she combined these influences with the influence of postimpressionist French painting in the attempt to produce a literature which should consist in the arrangement of fragments of continuous consciousness in patterns comparable to the compositions of the most abstract paintings of Braque and Picasso. There is, in other words, a distinct esthetic evolution in Miss Stein that makes her very difficult to explain in a single generalization. All that need be pointed out here is that, for her, reality resides in the timeless consciousness rather than in space, that she has based her form and her style on the reproduction of this consciousness without the intervention of the logical.

Of all the writers of our period who have dealt with time, James Joyce has shown the deepest and richest ingenuity in its treatment. Even in its form *Ulysses* makes an implicit statement about the difference between the two kinds of time: in less than twenty-four hours and in the single city of Dublin, Leopold Bloom experiences as many adventures of the mind and the soul as his prototype Odysseus in his ten years' voyaging in the Aegean. Here the disparity between physical and what we have called real time is objectively realized for us by a subtle formal contrast. Moreover, Joyce has evolved a style which records the instantaneous impact of outer reality on the inner mind with the exactitude of the seismograph recording the earth's vibrations. Here are the opening lines of the Proteus episode, in which Stephen Dedalus is walking along a beach outside Dublin:

> In the distance along the course of the slow-flowing Liffey slender masts flecked the sky, and more distant still, the dim fabric of the city lay prone in haze. Like a scene on some vague arras, old as man's weariness, the image of the seventh city of Christendom was visible to him across the timeless air, no older nor more weary nor less patient of subjection than in the days of the thingmote . . . so timeless seemed the gray warm air, so fluid and impersonal his own mood, that all ages were as one to him.

Here, past experience (including anything he has ever read, Dante and Bishop Berkeley), present experience—the sensations

surrounding him on the beach—and future directions (the movement of the mind toward understanding) are blended like sky,
sea, and sand in the outer world.

But I should like to turn from *Ulysses*, with which most people
are sufficiently familiar, to the work Joyce has not yet completed
and which is beginning to take on something of the property of
time itself. From the sections that have already appeared it would
seem that in his *Work in Progress* Joyce proceeds from the rendition of the individual consciousness to that of the whole race, to
what the school of Jung calls the collective consciousness and
which, only the other day at Harvard, Jung maintained is inherited in the strict sense. This sense that the individual includes
in his own psychic makeup the whole past history and experience
of his race is already present in *A Portrait of the Artist as a Young
Man* and *Ulysses*.

As far as one can now determine, Joyce's new work deals not
with any single nameable character, but a kind of hypothetic
character who is the soul of the race. In his semi-waking state, all
history merges and blends—historical and legendary figures such
as Helen of Troy, Brunhild, Deirdre, and Peaches Browning are
telescoped into one archetypal symbol of feminine destructive-
ness. The effect of certain episodes is of a humor of an order and
on a scale never before attempted in literature: the humor that
resides in the long view of history by a certain type of mind.
Unfortunately, Joyce has carried his notion of telescoping time
even into his language; for language too has its history, is made
up of ever changing fractions of the past.

I shall conclude this survey with Mann because in his current
unfinished work he is doing essentially the same thing. Mann
began as a writer influenced by the scientific time-view; for his
first book, *Buddenbrooks*, is a chronological account of the rise
and fall of a family of German merchants. Toward the end, however, this family produces an artistic temperament, and the book,
like the family, disintegrates into the subjective. *The Magic
Mountain* finds its title in that space-object which is at once the
symbol of permanance or anti-time and of detachment or im-

munity from the ordinary preoccupations of life, which include time. The book also emphasizes the disparity between the seven years that Hans Castorp spends at the sanatorium and the lifetime of intellectual and spiritual experience which he undergoes there. It is possible to relate the theme of the book, which is a dialogue between life and death, to the general theme of death. But Mann has not allowed his theme to determine his style and form as did Joyce and Proust. He is more comprehensible and therefore more popular than they. Mann *talks* about time frequently and with great clarity, but he does not *realize* it through his characters.

The opening of *Joseph and His Brethren* consists of a long essay on the timelessness of human history. Taking the biblical figure of Joseph, Mann treats the typical experience of a certain kind of temperament in every time and place. It should be added that it is not the irony of the comedy or the sameness of human history that impresses Mann so much as the survival through great sacrifice of certain fundamental human values.

All that has been accomplished in this hasty and superficial survey perhaps has been an indication of the metaphysical approach to literature. It has the advantage of allowing one, as we have seen, to treat the form and substance of works as one thing, arising out of an identical attitude. Also it renders unnecessary the unreal and tiresome parcelling out of literary history into movements like symbolism, impressionism, expressionism, and the rest.

But there is an objection to the method that will undoubtedly be raised and will have to be faced. It is, of course, an objection by a branch of scientific materialism that metaphysical attitudes, like the attitudes toward time here described, are ultimately traceable to socio-economic necessities. There is one, and one very potent, answer that can be made to this, and that is that materialism itself is the result of a metaphysical attitude, a particular view of the nature of time and space. To explain the attitudes of others as the consequence of automatic socio-economic conditioning while assuming that one's own are the essence of eternal truth, is either to claim divine inspiration or to be illogical, each of which is equally offensive to the materialistic mind.

A resolution of this conflict can only be attained when it is recognized that literature is inclined toward one view of reality and science toward another. Each has been able to accomplish marvelous results out of its assumptions; and each will probably continue to do so if both consider themselves as parallel rather than as rival ways of getting at truth.

But there is, it must be granted, some justification for those critics who charge the writers whom we have just discussed with having retreated from the realities, by which they mean political and economic realities, of their time and place into the exploration of the individual's personality. The only trouble here is the use of the term reality; for Proust and Joyce and Mann, the conflicts of their own temperaments were just as real as the class struggle of Marxist analysis. What is meant, rather, is that they did not cease to be artists and become propagandists or men of action engaged in changing the surface of historical reality. And the only answer to this is that, if they had, they would have ceased to be artists and become something else; they would have denied their function. Yet social criticism is on the right track when it complains of a shifting of the background or objects of experience from an outer world of concrete experience to an inner world of spiritual or psychological experience. The writer is at his best, or shall we say his healthiest, when there is a reciprocal interplay between the inner and the outer worlds, even when his objects are not found within himself. In Homer, in Shakespeare, in Dante, there is a world of tangible fact and substance, social and universal, and there is also a world of inner contemplation and illumination. The balance has been lost in modern literature; it began to be lost in the last terrifying plays of Shakespeare. The real problem of the social critic is to direct his attention to the establishment of a world with which the artist can resume communications; one which he need not regard with disgust, contempt, or indifference—in a word, one which he finds more congenial than that with which the great masters of our time have been confronted. This is the only hope for our literature, as it is for all the other forms of our culture.

A Note on Myth

[*1938*]

The most important of the discoveries made by modern anthropology through the scientific mode of cognition is, in my opinion, the fact that men everywhere in the world are governed by a quite different mode of cognition.

To this mode any number of labels may be applied, but "mythical" has the advantage of suggesting the concrete form in which it is to be discovered in all the literatures of the world. Myth, like science, is at once a method and a body of ordered experience. And it is in the sense of a method that I undertook to employ it as a means of formal interpretation in "Thomas Mann: Myth and Reason." * It has been my opinion, and I believe that it is the opinion of more and more people in England and America, that literature has long been suffering from the ravages of what might be called the Scientific Fallacy in criticism. This is the fallacy which has led in our time to that twofold process of reduction which consists first in reducing literature to its abstract content and then in reducing this content to one or another of the scientific categories. Of course if we are to assign a beginning to the tendency we must go back to the monumental distortions of Taine in the mid-nineteenth century. But I believe that the tendency, insofar as the vague materialism of Taine has sharpened

* See below, p. 213.

into an ever more narrow political doctrine, has reached its climax of ineptitude in our time.

For it must be repeated that the real objection to the application of science to art and literature is not to science as such but to its fundamental inappropriateness in these realms. Unfortunately, it is much less difficult to say what literature is not than to say what it is: the anatomy of the imagination will probably remain the last challenge to the scientific mind. But we *can* say that although the literary work is something material in the sense that it must have a vehicle—the "context"—the work itself represents a formal transcendence that cannot be deduced from any of its parts. This is more simply expressed in the formula that *what* a writer says is only relatively important. And this is the teasing fact that the abstracting type of intellect is unable or unwilling to accept. The scientific method is necessarily limited to the subject matter of a work, which includes of course the opinions, views, and judgments of a writer, along with their concrete expressions, because science is a method which requires a temporary hypothetical spatialization of its object. The procedure of the so-called scientific critic of literature is the following: the isolation of one or another aspect of the object, the reference of this aspect to an already completed scientific or quasi-scientific structure of logic (philosophical, psychological, or political), and the evaluation of the whole object in terms of the latter. (Thus, André Malraux's latest novel is reduced to a political phenomenon, analyzed in terms of Marxist political philosophy, and rejected by the critic as being inconsistent with this philosophy.) The apparent effort is to replace the original concrete esthetic structure by an altogether abstract structure of thought. But, as a matter of fact, the esthetic structure has not been affected at all. It retains its original imponderable character.

An adequate or comprehensive method of literary interpretation would have to begin with the recognition of this imponderable character of the aspects involved in any whole literary organism. For a work of literature, which is the constatation of the organic processes of the imagination, is capable of being grasped only in terms of its own inner pattern of movement—in terms like expansion and contraction, tension and rest, conflict and resolution. Where but from literature itself can we hope to derive an appropriate mode for such an analysis? From the study of the important works of the literary past there emerges a pattern of development of such distinctness and regularity that we are compelled to accept it as a *norm* for all the rest. This norm is the pattern described by the successive stages in the dialectic struggle between matter and form represented in its most vivid and concentrated human terms in the classic myth. To employ this pattern of development as a method for criticism is of course actually to establish an analogy between what is ideal, the abstract formal process, and what is real, the particular work in question. Insofar as it is an analogical method it bears a resemblance to the so-called method of fourfold interpretation of the medieval schoolmen, with their reading of works on the separate levels of the literal, the allegorical, the moral, and the anagogical. But the important difference is that while the analogy established by the schoolmen was always with a *particular* myth of the past the analogy here is simply with the general formal structure of the myth.

Is such a method an absolute? The answer must be that as a method it is an absolute exactly to the extent that the scientific method is an absolute. It is one of the modes of cognition, and as such must be accepted as valid within the field of its application. One cannot disagree with the contention that the legitimacy of a method is to be tested by its results. There is the point of view always from which no mode of human perception can lay safe claims to being an absolute. And all that is maintained here is that the "mythical" is the most relevant approach to literature because it is most faithful to the object: it produces more "integrated" results.

In the complete myth is projected a concrete and dynamic rehearsal of the dialectic struggle between the principle of matter and the principle of form. Reason, which is in one sense on the side of form, is in another sense, through its identification with will, on the side of matter. "Pure" reason, by which is meant the divorcing of the logical faculty from the other human faculties, ends up by becoming just as much a force for disruption as pure matter. The human organism at any given moment is the precariously sustained equilibrium between these two opposed principles of force, and the myth is its complete expression. It seems to me that there is nothing in this account that is in the least hostile to the spirit of science insofar as science is a method devoted to the study and control of the laws of matter. But it does place scientific reason in a dynamic relation to something else— to the laws governing the moral and psychological economy of the organism as a whole.

Now the reason that some people respond even to the sound of the word myth with horror and trepidation is that they confuse the notion of myth as the particular equilibriums of the past with the notion of myth as a process. They fail to recognize that for society, as for the individual, the materials of experience undergo an unbroken process of modification and change. If the individual does not achieve a fresh reordering of these materials, as Freud has explained, he will relapse into a former state of equilibrium, which is indistinguishable from the state of death. In the same way every myth, which corresponds to the once strenuously accomplished equilibrium of a culture, becomes in time inadequate to the situation, something dead, and therefore "false and dangerous." Any myth constructed in our time which should fail to take into account the development of the scientific impulse together with all its triumphs of the laboratory would indeed be a retrogression into the false stability of the grave. We must conclude with Rimbaud—*tenir le pas gagné*. In brief, it must be understood that while every myth corresponds only to a temporary resolution of a conflict, the conflict itself is ever alive, ever becoming involved in new terms of experience, and ever seeking a resolution. In every epoch there are the old myths of the past, haunting the present like a fixation of childhood, and the new myths struggling to be born. And it is a mistake not to be able to tell them apart.

This is not the place to describe the role of myth in social and political organization. At the moment the triumph of the myth, the dead and false myth, almost everywhere in the world, and with it the imminent destruction of all those values which Western Europe had earned through its agony of three centuries, should be enough to persuade us of its reality. It should teach us that in history, as in finance, bad myths tend to drive out good myths, and that our only salvation lies in a purification of our symbols toward the creation of a new myth which will correspond to the stage at which the more conscious and responsible actions of mankind have arrived.

In my essay on Mann I attempted to show that in our romantic, liberal, bourgeois culture the so-called artist type alone has exhibited both in his life and his work the problems involved in being and the proper mode of their resolution. My final point was that in the figure of Joseph this artist type finally attains his complete integration through an identification of his personal destiny with the highest spiritual ideals and aspirations of the race. This was not to suggest a too facile identification of the artist as man with the artist as symbol. Whatever particular weaknesses, follies, or errors of judgment the artist may commit as a man do not affect the symbolic value of his work. This was what I intended by declaring that, in the last analysis, Joseph is a figure of the imagination. And perhaps it would be better to have said the moral imagination. In that realm the potential is realized with a purity and vividness with which it can never unfortunately be realized in actuality; it is romantic to think that it might be; and it has become time for us to replace our romanticism with a recognition of this fact. For without symbols we are lost; we are without any means of integrating thought and action, therefore without direction. We may live in the colorless world provided by a purely scientific and valueless view of life for a certain length of time. But the moment must come when the old exiled symbols, dressed up in their gaudy shrouds, will reappear across this world and claim it for their own—unless they are met with a strong resistance.

Myth, Method, and the Future

Honneur des Hommes, Saint Langage,
Discours prophétique et paré,
Belles chaînes en qui s'engage
Le dieu dans la chair égaré,
Illumination, largesse!
—Paul Valéry *

[1946]

Although conscious preoccupation with the myth has never been so widespread and intense as at the moment, it has never really waned throughout the ages, however much it may have seemed to during certain epochs. Jessie Weston, in a book that by now everybody has read, has shown beyond doubt to what extent the pre-Christian initiation pattern survived through the Middle Ages in the Grail romances. And certainly some of the greatest minds of the Renaissance—Pico, Bruno, and Vico—were instinctively more attracted to the great myths of the past (particularly Bruno, whose *Triumphant Beast* served Joyce as one of the models for *Finnegans Wake*) than to the abstract improvisations of the schoolmen. *Shakespeare's Mystery Play* (a book by Colin Still, which unfortunately not enough people have read) defends brilliantly the thesis that the Elizabethan mind was still so saturated with the old memories that *The Tempest* is best comprehended in terms of the ritual pattern. Even in the so-called Age of Reason the unlaid ghosts of the Age of Mystery rumbled unquietly beneath the deceiving surface. Masonism, Illuminatism, Swedenborgianism were among the numerous cult movements which had their origin in the eighteenth century, preparing the way for the full romantic revolt against the sway of "Bacon, Newton, and Locke."

* From "La Pythie," in Paul Valéry: *Oeuvres*, Paris, Gallimard, 1957, p. 136

What actually happened with Blake and the Romantics was the frank and open re-admission of the myth into the Western consciousness. Since their time the history of the myth has consisted of shifting emphases within a more or less uniform pattern. For example, Faust, the hero all "will-to-know," heir of the Machiavellian phase of the Renaissance, yields to Prometheus, the hero all "will-to-do," * precisely as the Western mind gave itself more and more to material power in all of its forms—war, imperialism, and money. It is this which is unfolded in the grand manner in the Siegfried cycle, in which the modern *daimon* of money is embodied in the ancient symbol of the dragon—Fafnir. But by the middle of the century there is another shift—from man-against-Nature, or man-against-society (except for a few naturalists and the Marxists), to man-against-himself. This found its inevitable expression in the revival, by all the French Symbolists up to and including Proust, of the Narcissus legend, with its associated symbols of pool, mirror, and solitary swan. With Yeats, George, Joyce, and Mann, there is of course no longer any question of the degree of conscious deliberation with which our most important writers have turned to the myth for their various purposes: their works are woven of the whole cloth.

And that is the point of this perhaps unnecessary historical excursus. We have today reached the point at which we are interested not so much in the substance of particular myths as in the essential pattern or structure of myth in general. Indeed, we have come to wonder whether the word should be used in the plural at all. Perhaps there is, after all, only *one* myth—the Myth. And in that case the effort of the intellect can only be to determine more clearly its outline; to distinguish its order, if one prefers to consider it rather as a process; in brief, to establish what might be called its categories. Until this is accomplished we shall not be able fully to realize all its uses for the richer interpretation of our literature and arts, not to mention our

---

* The Satanic Man, especially in his later refinements, a Julien Sorel or a Raskolnikov, represents a fusion of the two in the hero who would conquer society by a process of "out-witting."

culture and individual selves. We must sharpen ever more finely the tools which it offers to our understanding. Here psychoanalysis has been helpful, largely in providing a vocabulary; anthropology and comparative religion have supplied materials and evidence. But these are disciplines in themselves, with their own divergent presuppositions and their own limiting reductions. What is possibly most in order at the moment is a thoroughgoing refurbishment of the medieval fourfold method of interpretation, which was first developed, it will be recalled, for just such a purpose—to make at least partially available to the reason that complex of human problems which are embedded, deep and imponderable, in the Myth.

> Littera *gesta docet, quae credas* Allegoria,
> Moralis *quid agas, quo tendas* Anagogia.

Of these four levels of meaning, surely the most important for us today is the last, the anagogical, which teaches us "whither we may turn ourselves." For it should be implicit in this note that if we are to be saved, which also assumes that we wish to be saved, it can only be through some reintegration of the Myth in terms of the heartbreaking concerns of the times. "The times are nightfall," Hopkins said long ago, and they grow worse from hour to hour. Yet, when really everything has been said, are the most overwhelming problems of our age ultimately different from what have been the greatest problems of the race from its dark beginnings—love and justice? And it is exactly with these two problems above all else that the Myth is concerned. It is the cartograph of the perennial human situation, the more appealing for being concrete, the more persuasive for being not subject to final analysis. The Myth provides us not merely with illustrations of destiny but with a guide to its better control and mastery—the anagogical. "We must love one another or die," as Mr. Auden warns us. In a regenerated Myth alone we may hope to find a beckoning image of the successful alliance of the twin virtues of love and justice.

II BRITISH AND AMERICAN LITERATURE

The Lesson of the Master

[*1931*]

It is perhaps another evidence of his genius that Henry James, like certain other great writers of the past, has come to mean something different to each of the successive literary generations that have taken up his work. What James meant to the readers of *Harpers* and the *Atlantic* in the eighties and nineties, what he meant to the generation of Mr. H. G. Wells, or to the generation of Mr. T. S. Eliot and Mr. Ezra Pound, was probably not any of the things that he means, or may come to mean, to the generation in which we are naturally much interested—the present one. So abundant are the implications of his work that he is capable of being read—or misread—to suit the needs of widely different classes of readers, of distinct periods of literary taste; capable also of being "used," in a very real sense, as Shakespeare was used by the German romantics of the eighteenth century, or as Baudelaire is now being used by a whole wing of contemporary French and American poets. Of what possible "use" in this sense may James prove to be to the present generation of novelists? What lesson may this formidable and often-disputed master offer to the inheritors of his craft in our time? If his example includes anything of value special to them, if his strength corresponds to any of their numerous weaknesses, he should be appropriated at once, reinstated in the direct current of our letters.

It happens, moreover, that James is in immediate need of some sort of reinstatement. At the moment, he remains suspended in that vague limbo of disrepute to which the last generation of Freudian critics so often consigned their victims. He is easily the most tolerated author of his size in modern literature. The elaborate execution which Mr. Van Wyck Brooks performed in *The Pilgrimage of Henry James* was simply the final blow in the long catastrophe of his reputation. For more than forty years James had been chiefly read by people who admired him for hardly any more palpable reason than the vague penumbra of gentility which surrounded his pages. The close of his life was rendered positively unhappy (as we know from his letters) by the ribald humors of a new order which dismissed him as nothing short of a pompous old fool. Mr. Wells's brutal parody in *Boon* served to lay the ghost for prewar England. All that remained for Mr. Brooks in 1925 was to dispose of James in a more comprehensive fashion and in terms that should be more effective for the period. What Mr. Brooks did to James's reputation, however, is important, for the semi-ridiculous, semi-tragic figure that he created is the most popular conception of him at the moment.

For Mr. Brooks, it will be recalled, James offered nothing more or less than a case history. Here was an example of an American who had sacrificed not only his promise as an artist but also his identity as an individual in the fruitless effort to adjust himself to an alien culture. All the habits of James's mind—"the caution, the ceremoniousness, the baffled curiosity, the nervousness and constant self-communion, the fear of committing himself"—are traceable to the long years he spent in England, where he had never been anything but "an enchanted exile in a museum-world." A self-conscious guest in a house where he had never been at home, James reflected even in his style "the evasiveness, the hesitancy, the scrupulosity of an habitually embarrassed man." The diagnosis becomes steadily more emphatic toward the end. In James's later writings Mr. Brooks can discern no more than "the confused reveries of an invalid child." It is as if the author of *Roderick Hudson* and *The Portrait of a Lady* had developed at the last into a kind of "impassioned geometer—or, shall we say, some vast arachnid of art, pouncing upon the tiny air-blown particle and wrapping it round and round." What stands out most remarkably today in this analysis is a single statement which throws ever so much more light on Mr. Brooks than it does on Henry James: "What interested him [in his novels] was not the figures but their relations, the relations which alone make pawns significant."

To Mr. Brooks and his generation, as such a remark implies, an interest in relations was almost certain evidence of sterility in a writer. To concentrate on relations was to be faced immediately with the problems of value on which they hinged, and to betray an interest in any such problems was to be rendered more than a little suspect at the time. It was genuinely difficult for Mr. Brooks to conceive how a writer of James's manifest intelligence could have considered the relations of his "figures" more important than the movements of pawns in a game. It was difficult because it was almost impossible for his generation to recognize the existence of values or the part they usually play in vital literary creation. Even a game, it was forgotten, must have its rules; and for a game to be properly absorbing, for either player or spectator, the values assigned the rules must be accepted, temporarily at least, with something like seriousness. For James himself the rules did exist, and he accepted them with a passionate seriousness. Before ever they were apprehended by his mind, they were *felt*, and with enough intensity of feeling to provide the center, the very foundation of his artistic task. The "pawns" of his game, however inanimate they may sometimes seem in other respects, are always alive, even violently alive, in that portion of their being which James chose to explore and represent, because he believed it to be the richest and "most finely contributive" of all—the conscience.

By such a term as conscience one need not understand anything more definite than James himself intended by the term— that region of the mind, that area of our habitual mental activity, which is reserved for the recognition and solution of moral conflicts. At least to the extent that his "figures" do, every one of them, function in this region are they worthy of being called *characters*—or the label is without meaning. Often, it is true, the relations, situations, or patterns in which the somewhat special experience of their creator involves them are so unique or complex, so extremely tenuous, as to make them seem to respire a little outside the usual zone of verisimilitude. But the comparison with a geometer is inaccurate if it refers to anything but the hard and luminous detachment with which a given intellectual terrain is surveyed. For James the conscience that controlled the actions of his personages was something real and concrete; the values which determined for Fleda Vetch and Lambert Strether and Milly Theale the solution of their delicately attenuated problems were for him *true* values. For James's reader, however, who is primarily concerned with the interest that these problems afford, with their possible esthetic result, there is no such obligation to accept these particular values as true. For him it is simply necessary to accept their reality in the minds of the characters, to imagine, if only for the time being, that they *might* be considered true, for the sake of the satisfaction that their representation provides in an orderly execution of a work of art.

For various reasons this was an effort of the imagination that few in the last generation showed themselves able or willing to make. Perhaps the chief reason was the particular psychological absolutism of the time, which submerged personality beneath that plane of conscious judgment which for James and others before him had constituted the real domain of character. The belief in character that had sustained James was not recognized because it was not understood; and his fervid explorations could only be explained as the mystifying vagaries of someone who had ventured too far outside the normal bounds of experience. He could be accounted for only as a kind of exquisite monster, as the victim of some fundamental lesion of personality or—as the critics would have it—as a psychological "case." The formula was ready at hand and it was rich in possibilities of embroidery. Everything in James's mind and work—his characters, his themes, his form and style even—became immediately clear when it was once remembered that he was an American who had spent most of his adult years in Europe.

Whatever truth there may be in this formula as applied to other native American writers who have forsworn their country for the warm securities of European culture, one may question its validity as a total explanation of all that characterized Henry James as a man and an artist. Some of the more superficial biases of his mind, some of the minor idiosyncrasies of his style, can doubtless be traced to the influence of his prolonged residence in England. But one might show the equivalent consequences for his contemporary, William Dean Howells, of a migration from Ohio to Boston at about the same period. Unquestionably also, in his choice of backgrounds, characters, and the situations in which he placed them, James was affected for better or worse by the particular foreign milieu in which he happened to pass the greater part of his life. If certain subjects, like that of American "innocence" caught in the toils of European duplicity, recur constantly throughout his work it is merely because these subjects repeated themselves so often in the course of his experience and therefore became the most familiar patterns of reality available to him. To complain of these subjects, however, on the grounds that they are too narrow, or too special, or too refined, is illegitimate. It is to decline to play what James himself called "the fair critical game with an author," which is to grant him his postulates. "His subject is what is given him—given him by influences, by a process, with which we have nothing to do; since what art, what revelation, can ever really make such a mystery, such a passage as the private life of the intellect, adequately traceable for us? His treatment of it, on the other hand, is what he actively gives; and it is with what he gives that we are critically concerned."

Behind and above everything else was Henry James's mind, with its special quality, endowment, and direction. What is all too seldom realized, for it alone would discredit Mr. Brooks's thesis, is that the main set and direction of that mind was already well established long before James ever made his decision to settle in England. Already he had formulated, in a review of Walt Whitman written in 1865, what was to be the principle of his artistic creed for the whole of his career: "To be positive, one must have something to say; to be positive requires reason, labor, and art; and art requires above all things a suppression of one's self to an idea." The real problem before him in those early wander years was not the quest of some place that might change or modify the native bent of his mind, but one that should offer to his mind greater opportunities for play, a richer field in which to grow and expand, a more *plausible* background for the working out of his particular "idea." It was a problem of nutrition. And it was only after a trial-and-error process—for there was the important experiment of his year in Paris—that he hit upon the country that seemed most suitable to his purpose.

It might quite as easily be shown that the truth is the exact opposite of what Mr. Brooks and others have contended: that for James residence in England, rather than being a source of sterility and corruption, was an indispensable condition of fulfillment. Since these critics had made up their minds not to occupy themselves with his work, with what as an artist he had "given," they might equally well have considered the reverse of the medal: What would have happened to James if he had turned to the society that awaited him in the Boston or New York of the late nineteenth century? Would James, with his peculiarly refined sensibility, have escaped an ordeal less intense than that which Mr. Brooks has elsewhere traced in the career of Mark Twain? Indeed, there was hardly any means of salvation for the artist in Mr. Brooks's scheme of nineteenth-century America. Upon further reflection Mr. Brooks might well have concluded that in one sense there is never any salvation for the artist—at any time or in any place. His only chance of fulfillment is to be as good an artist as he can under the conditions of his time and the limitations of his own temperament. But such a view would lead instantly to an entirely different kind of criticism. One would have to concentrate more directly on the study and evaluation of a writer's work.

The specific question which we set out to examine was in what sense and to what extent may James's example have any special meaning for the novelists of our generation. How, we may inquire, may he show them the way to make their work more deeply and broadly *interesting?*

For the sole obligation of the novel, its one excuse for being, as James insisted, is that it be interesting. The question which such a demand leaves in the mind is, of course, what, properly speaking, constitutes the interest of a novel? Fortunately, in his essays, prefaces, and letters James has provided us with a complete and lucid exposition of his own view of the problem. There is life obviously, which is the novel-writer's material, and there is art, which consists of the special use that he makes of his material. Life is common, inexhaustible, chaotic—a "splendid waste," to use James's fine phrase. It is art alone that gives it beauty and meaning, through the form and expression with which the creative mind endows it, for "expression is creation and makes the reality." To be interesting, therefore, a novel must give or lend something to the "splendid waste" which is life. That something is "composition," the design which the artist makes out of the scattered and unchecked flow of his impressions and responses. Without such design the novel would have no identity as an art form, no value as a projection of reality, and hence no meaning to the mind or the imagination. "I hold that interest may be, *must be*, exquisitely made and created, and that if we don't make it, we who undertake to, nobody and nothing will make it for us," James wrote to Wells at the close of his life. And in the same letter he makes an even more complete avowal of his belief in the unique and absolute value of the artistic process: "It is art that *makes* life, makes importance, for our consideration and application of these things, and I know of no substitute whatever for the force and beauty of its process."

The various alternatives to this view of the novelist's special rôle and function are necessarily vague and contradictory. There are for example the exponents of "life"—of life *tout court*, of life at any cost. What precisely, however, do these people mean? If the novel is to be classified at all it is as an art form, and if art means anything it means the process by which the materials of life are arranged and fused into a unity. It is only through its unity that the meaning and value of a given work of art are to be discovered. A novel with insufficient evidence of unity represents mere arbitrariness, or ineptitude, or the surrender of the mind to the rich disorder of nature. It is possible, James admitted, to reproduce life—its substance and even its quality, its imponderable multiplicity—but without art ("composition") the result would be devoid of meaning. "There may in its absence be life, incontestably, as *The Newcomes* has life, as *Les Trois Mousquetaires*, as Tolstoy's *War and Peace* have it; but what do such large loose baggy monsters, with their queer elements of the accidental and the arbitrary, artistically *mean*. . . . There is life and life, and as waste is only life sacrificed and thereby prevented from 'counting,' I delight in a deep-breathing economy and an organic form."

Yet it would be wholly wrong to interpret such a statement as merely another expression of the "art for art's sake" doctrine which was so loudly articulated in James's own lifetime and to which he objected from the beginning. While James was firm in his recognition of esthetic values he was definitely not an esthete —that is to say, one for whom the means is also the end. For James even the patterns of art owe their initial suggestion to reality. Even composition depends on the existence of elements already present in life, elements capable of being drawn together with greater tightness, concentration, and beauty through the artistic process. Form is not therefore something distinct from life, but the arrangement of something already there, or at least there for the artist's specially trained observation. Unlike the real esthete, James distrusted all constructions of the mind which did not derive from their parallel somewhere in experience. "Never can a composition of this sort," he writes of *The Ambassadors*, "have sprung straighter from a dropped grain of suggestion, and never can that grain, developed, overgrown and smothered, have yet lurked more in the mass as an independent particle." And surely *The Ambassadors* is a good enough example of his later more complex and "geometrical" style! Whatever were the limitations of his experience his brain was never, like Mallarmé's for example, haunted by the memory of azure skies shut out, never drained of content

> Comme le pot de fard gisant au pied d'un mur.*

But what, since we have only mentioned them, are the elements of those patterns which life is made to assume in the imagination of the artist? Since they can be observed they must be objective; and objective patterns of human life can be built on one thing only, action. Action, to James, is therefore the "soul of the novel." All else is subordinate—description, "local color," incidental ideas, everything in fact not strictly related to the progressive explication of the central narrative core. At the same time the highest interest cannot be created by action alone, that is, action considered for its own sake. If incident is the illustration of character, character itself is the determination of incident. What is always really interesting is character, and that can only be fully understood through an imaginative reconstruction of the motives that precede action in the mind. The external patterns of life—and this is commonplace enough—have significance only insofar as we are made acquainted with the complex and never to be wholly apprehended background of motives behind them.

The moment we speak of motives we are headed straight into the whole field of difficulties whose attempted solution afforded the passion of James's task as an imaginative artist. These are, in a word, all those difficulties which are set up by the necessity of the individual to adjust himself to some moral order. The most interesting patterns of art are in fact just those the novelist is able to construct out of the often wasted, unrealized possibilities

* From "L'Azur," in his *Poésies*.

thrown up by these predicaments in life. Motives exist in all their confused and multiple variety; sometimes, but rarely, they fall into design of their own accord; it is the novelist's special business to see that what is thus accidental is always achieved. His business is with the motives behind conduct because they are what make fiction, as they make life, difficult—and, so, interesting. For that reason James exclaimed at "the moral timidity of the usual English novelist, with his (or with her) aversion to face the difficulties with which on every side the treatment of reality bristles." To shun these difficulties was in fact to miss the peculiar excitement on which, in the last analysis, everything depended.

To imply solution of any absolute sort is of course to assume a standard, a criterion to which in the end all problems may be referred. Here it will have to be enough to say that by a moral order James understood some body of felt values existing through one or another process of absorption in the individual's mind. For the individual's adjustment to be imperative these values must not only exist, but exist in a strong and potent way. Without this assumption of values as something felt one cannot make the assumption of art; for one cannot otherwise account for the extreme intensity of those conflicts around which the artist in fiction erects his constructions. Nor can one explain the quite real importance which these imagined conflicts take on in the reader's interest. Against some background of felt values, therefore, every individual conflict must be set; and on some such individual conflict the scheme of every novel must rest.

In these terms, plot, for example, becomes more easily definable: it is the abstract curve of the moral drama being enacted in the mind or conscience of a character. It is quantitatively all that development, growth, and expansion of "the dropped grain of suggestion" which has excited in the first place the novelist's passion for difficulties. In the same way, it may be seen how esthetic values are necessarily subordinated to other values anterior to them in reality. Subordinated is perhaps hardly the word—for the two kinds of values are really so identified as to be altogether indistinguishable. The esthetic pattern *is* the moral pattern—or the beginning, middle, and end of all that has taken place in the active conscience of the individual.

Unlike almost all of his fellow novelists in English, James served a deliberate apprenticeship during which he learned everything he could about the nature and function of his craft. Before writing as he did write (for, once established, his style and method progressed only in refinement) he had surveyed the field, measured the hazards, and envisaged all the possible alternatives. In his own lifetime he had the opportunity to study all the later mutations of the novel-form—the English Victorians (with their "fluid puddings") and the Russians, French realism and naturalism, and two whole epochs of pure estheticism. During his memorable year in France he learned so much about what the novel as novel might be that a contemporary French critic like M. Gide finds his work too much in the native tradition to captivate his taste. But he also learned, from Flaubert especially, the ultimate emptiness of even the most perfect work of art that pretended to an absolute moral indifference. From the Goncourts he learned that mere *décor*, no matter how sumptuous, was a poor substitute indeed for motivated human action. (Thus, years afterwards, writing *The Spoils of Poynton*, he avoids offering any detailed description of the furniture and other objects which are actually the source of the drama.) Most of all, from Zola, he learned that art and science were two different quantities, and that art at least was a quantity that was not to be amassed through perspiration alone. Of the group as a whole his indictment is significant: "The conviction that held them together was the conviction that art and morality are two perfectly different things and that the former has no more to do with the latter than it has with astronomy or embryology."

Because he had eliminated all these alternatives James may be said to have escaped all the blunders and excesses to which the novel after him was condemned. He himself could hardly have foreseen that so long after his pointed remark about Zola—"if he had as much light as energy, his results would be of the highest value"—the same process of burrowing in the dark would be resumed by Mr. Theodore Dreiser. Hardly less could he have guessed that estheticism would one day fade away into the pallid *fabliaux* of Mr. James Branch Cabell and the variegated pastiche of Mr. Thornton Wilder. But he must certainly have realized that naturalism carried far enough was bound to result in a subjectivism that should be opposed by its very nature to the traditions of an ordered art. He was certainly aware that to desert the living world of action was to descend to a region where anything resembling order was impossible. Did he not refer to impressionism like that of D'Annunzio as "the open door to the trivial"? Impressionism in our day is called by a different name, but the Jamesian objection is still valid. Psychoanalysis in fiction is simply impressionism supported by a method; and impressionism in the novel has meant the same abandonment of character at the level where its possibilities for the artist are most interesting. For James as an artist, order, the assumption of order, was essential; and to submerge beneath the plane where order was possible was merely to renounce for primordial chaos one's aspirations, to become lost in the "splendid waste."

The real difficulty in our time has of course been values. The old ones are no longer capable of generating enough conviction in actual living to justify their continued representation in fiction and the new have been found uniformly insufficient. Here, it must be granted, James can hardly be expected to offer any more immediate succor than has been thus far offered by contemporary life. But as he has already revealed the necessity and the exact function of values in narrative art he can now do much to prevent a certain confusion in regard to the novelist's proper relation to them.

Nothing in James's own example or declaration, let it be said, allows us to understand that it is ever the business of the novelist to establish values. As he assumed them from the society of the period in which he lived, so must those who follow after him in the path of the novel assume them from the moral consciousness of their own time. The contemporary writer can only hope to discover in the complex welter of our time those standards of judgment which emerge with sufficient strength and frequency to stand the test of being submitted to the artistic process. He must search, observe, experiment, and then make his test with the almost certain prospect of defeat for a considerable time to come. It may be that for some years he will have to be content to operate without nearly so cohesive a body of felt values as obtained in the past. He may be compelled to devote himself to the rapid atrophy and decline of those values in the present; to the issues caused by their dramatic refusal to be displaced; or to the equally dramatic effort of those new values which gradually assert themselves in the future. Any one of these courses would be more truly creative, according to the Jamesian point of view, than the blind appropriation of values which are no longer felt because they are no longer sufficiently alive.

What the writers of our time can learn from James is not anything distinctly represented in his achievement; is nothing implicit in his style or method, which are both too personal ever to be duplicated; not his "philosophy," not even the assumptions about human character which were for him the source of so much eloquence. What they can learn from him is the deepest meaning of the phrase "the integrity of the artist." He can show them to what an essential degree the artist is dependent on something anterior to himself in life; how the truest values of art are never to be dissociated from the most potent values of the world about him; and how, although the particular values of the one are always in one sense relative to those of the other, the single constant in the whole relationship is the fact of the artistic impulse. And as a last check on the possible interpretation that all this implies a certain dangerous relativity of values for art, he has written: "There is one point at which the moral sense and the artistic sense lie very close together; that is in the light of the very obvious truth that the deepest quality of a work of art will always be the quality of the mind of the producer . . . that seems to me an axiom which, for the artist in fiction, will cover all needful moral ground."

The Altar of Henry James

[1943]

This is, perhaps, an unfortunate title; it does not refer, for example, to the increasing number of people who have been throwing themselves at the feet of Henry James in the last few years. At least a half dozen full-length studies of his work are in preparation; not all of his books are easily available on the market; his reputation is higher than at any moment in his own lifetime. It is clear enough that to the present generation he means something more than to the generation of Van Wyck Brooks and Lewis Mumford or to the addled and intolerant generation of the thirties. Also clear is that what he means is something different. To say what this something is in every case is, of course, impossible. What this article undertakes is to suggest that if he makes such a great appeal to so many of us today it must be because there lies at the center of his work something that corresponds to our deepest contemporary needs and hopes. It raises the question of what was James's *own* altar—or, if one prefers, the particular object of piety to which he was able to devote himself at the end.

All this is to strike the religious note; and indeed, since we have no better word for the kind of passionate and responsible sense of human things that James possessed, he must be accounted a religious man. In this he simply followed his astonishing father, who ached out a lifetime trying to reconcile a heritage of respectability and good sense with a taste for Swedenborgian mysticism. Nor was he essentially unlike his brother William, whose too sudden plunge into the darker cellars of the personality during the period of his breakdown frightened him into a loud and quasi-religious philosophy of optimism. All the Jameses were religious. The important thing about Henry is that he was an artist; that is, he had to work in a concrete medium and in a more or less fixed craft which did not permit him the consolations of shaking his head over Brook Farm experiments or becoming the Socrates of the Chautauquas. It meant that he could not evade the really great questions because these questions were stubbornly embedded in the very materials of his craft—the lived and observed human situation.

For us it means that if we are to look for what is essential in James we are not likely to find it on the surface of his writing. (This is probably what T. S. Eliot means by the remark, "James had a mind so pure that no idea could violate it.") As in any authentic artist, the "meaning" in James is contained in the total arrangement and order of his symbols, and in the novel everything —people, events, and settings—is capable of being invested with symbolic value. In only a few novelists like Turgenev, Joyce, and the Mann of "Death in Venice" are meaning and literal statement so indivisible; the great works of the last period, *The Ambassadors* and *The Golden Bowl*, are put together, if not like a vastly exfoliated lyric, like one of the final plays of Shakespeare. And to approach them in the manner of Caroline Spurgeon or G. W. Knight on Shakespeare is almost certainly to uncover conflicts of feeling that are more often than not belied by the overt urbanity of style. It is also to raise the question of how much is conscious, how much unconscious, in any artist's work—in James's case, the often noted element of ambiguity. Is it merely an accident, for example, that in an early work like *The Portrait of a Lady* all the great climaxes in Isabel Archer's career—from her refusal of the English lord to her final flight from Caspar Goodwood—are made to occur in a garden? If an accident it was a fortunate one, for the garden symbol provides a wonderful point of concentration for the widest possible number of associations—the recollection especially of the famous Garden in which one of Isabel's ancestresses was also confronted with the fruit of the tree of the knowledge of good and evil. It enables us to arrive at the formula, nowhere explicit in the book, that the real trouble with Isabel is that she is someone who will have none of the bitter fruit and runs from the garden in panic. And it might lead us to an even wider formula regarding James's own attitude toward these matters at this point in his development.

For the symbolic approach to James, besides lifting the burden of the mystery of individual works, makes possible a more organic study of his growth and achievement than the usual chronological division of his career into three periods. If the garden symbol began as an accident, for example, it persists with remarkable frequency; and it is submitted to a series of drastic modifications. In *The Portrait of a Lady* it is clearly ambivalent. On the one hand, it is all that rich if uncertain promise of beautiful fulfillment that life is opening up to Isabel—wealth, marriage, Europe. On the other, it is the dwelling place of the unknown terror that is actually in herself—the terror of experience, which at the end she rationalizes in terms of moral obligation. If the novel ends with such manifest ambiguity it is because James himself has not yet resolved certain issues in his mind and temperament. In the novels and tales of the nineties, the so-called "middle period," the symbol is first split wide asunder into its two aspects, then one of them is made to dominate. When the governess in *The Turn of the Screw* begins her afternoon walk in the garden everything is calm and radiant and peaceful. It is with the force of a shock, she tells us, that it suddenly becomes transformed for her into a scene of desolation and death. Once again we know that this is a case of projection; the garden is all that alarming and unsuspected side of her nature which she cannot accept because she believes it to be evil. Nor do we feel that James accepts it; evil, working in the guise of zeal, is triumphant; and the story adds up to another terrifying treatment of the Othello motif, the infinite amount of mischief done in the world, in the name of goodness, by self-blinded innocence. Even more terrifying perhaps, in its nightmarish cancellation of all normal motives, is *The Other House*, in which nearly all the action occurs in a garden. James did not include this in the New York edition; it is the one altogether evil book that he ever wrote. But it sounds the depths of what must have been in his life a period of the most torturous metaphysical panic and moral despair. Without such a sojourn in the abyss as it represents he would never have attained to the full-bodied affirmation of the last and greatest period. Like Strether in *The Ambassadors*, he wins through, by a long and difficult "process of vision," to an acceptance of human life as it is lived—qualified, of course, by a revalidation of the naively grasped moral certitudes of his youth. It is in Gloriani's garden that Strether makes the celebrated speech with the refrain, "Live, live while you can!" But life now is to be lived always with the wary knowledge of the shadows lurking ever in the dark corners of the garden.

To point out that the full import of James is to be derived only from some such weighing of his major symbols is not to deny that throughout his work he does let drop explicit judgments and opinions on important matters, although never, like Tolstoy or Proust, to the temporary abnegation of his rôle. It so happens that in one of the final stories of the middle period—not one of the best known or most admired—he has given us what may be taken as something like a testament of belief. *The Altar of the Dead* is unique in the James canon, fluttering on the edge of a morbid emotionalism and sustained only by a marvelous tonality of style. It is also a masterpiece of its kind in English—the long short story or novella. But for our purpose it is significant because it is the only one of James's works in which a character is made to come face to face with the problem of religion.

Its hero, one of those sensitive middle-aged gentlemen whom James apologizes for writing about in the nineties, shocked by the callousness of a friend who remarries too soon after his first wife's death, dedicates himself to keeping up the memory of his dead friends. "What came to pass was that an altar, such as was after all within everybody's compass, lighted with perpetual candles and dedicated to these secret rites, reared itself in his spiritual spaces. He had wondered of old, in some embarrassment, whether he had a religion; being very sure, and not a little content, that he hadn't at all events the religion some of the people he had known wanted him to have. Gradually this question was straightened out for him—it became clear to him that the religion instilled by his earliest consciousness had been simply the religion of the Dead." Difficulties begin when quite by accident he enters a church and is tempted to light real candles before the real altar of a religion in which he does not believe. For he soon acquires a companion in mourning—a woman given to the same rites for a dead friend. In time it turns out that this friend, who had actually been her ruin, is also the one man among his friends whom the hero cannot commemorate because of some betrayal in the past. This coincidence threatens their relationship; they can no longer pay tribute at the same altar. A resolution is managed only when the hero realizes that the true "religion of the Dead" requires that we remember even our enemies—just because they were once part of ourselves and helped make us what we are.

What does James intend by this strange and tenuous parable, which he himself refers to as a "conceit"? It is, as he tells us in a preface, an instance of the "exasperated piety" of the Londoner of his time: "an instance of some such practised communion was a foredoomed consequence of life, year after year, amid the densest and most materialized aggregation of men on earth, the society most wedded by all its conditions to the immediate and finite." It is a commentary on the pathetic desolation of the individual in our society—a desolation shared by both the living and the dead. Toward the dead it expresses the same kind of sympathy that we find in Baudelaire's

> Les morts, les pauvres morts, ont de grandes douleurs,
> Et quand Octobre souffle, émondeur des vieux arbres,

> Son vent mélancolique à l'entour de leurs marbres,
> Certe, ils doivent trouver les vivants bien ingrats.*

And in its emphasis on the still potent influence that the dead can exercise on the living, it recalls Joyce's fine story, "The Dead." As to the living, or the living-dead, it explains their desolation as the absence of any ritual by which some principle of continuity in human experience may be recognized and observed. For it is continuity that is represented as the basis of everything—of personality, friendship, morality, and civilization itself. Without some sense of it the individual is no more than a moment in time and a speck in space; he has nothing by means of which he can define his own identity.

What James tells us, finally, is that we exist only by virtue of the existence of others, living and dead, with whom we have had relations. The individual, in the language of modern physics, is only an "event," to be defined in terms of a given field of forces. These relations or forces bring with them certain obligations, and the greatest of these is the formal act of commemoration. It is not morbidity that prompts James to write: "The sense of the state of the dead is but part of the sense of the state of the living; and, congruously with that, life is cheated to almost the same degree of the finest homage (precisely this our possible friendships and intimacies) that we fain would render it." We pay respect to the dead because they enhance the state of the living, and the dead is of course a metaphor for the whole tradition of civilized humanity of which we are a part and in terms of which we must ultimately be measured. This sense of the continuum between past and present, between all who share the memory of a common experience, is now known to be at the base of every religion in the world. For James it is a very real religion, although wholly without any theological cast. Or, if we prefer, he emerges as one of our great humanists, the greatest perhaps, because his humanism was grounded in such a rich tragic experience. And, in that

* From "La servante au grand coeur d'ont vous étiez jalouse," *Les Fleurs du Mal*, cɪɪɪ.

case, his altar—what would it be but the sometimes splendid and exultant, sometimes mangled and ignoble, body of humanity stretched out in imagination in time and space? At a moment when loss of continuity is our gravest threat, when personality is everywhere at a discount, when all consequent values dissolve in the general terror, it is probably no great wonder that more and more people are turning to Henry James.

Virginia Woolf
and the Novel of Sensibility

Life is not a series of gig-lamps symmetrically arranged; but a luminous halo, a semi-transparent envelope *surrounding us from the
beginning of consciousness to the end.*

[1932]

Not only in rhythm and tone but also in the imponderable vagueness of its diction this statement has a familiar ring to the modern
ear. The phrases in italics alone are sufficient to suggest its proper
order and place in contemporary thought. For if this is not the
exact voice of Henri Bergson, it is at least a very successful imitation. Dropped so casually by Mrs. Woolf in the course of a dis-
sertation on the art of fiction, such a statement really implies an
acceptance of a whole theory of metaphysics. Behind it lies all
that resistance to the naturalistic formula, all that enthusiastic
surrender to the world of flux and individual intuition, which has
constituted the influence of Bergson on the art and literature of
the past thirty years. Whether Mrs. Woolf was affected by this
influence directly, or through the medium of Proust or some other
secondary source, is not very important. The evidence is clear
enough in her work that the fundamental view of reality on
which it is based derives from what was the most popular ideology
of her generation. What is so often regarded as unique in her
fiction is actually less the result of an individual attitude than of
the dominant metaphysical bias of a whole generation.

For members of that generation concerned with fiction the
philosophy of flux and intuition offered a relief from the cumber-
some technique and mechanical pattern of naturalism. (Against

even such mild adherents to the doctrine as Wells and Bennett Mrs. Woolf raised the attack in *Mr. Bennett and Mrs. Brown.*) Moreover, the new philosophy opened up sources of interest for the novel which allowed it to dispense with whatever values such writers as George Eliot and Henry James had depended on in a still remoter period. Like naturalism, it brought with it its own version of an esthetic; it supplied a medium which involved no values other than the primary one of self-expression. Of course one cannot wholly ignore the helpful cooperation of psychoanalysis. But to distinguish between the metaphysical and the psychological origins of the new techniques is not a profitable task. It is not difficult to understand how the subjective novel could have derived its assumptions from the one field, its method from the other. And the fusion between them had been completed by the time Mrs. Woolf published her little pamphlet. Everybody, in Rebecca West's phrase, was "doing" a novel in the period immediately following the World War. Everybody, that is to say, was writing a quasi-poetic rendition of his sensibility in a form which it was agreed should be called the novel.

Possessing a mind schooled in abstract theory, especially alert to the intellectual novelties of her own time, Mrs. Woolf was naturally attracted by a method which in addition to being contemporary offered so much to the speculative mind. But the deeper causes of the attraction, it is now evident, were embedded in Mrs. Woolf's own temperament or sensibility. The subjective mode is the only mode especially designed for temperaments immersed in their own sensibility, obsessed with its movements and vacillations, fascinated by its instability. It was the only mode possible for someone like Proust; it was alone capable of projecting the sensibility which, because it has remained so uniform throughout her work, we may be permitted to call Mrs. Woolf's own. Here it happens to be Bernard, in *The Waves,* speaking:

> A space was cleared in my mind. I saw through the thick leaves of habit. Leaning over the gate I regretted so much litter, so much unaccomplishment and separation, for one cannot cross London to see a friend, life being so full of engagements; nor

take ship to India and see a naked man spearing fish in blue water. I said life had been imperfect, an unfinished phrase. It had been impossible for me, taking snuff as I do from any bagman met in a train, to keep coherency—that sense of the generations, of women carrying red pitchers to the Nile, of the nightingale who sings among conquests and migrations . . .

But this might be almost any one of Mrs. Woolf's characters; and from such a passage we can appreciate how perfectly the subjective or "confessional" method is adapted to the particular sensibility reflected throughout her work.

And if we require in turn some explanation for this hieratic cultivation of the sensibility, we need only examine for a moment the nature and quality of the experience represented by most of her characters. From *The Voyage Out* to *The Waves* Mrs. Woolf has written almost exclusively about one class of people, almost, one might say, one type of individual, and that, a class or type whose experience is largely vicarious, whose contacts with actuality have been for one or another reason incomplete, unsatisfactory, or inhibited. Made up of poets, metaphysicians, botanists, water-colorists, the world of Mrs. Woolf is a kind of superior Bohemia, as acutely refined and aristocratic in its way as the world of Henry James, except that its inhabitants concentrate on their sensations and impressions rather than on their problems of conduct. (Such problems, of course, do not exist for them since they rarely allow themselves even the possibility of action.) Life for these people, therefore, is painful less for what it has done to them than for what their excessive sensitivity causes them to make of it. Almost every one of them is the victim of some vast and inarticulate fixation: Mrs. Dalloway on Peter Walsh, Lily Briscoe in *To the Lighthouse* on Mrs. Ramsay, everyone in *The Waves* on Percival. All of them, like Neville in the last-named book, are listening for "that wild hunting-song, Percival's music." For all of them what Percival represents is something lost or denied, something which must remain forever outside the intense circle of their own renunciation. No consolation is left them but solitude, a timeless solitude in which to descend to a kind of self-induced nirvana. "Heaven be praised for solitude!" cries Bernard toward the close of *The Waves*. "Heaven be praised for solitude that has removed the pressure of the eye, the solicitation of the body, and all need of lies and phrases." Through solitude these people are able to relieve themselves with finality from the responsibilities of living, they are able to complete their divorce from reality even to the extent of escaping the burden of personality. Nothing in Mrs. Woolf's work serves as a better revelation of her characters as a whole than these ruminations of Mrs. Ramsay in *To the Lighthouse*:

> To be silent; to be alone. All the being and the doing, expansive, glittering, vocal, evaporated; and one shrunk, with a sense of solemnity, to being oneself, a wedge-shaped core of darkness . . . When life sank down for a moment, *the range of experience seemed limitless*. . . . Losing personality, one lost the fret, the hurry, the stir; and there rose to her lips always some exclamation of triumph over life when things came together in this peace, this rest, this eternity . . .

What Mrs. Ramsay really means to say is that when life sinks down in this manner the range of *implicit* experience is limitless. Once one has abandoned the effort to act upon reality, either with the will or the intellect, the mind is permitted to wander in freedom through the stored treasures of its memories and impressions, following no course but that of fancy or simple association, murmuring Pillicock sat on Pillicock's Hill or Come away, come away, Death, "mingling poetry and nonsense, floating in the stream." But experience in this sense is something quite different from experience in the sense in which it is ordinarily understood in referring to people in life or in books. It does not involve that active impact of character upon reality which provides the objective materials of experience in both literature and life. And if it leads to its own peculiar triumphs, it does so only through a dread of being and doing, an abdication of personality and a shrinking into the solitary darkness.

Because of this self-imposed limitation of their experience, therefore, the characters of Mrs. Woolf are unable to *function* anywhere but on the single plane of the sensibility. On this plane alone is enacted whatever movement, drama, or tragedy occurs in her works. The movement of course is centrifugal, the drama unrealized, the tragedy hushed. The only truly dramatic moments in these novels are, significantly enough, precisely those in which the characters seem now and again to catch a single, brief glimpse of that imposing world of fact which they have forsworn. The scenes we remember best are those like the one in *Mrs. Dalloway* in which the heroine, bright, excited, and happy among the guests at her party, is brought suddenly face to face with the fact of death. Or like the extremely moving one at the end of *To the Lighthouse* in which Lily Briscoe at last breaks into tears and cries aloud the hallowed name of Mrs. Ramsay. In such scenes Mrs. Woolf is excellent; no living novelist can translate these nuances of perception in quite the same way; and their effect in her work is of an occasional transitory rift in that diaphanous "envelope" with which she surrounds her characters from beginning to end.

For the novelist of sensibility the most embarrassing of all problems, of course, has been the problem of form. From Richardson to Mrs. Woolf it has been the problem of how to reconcile something that is immeasurable, which is what experience as *feeling* very soon becomes, with something that is measured and defined, which has remained perhaps our most elementary conception of art. In the eighteenth century the impulse toward reconciliation was undoubtedly less acute than it has become today: Richardson and Sterne were working in a medium which did not yet make serious pretensions to being opposed to poetry and drama as a distinct form. There was not yet a Flaubert or a Tolstoy, a Turgenev or a Henry James. Feeling was enough; and feeling was allowed to expand in volumes whose uncontrollable bulk was an eloquent demonstration of its immeasurability. But when at the turn of the present century, under distinguished philosophical auspices, feeling was restored to the novel, when the sensibility finally triumphed over the floundering nineteenth-

century Reason, no such artistic insouciance was possible for anyone at all conscious of the literary tradition. In Proust we see
the attempt to achieve form on a large scale through the substitution of a purely metaphysical system for the various collaps-
ing frameworks of values—religious, ethical, and scientific—on
which the fiction of the nineteenth century had depended. In
Joyce it is through a substitution of quite a different kind, that
of a particular myth from the remote literary past, that the effort
is made to endow the treasures of the sensibility with something
like the *integritas* of the classical estheticians. And in the case of
Mrs. Woolf, who is in this respect representative of most of the
followers of these two great contemporary exemplars, the pursuit
of an adequate form has been a strenuous one from first to last.

In her earliest two books, to be sure, this strain is not too
clearly apparent. But *The Voyage Out*, although an interesting
novel in many respects, is notably deficient in what we usually
designate as narrative appeal. In retrospect the excellence of the
dialogue, the skill with social comedy, the objective portraiture
of character—all traditional elements which Mrs. Woolf has since
chosen to discard—seem remarkable. But already one can observe
a failure or reluctance to project character through a progressive
representation of motives, which provides the structure in such
a novelist as Jane Austen, for example, whom Mrs. Woolf happens to resemble most in this novel. For an ordered pattern of
action unfolding in time Mrs. Woolf substitutes a kind of spatial
unity (the setting is a yacht at sea and later a Portuguese hotel),
a cadre, so to speak, within which everything—characters, scenes,
and ideas—tends to remain fixed and self-contained. This would
be an altogether true description if it were not for the promise of
some larger development in the love affair that emerges at the
end. But even here, in Mrs. Woolf's first novel, no fulfillment is
allowed; death is invoked; death supplies a termination which
might not otherwise be reached, since none is inherent in the
plan. *Night and Day* represents an effort to write a novel on a
thoroughly conventional model, and the result is so uncertain
that we can understand the rather sudden turning to a newer

method. It is as if Mrs. Woolf had persuaded herself by these experiments (how consciously we may judge from her essay *Mr. Bennett and Mrs. Brown*) that her view of personality did not at all coincide with the formal requirements of the conventional novel. Of course she was not alone in this discovery, for there already existed the rudiments of a new tradition, whose main tendency was to dispense with form for the sake of an intensive exploitation of method.

Despite the number of artists in every field who assume that an innovation in method entails a corresponding achievement in form, method cannot be regarded as quite the same thing as form. For the novelist all that we can mean by method is embraced in the familiar phrase "the point of view." As his object is character, his only method can be that by which he endeavors to attain to a complete grasp and understanding of that object. "Method" in fiction narrows down to nothing more or less than the selection of a point of view from which character may be studied and presented. The drastic shift in the point of view for which Henry James prepared English fiction has undeniably resulted in many noticeable effects in its form or structure. But it is not yet possible to declare that it has resulted in any *new* form. Dorothy Richardson, in the opening volume of *Pilgrimage*, was among the first to apply this new method, but in none of the volumes which followed has she allied it to anything like a consistent form. What Mrs. Woolf absorbed from Miss Richardson, from May Sinclair, and from James Joyce, all of whom had advanced its use before 1918, was therefore only method, and not form. In the collection of sketches called *Monday or Tuesday* Mrs. Woolf definitely announced her affiliation with the new tradition. But such pieces as "Kew Gardens" and "The Mark on the Wall" were so slight in scope that they could make their appeal (like the essays of Lamb, for example) without the aid of any formal order or plan. Not until *Jacob's Room* does Mrs. Woolf attempt to use the method at any length, and in this book, with which her larger reputation began, we can first perceive the nature of the problem suggested by her work.

In one sense, the structure of *Jacob's Room* is that of the simplest form known to storytelling—the chronicle. From its intense pages one is able to detach a bare continuity of events: Jacob goes to the seashore, to Cambridge, to Greece, to the War. But what his creator is manifestly concerned with is not the relation of these events to his character, but their relation to his sensibility. The latter is projected through a poetic rendering of the dreams, desires, fantasies, and enthusiasms which pass through his brain. The rendering is poetic because it is managed entirely by images, certain of which are recurrent throughout—the sheep's jaw with yellow teeth, "the moors and Byron," Greece. The theme also would seem to be a kind of poetic contrast between the outward passage of events and the permanence of a certain set of images in the mind. It happens that there is enough progression of outward events to give the book about as much movement as any other biographical (or autobiographical) chronicle. But one cannot point to any similar movement, any principle of progressive unity in the revelation of all that implicit life of the hero which makes up the substance of the book. As a sensibility Jacob remains the same throughout; he reacts in an identical fashion to the successive phenomena of his experience. Since he reacts only through his sensibility, since he does not act directly upon experience, he fails to "develop," in the sense in which characters in fiction usually develop. Instead of acting, he responds, and when death puts an end to his response, the book also comes to an end. "What am I to do with these?" his mother asks at the close, holding up an old pair of shoes, and this bit of romantic pathos is all the significance which his rich accumulation of dreams and suffering is made to assume in our minds.

In *Mrs. Dalloway* there is a much more deliberate use of recurrent images to identify the consciousness of each of the characters. The effort is not toward an integration of these images, for that would amount to something which is opposed to Mrs. Woolf's whole view of personality. It is toward no more than the emphasis of a certain rhythm in consciousness, which is obviously intended to supply a corresponding rhythm to the book as a whole. Moreover, in this work use is made for the first time of an enlarged image, a symbol that is fixed, constant, and wholly outside the time world of the characters. The symbol of Big Ben, since it sets the contrast between physical time and the measureless duration of the characters' inner life, serves as a sort of standard or center of reference. But neither of these devices, it should be realized, has anything directly to do with the organization of character: rhythm, the rhythm of images in the consciousness, is not the same thing as an order of the personality; the symbol of Big Ben is no real center because it exists outside the characters, is set up in contrast with them. By means of these devices carried over from lyric poetry, a kind of unity is achieved which is merely superficial or decorative, corresponding to no fundamental organization of the experience.

In her next book, however, Mrs. Woolf goes much further toward a fusion of character and design. *To the Lighthouse*, which is probably her finest performance in every respect, owes its success not least to the completeness with which the symbol chosen is identified with the will of every one of the characters. The lighthouse is the common point toward which all their desires are oriented; it is an object of attainment or fulfillment which gives direction to the movements of their thought and sensibility; and since it is thus associated with them it gives a valid unity to the whole work. Moreover, alone among Mrs. Woolf's works, *To the Lighthouse* has for its subject an action, a single definite action, "going to the lighthouse," which places it clearly in the realm of narrative. In fact, as narrative, it may be even more precisely classified as an incident. The sole objection that might be raised on esthetic grounds is whether Mrs. Woolf's method has not perhaps caused her to extend her development beyond the inherent potentialities of this form. The question is whether such a narrow structure can support the weight of the material and the stress of its treatment. More relevant to the present question, however, is the consideration that so much of the success of the book rests on the unusually happy choice of symbol, one that is very specially adapted to the theme, and not likely to be used soon again. Not many more such symbols occur to the imagination.

Certainly Mrs. Woolf does not make use of the same kind of symbol in her next novel; for in *The Waves* she returns to the devices of rhythm and symbolical contrast on which she depended in her earlier books. (*Orlando* is not a novel, but a "biography," and has only to follow a simple chronological order. Whatever hilarious variations its author plays on the traditional concept of time do not affect her adherence to this simple order.) In *The Waves* Mrs. Woolf again presents her characters through the rhythm of images in the brain, again bases her structure on a contrast between these and a permanent symbol of the objective world. There is, first of all, the image or set of images which serves as a motif for each of the characters; for Louis, a chained beast stamping on the shore; for Bernard, the willow tree by the river; for Neville, "that wild hunting-song, Percival's music." And also there is the cumulative image of each of their lives taken as a whole, set in a parallel relationship to the movements of the sea.

Such a parallel, of course, is not an unfamiliar one. "Dwellers by the sea cannot fail to be impressed by the sight of its ceaseless ebb and flow," remarks Frazer in *The Golden Bough*, "and are apt . . . to trace a subtle relation, a secret harmony, between its tides and the life of man." What is unique is Mrs. Woolf's effort to expand what is usually no more than an intuition, a single association, a lyrical utterance to the dimensions of a novel. In one sense this is accomplished by a kind of multiplication: we are given six lyric poets instead of the usual one. For what Mrs. Woolf offers is a rendering of the subjective response to reality of six different people at successive stages in their lives. We are presented to them in childhood, adolescence, youth, early and late middle age. "*The waves broke on the shore*" is the last line in the book, and from this we are probably to assume that at the close they are all dead. Such a scheme has the order of a chronicle, of a group of parallel biographies, but Mrs. Woolf is much more ambitious. Each period in her characters' lives corresponds to a particular movement of the sea; the current of their lives at the end is likened to its "incessant rise and fall and rise and fall again." In addition, the different periods correspond to the changing position of the sun in the sky on a single day, suggesting a vision of human lives *sub specie aeternitatis.* (The ancillary images of birds, flowers, and wind intensify the same effect.) The theme is best summed up by one of the characters in a long monologue at the end: "Let us again pretend that life is a solid substance, shaped like a globe, which we turn about in our fingers. Let us pretend that we can make out a plain and logical story, so that when one matter is despatched—love, for instance—we go on, in an orderly manner to the next. I was saying there was a willow tree. Its shower of falling branches, its creased and crooked bark had the effect of what remains outside our illusions yet cannot stay them, is changed by them for the moment, yet shows through stable, still, with a sternness that our lives lack. Hence the comment it makes; the standard it supplies, the reason why, as we flow and change, it seems to measure." In conception and form, in method and style, this book is the most poetic which Mrs. Woolf has yet written. It represents the extreme culmination of the method to which she has applied herself exclusively since *Monday or Tuesday.* It is significant because it forces the question whether the form in which for her that method has resulted is not essentially opposed to the conditions of narrative art.

But this form is unmistakably that of the extended or elaborated lyric; and criticism of these novels gets down ultimately to the question with what impunity one can confuse the traditional means of one literary form with the traditional means of another. This is no place to undertake another discussion of the difference between poetry and prose—or, more particularly, the difference between the lyrical and the narrative. It is a difference which we immediately recognize, and which criticism has always rightly recognized, even when it has not been altogether certain of its explanations. The least sensible of these explanations has undoubtedly been that which would make us believe that the difference between them is *qualitative*—that poetry deals with different things from prose, with the implication that the things of poetry are of a higher order than those of prose. This is a snobbery which, fortunately in one sense, has been pretty well removed in our time, although unfortunately in another it has led to a different kind of confusion. And this is the confusion which consists in removing any *formal* distinctions between the two modes.

The objection to the lyrical method in narrative is that it renders impossible the peculiar kind of interest which the latter is designed to supply. By the lyrical method is meant the substitution of a group of symbols for the orderly working-out of a motive or a set of motives which has constituted the immemorial pattern of narrative art. Perhaps the simplest definition of symbols is that they are things used to stand for other things; and undoubtedly the most important part of such a definition is the word "stand." Whatever operations of the imagination have gone on to produce them, symbols themselves become fixed, constant, and static. They may be considered as the end-results of the effort of the imagination to fix itself somewhere in space. The symbol may be considered as something *spatial*. Symbols are thus ordinarily used in lyric poetry, where the effort is to fix ideas, sentiments, or emotions. By themselves, of course, symbols in poetry are no more than so many detached, isolated, and unrelated points in space. When projected separately, as in the poetry of the Imagist school, or in too great confusion, as in much contemporary poetry, they do not possess any necessary meaning or value to the intelligence: the worlds that they indicate are either too small or too large to live in. Moreover, whether separate or integrated into a total vision, symbols are capable of being grasped, like any other objects of space, by a single and instantaneous effort of perception. The interval of time between their presentation and our response to them is ideally no longer than the time required for our reading of a poem. Even when their presentation is like a gradual exfoliation, as in certain poems by Donne and Baudelaire, for example, that time is never allowed to be too greatly prolonged. We do not require Poe's axiom that all lyrics must be brief to understand why they must be so. The symbols on which they are constructed can be perceived in a moment of time.

When narrative based itself on a simple chronological record of action, it was assured of a certain degree of interest. When, later, it based itself on an arrangement of action which corresponded to an orderly view of life or reality, it attained to the very high interest of a work of art. As long as it based itself firmly on action according to one pattern or another, it was certain of some degree of interest. To understand the nature of the satisfaction which we seem to take in the representation of reality in a temporal order we should have to know more about certain primitive elements of our psychology than science has yet been able to discover. It is enough to recognize that whatever the reasons this satisfaction is rooted in our sense of *time*. It is enough to realize that this is the basis of the appeal which narrative has made through the whole history of fiction, from the earliest fables of the race to the most complex "constructions" of Henry James. For this reason, for example, description has always occupied a most uncertain place in fiction. Description, which deals with things rather than events, interposes a space world in the march of that time world which is the subject of fiction. For this reason the use of poetic symbols in fiction, as in all Mrs. Woolf's work since *Monday or Tuesday*, seems to be in direct contradiction to the foundations of our response to that form.

Because it is in an almost continuous state of moral and intellectual relaxation that Mrs. Woolf's characters draw out their existence, they can be projected only through a more or less direct transcription of their consciousness. Such a qualification is necessary, however, for the method here is rarely if ever as direct as that of Joyce or his followers. Between the consciousness and the rendition of it there is nearly always interposed a highly artificial literary style. This style remains practically uniform for all the characters; it is at once individual and traditional. The effect of its elegant diction and elaborately turned periods is to make one feel at times as if these sad and lonely people were partly com-

pensated for the vacuity of their lives by the gift of casting even
their most random thoughts in the best literary tradition. For
some of them, like Bernard in *The Waves* (or is it the author
herself speaking?), language is more than a compensation; it has
an absolute value in itself: "A good phrase, however, seems to
me to have an independent existence." Others may go to religion,
to art, to friendship, but Mrs. Woolf's people more often than
not go "to seek among phrases and fragments something unbroken." It is as if they seek to net the world of time and change
with a phrase, to retrieve the chaos with words. For this reason
the presentation of character by Mrs. Woolf gets down finally
to a problem of style, to the most beautiful arrangement of beautiful words and phrases.

Here also Mrs. Woolf is pre-eminently the poet; for as an un-
willingness to use motives and actions led to her substitution of
poetic symbols in their stead, so is she also compelled to use a
metaphorical rather than a narrative style. In this practice of
course she is not without precedent; other novelists have relied
on metaphor to secure their finest effects of communication. But
while such effects are ordinarily used to heighten the narrative,
they are never extended to the point where they assume an independent interest. In Mrs. Woolf's books metaphorical writing
is not occasional but predominant; from the beginning it has
subordinated every other kind; and it was inevitable that it should
one day be segmented into the purely descriptive prose-poems of
The Waves.

No sooner is the essentially poetic character of this writing admitted than one is confronted with the whole host of problems
associated with the general problem of imagery in poetry. It happens, however, that the peculiar use of imagery in Mrs. Woolf's
prose suggests among other things a particular distinction, and
one which has not been often enough made, although it was recognized by both Coleridge and Baudelaire, a distinction between
two kinds of sensibility.

Of the two kinds of sensibility that we can identify in examin-
ing works of poetry the first would seem to be incapable of re-

ceiving impressions except through the prism of an already acquired set of language symbols. It is as if poets with this type of sensibility are uncontrollably *determined* in the kind of response they can make to reality. And because they are so determined in their initial response they are determined also in their manner of expression. The original language-symbols, acquired through culture, training, or unconscious immersion in some tradition, are infinitely perpetuated in their writing. At its worst such writing is anemic and invertebrate, like the minor verse of any period or like the earlier work of many excellent poets. In such verse the language gives the effect of having occasioned the feeling more often than the feeling the language. At its most sophisticated, however, this verse is capable of achieving a certain superficial quality of distinction all its own. It is a quality of distinction undoubtedly made possible by the reduced effort to discover precise images to convey very definite and particular sensations or emotions. It may consist in the pure musicalization of language through the draining of all specific content from the imagery that we find in Mallarmé or (on a lower plane) in Swinburne. Or it may consist in that plastic manipulation of surfaces which is another department of the interesting verse of any period. The effect in either case is the same, that of a resuscitation rather than a re-creation of language.

The other type of sensibility, of course, is in the habit of receiving direct impressions, of forming images which possess the freshness, uniqueness, and body of the original object. It has the faculty of creating new language-symbols to convey what it has perceived or, as sometimes happens, of re-creating traditional symbols with enough force to make them serve again. (For used symbols are capable of being recharged, so to speak, under the pressure of the new emotion they are called upon to convey.) Only when the original perception is solid and clear is it able to crystallize into images capable of transmitting emotion; and only when the emotion is adequate are these images capable of creating or re-creating language. The difference is between language which is made its own object and language which is made to realize emotion by evoking particular objects of concrete experience. It is the difference between writing which secures a certain effectiveness through being recognizable in a particular tradition and writing which is an exact verbal equivalent for a precise emotion or set of emotions. It is the difference, among the writers of our time, between Sara Teasdale and Marianne Moore, or between Thomas Wolfe and Stephen Crane. And in the most characteristic lines of the best writers of any time it is this latter kind of sensibility that we can see at work. We see it in Antony's rebuke to Cleopatra:

> I found you as a morsel, cold upon
> Dead Caesar's trencher

or in Baudelaire's

> J'ai cherché dans l'amour un sommeil oublieux;
> Mais l'amour n'est pour moi qu'un matelas d'aiguilles *

or in Yeats's

> I pace upon the battlements and stare
> On the foundations of a house, or where
> Tree, like a sooty finger, starts from the earth.†

In prose fiction, when the language approaches the precision and density of poetry, it is a result of the same necessity on the part of author or character, under stress of exceptional feeling, to seize upon his experience for the particular image or images necessary to express his state. The only difference is that the images of fiction are likely to be less remote, less "difficult" perhaps, than those of poetry. And the reason of course is that the images are likely to arise out of the immediate background of the novel. No better example of this can be offered than in the speech

* From "La Fontaine de Sang," *Les Fleurs du Mal*, cxviii.
† From "The Tower," *Variorum Edition of the Poems of W. B. Yeats*, New York, Macmillan, 1957.

in *Wuthering Heights* in which Catherine, in her delirium, shakes the feathers out of her pillow:

> That's a turkey's . . . and this is a wild duck's; and this is a pigeon's. Ah, they put pigeons' feathers in the pillows—no wonder I couldn't die! . . . And here is a moor-cock's; and this—I should know it among a thousand—it's a lapwing's. Bonny bird; wheeling over our heads in the middle of the moor. It wanted to get to its nest, for the clouds had touched the swells, and it felt rain coming.

In Mrs. Woolf's novels, as replete with imagery as they are, the effect is never quite the same as in this passage from Emily Brontë. The images that pass through her characters' minds are rarely seized from any *particular* background of concrete experience. There are few of them which we have not encountered somewhere before. They belong not so much to the particular character as to the general tradition of literature. The effect is of an insidious infiltration of tradition into the sensibility. And this effect is the same whether it is a straight description by the author, as in *To the Lighthouse*:

> The autumn trees, ravaged as they are, take on the flash of tattered flags kindling in the gloom of cool cathedral caves where gold letters on marble pages describe death in battle and how bones bleach and burn far away on Indian sands. The autumn trees gleam in the yellow moonlight, in the light of harvest moons, the light which mellows the energy of labour, and smooths the stubble, and brings the wave lapping blue to the shore.

or a presentation of mood, as in *Mrs. Dalloway*:

> Fear no more, says the heart. Fear no more, says the heart, committing its burden to some sea, which sighs collectively for all sorrows, and renews, begins, collects, lets fall. And the body alone listens to the passing bee; the wave breaking; the dog barking, far away barking and barking.

or a translation of ecstasy, as in *The Waves:*

> Now tonight, my body rises tier upon tier like some cool temple
> whose floor is strewn with carpets and murmurs rise and the
> altars stand smoking; but up above, here in my serene head,
> come only fine gusts of melody, waves of incense, while the
> lost dove wails, and the banners tremble above tombs, and the
> dark airs of midnight shake trees outside the open windows.

From such examples it should be apparent to what extent the
sensibility here is haunted by the word symbols of the past. The
consciousness of each of these characters is a Sargasso Sea of
words, phrases, broken relics of poetry and song. The phrases
which rise to the surface are like bright shells resonant with the
accumulated echoes of their past histories. Some of them have
the familiar charm of cherished heirlooms; only a few retain completely whatever power to stir the imagination they may once
have had. Almost all of them depend for their effect on their
associations to the cultivated mind rather than on their ability to
evoke the fullness and immediacy of concrete experience. And
the reason of course is that there is insufficient experience of this
sort anywhere reflected in the course of Mrs. Woolf's work.

It is also clear in such passages how Mrs. Woolf has come more
and more to cultivate language for its own sake, to seek in phrases
some "independent existence" which will give them an absolute
beauty in themselves. But detached from experience as they are
they attain to no more substantial beauty than that of a charming
virtuosity of style. It is not the beauty but the cleverness of Mrs.
Woolf's writing which is responsible for the final effect on the
reader. "No woman before Virginia Woolf has used our language
with such easy authority," wrote the late Sara Teasdale. Indeed
few writers of either sex have written English with the same
mastery of traditional resources, the same calculated effectiveness,
the same facility. And when this facile traditionalism is allied
with an appropriate subject, as in a frank burlesque like *Orlando,*
the result is truly brilliant. It is only when it is used as the vehicle
for significant, serious thoughts and emotions, as in the larger

portion of Mrs. Woolf's work, that its charm seems false, its authority invalid, and its beauty sterile.

It is only fair to point out what would seem to be a sincere self-questioning in the long monologue at the end of *The Waves*. Bernard, the inveterate phrasemonger, recalling the scene in which he and his friends first heard of Percival's death, remembers that they had compared him to a lily. "So the sincerity of the moment passed," Bernard cries, "so it had become symbolical; and that I could not stand. Let us commit any blasphemy of laughter and criticism rather than exude this lily-sweet glue; and cover him over with phrases." Perhaps it is too much to read into this lapse into sincerity on the part of a single character a confession of dissatisfaction by the author with the kind of language that she has been using all along in her work. But while such an interpretation may be too eager there is at least the implication that she is aware that reality when it is encountered is something far too important to be covered over with beautiful phrases. The vague hope is thrown out that in her later work she may finally be tempted to give us Percival himself, that she may spare him from death and allow him a more solid existence than he ever enjoyed in the minds and memories of his friends.

But no sooner is this idea expressed than one is reminded of the profound changes that would have to happen in Mrs. Woolf's whole metaphysical outlook before any such hope could be realized. For every element of her work that we have considered—her form, her method of characterization, her style even—is affected at its root by the same fundamental view of personality. These elements of form and of style can hardly be expected to change as long as the view which determines them remains unchanged. And nothing in Mrs. Woolf's recent work, it must be admitted, justifies the belief that this view is likely to be changed in the near future.

[*1937*]

By this time so little that is fundamental remains to be said of the merits or limitations of Mrs. Woolf's narrative method that a review of her novel *The Years*, which is a reshuffling of elements already familiar to all readers of her work, is doomed to the same sort of repetitiousness from which that work itself has for some time suffered. Her admirers, writing in a style too suspiciously like her own to be altogether convincing, will revive the phrases about the beauty and the distinction and the ultimate truth to life of everything that Mrs. Woolf has written. And a few others, still disturbed by the persistence of these claims, will take the trouble to point out that each of them is capable of a little more exact definition—particularly the reference to the truth about life. They will doubtless protest that what we probably get in these distinguished novels is not so much life as a special vision of a special kind of life—a vision, moreover, that has been largely created, nurtured, and corroborated by the conditions of this life. "We receive but what we give," in Coleridge's well-known formula; and if Mrs. Woolf's impression of the years is what it is, it may be only because she has superimposed on them an impression that was, in the first place, the kind of impression that the Ramsays, the Pargiters, and the rest were forced to draw from their own experience. From this maddening shuttle of cause and effect, the rankest of determinisms, we are never released through that vigorous act of imagination by which the writer attempts to transcend the limiting conditions of his materials: the deep voice of Coleridge mumbling of the fusion of "*sum*ject" and "*oom*ject" is stilled like everything else by the resounding waters of time. So also in the set pieces of beautiful writing—precisely distributed here at the beginning of each of those divisions by which the immeasurable is arbitrarily measured—what we get thrown back at us, in this charming evocation of a summer day, this clever impersonation of a March wind, are images and words and phrases so hoarily incrusted in the characters' collective consciousness that nothing really fresh is added to our perception. And it is undoubtedly the total effect of language of this sort that is referred to by the somewhat vague term, distinction. It is now apparent that final evaluation of Mrs. Woolf's work must revolve monotonously around the question of the experience and the attitude toward experience of her typical characters. This is a standard imposed by her faithful refusal to oppose any attitude of her own by which we can measure them within the perspective of her work. And it is, needless to say, a standard that cannot be very successfully applied beyond a certain point. Either these people will be found to glow with a still potent charm of well-bred sensitivity or they will emit a most unpleasant smell as of something already quite dead and decayed.

All that is perhaps necessary in this review, therefore, is to consider the reshuffling that has taken place in the light of its possible consequences on the theme. For the book is of course another celebration of the flux, another slow passage down the most traversed river in modern fiction, another extended prose gloss on *Eheu! fugaces labuntur anni*. But where in *Jacob's Room* and *Orlando* the theme was rendered in terms of a single individual, and where in *Mrs. Dalloway* and *To the Lighthouse* the period covered was relatively short, we have here a chronicle of a whole typical middle-class English family, with their accumulating host of relatives and friends, from 1880 to the present. Such distinctions should not, however, be stressed too much; for in *The Waves* also Mrs. Woolf was concerned with tracing the destinies of a group of people over the whole course of their lives. The great difference would be that for the first time she is trying to maintain something like a balance between the outer and the inner reality, between the public and the personal, between the mechanical ticking of Big Ben and the sound of time's passing in the mind's ear. In this effort she has returned somewhat to the form and style of her very earliest novels; she has adopted a simple chronological order; and she has practically put a stop to the direction which reached its climax in *The Waves*.

The most immediate changes to be observed will be in fact the reduction of those prolonged subjective improvisations that have been so much admired in all Mrs. Woolf's more recent novels. From another point of view of course, this shift to a neater, more rapid, less mannered style will be welcomed. It promises, at least at the beginning, a corresponding modification of other important things—most notably the conception of human character as little more than a highly sensitized instrument for registering impressions. But this is unfortunately a promise that recedes in exact proportion to the characters' uniform failure, through the unfolding years, to exhibit anything resembling moral progress. Time goes on and on, but the Edwards, the Delias, the Eleanors, and the Kittys retain the same niceties, the same frustrations, the same terror of existence with which they began. All suffer from a malady of will that makes them as inappropriate to the purposes of fiction as to the bustle and dirt of the London streets.

Of all the symbolical scenes in the book none is more symbolical than the one in which a member of the Pargiter clan, looking out from the tastefully furnished room in the slums which she shares with her sister, is made to exclaim: "In time to come . . . people, looking into this room—this cave, this little antre, scooped out of mud and dung, will hold their fingers to their noses"—she held her fingers to her nose—"and say, 'Pah! They stink!'" With characters possessing such a view of themselves, Mrs. Woolf is hardly able to do very much that she has not already done, with consummate perfection, in the past. The present book merely throws into new relief the fact that no expansion of scale, no experimentation with method can lend meaning and significance where neither is implicit in the experience. It seems more than ever unlikely that Mrs. Woolf's talents, which are considerable in so many different departments of fiction, will develop to their full measure while she persists in limiting herself to purely formal variations on the same old dirgelike tune.

[1952]

Much of this scrutiny, especially the first section, written some twenty years ago, will inevitably seem dated to most readers today. Since her tragic death Mrs. Woolf's work has found its own secure and appropriate place in the literature of our time. That place has turned out to be neither so small nor so inconsequential as the prevailing tone here tends to predict, nor is it so large as certain of her admirers and imitators in the twenties hoped that it would become. Here again Time, of which no one in her generation in England was more painfully conscious, has altered or at least tempered literary judgment along with everything else. Time has established the balance.

For the pert severity of most of the objections to Mrs. Woolf's novels the only excuse that can be made, apart from the stock and always irrelevant one of youth, is that they did at the time seem to represent a kind of facile emotionalism and moral attenuation that could spell no good for the novel as a developing art form. But whatever threat they may have offered has long since disappeared; and, as a matter of fact, we are actually inclined to turn back with a certain nostalgia to those very qualities of delicacy and elegance at which we took offense and which have now, alas, almost universally departed from the novel. For example, it now seems undoubtedly a mistake to have raised the hackneyed charge of sterility, to make the frequent confusion between a writer's world and his treatment of it, to assume that because a writer chooses to write about so-called sterile people his own work is thereby necessarily sterile. In rereading the best of Mrs. Woolf's novels, one is today more likely to be impressed by the underlying vigor and zest about the whole essential business of human experience, amounting at moments to ecstasy, as in the closing lines of *To the Lighthouse* when Lily Briscoe turns to the canvas upon which she has been working throughout the book.

> There it was—her picture. Yes, with all its greens and blues, its lines running up and across, its attempt at something. It

would be hung in the attics, she thought; it would be destroyed. But what did that matter? she asked herself, taking up her brush again. She looked at the steps; they were empty; she looked at her canvas; it was blurred. With a sudden intensity, as if she saw it clear for a second, she drew a line there, in the centre. It was done; it was finished. Yes, she thought, laying down her brush in extreme fatigue, I have had my vision.

Yes, we now can recognize that Mrs. Woolf too had her vision, too narrow or special perhaps for most of us to share with patience and sympathy, but her own and authentic. And all that matters is the high and exquisite art by which she was able to render it.

Stephen Dedalus and James Joyce

[1934]

To say that undoubtedly the greatest advantage of having *Ulysses* on public sale in this country is that it enables more people to read the book is not such an obvious statement as it may at first sound. For Joyce's masterpiece, although it has certainly been the most reviled, the most admired, and the most generally discussed work of our generation, has been at the same time one of the least read—in the sense of a patient, conscientious, and thoughtful examination of its contents. Of course there has never been any reason to expect that it would be widely read by the popular reading public: it makes too many demands on the intellect, the sensibility, and the experience of the average reader. Nor will all the efforts to endow it with the fascination of the occult, which seems to be the object behind the many "keys," commentaries, and esoteric interpretations that have appeared, succeed in our enlightened age in earning for it the kind of reputation which the golden book of Vergil enjoyed in the Middle Ages. And even as an intellectual game, a substitute for the crossword puzzle, the book must remain an exercise for more or less superior wits. One does not refer, therefore, either to the so-called plain reader or to his guides in expressing the belief that *Ulysses* has not been as carefully studied as it might have been in the twelve years since its publication. The reference is rather to the number of serious and informed critics all during that period who have concentrated on one or another separate aspect of the work without attempting to weigh for us the meaning or final implications of the work as a whole.

The most common confusion into which discussion of the work has fallen is the result of the failure to distinguish between Stephen Dedalus, who is one of its three principal characters, and James Joyce, who is its author. It is a confusion that is not very difficult to understand; for Stephen Dedalus is not only one of the most perfectly realized characters in modern fiction but also the character with whom the modern reader can most easily identify himself. The influence of Joyce on other writers, for example, has been almost exclusively the influence of the character of Stephen Dedalus, and not of the characters of Leopold and Molly Bloom, although these two characters are certainly of equal importance in the structure of his work. In other words, the modern writer, finding in the mental and psychological state of Stephen as rendered by Joyce such a precise duplicate of his own, has been quick to assume that this must also be the permanent mental and psychological state of his creator. It has been too seldom recognized that quite apart from whatever special interest he may have as the Hamlet *de nos jours*, Stephen is one character among others in an objectively constructed work of fiction; that he is only a part of a whole, and not the whole itself; and even that whatever development of his character occurs is necessarily subordinate to the total development of the work. Now it need hardly be remarked that if a few of the many imitators of Joyce's style and method had shown some awareness of this fact we should probably have been spared that chaotic and artistically meaningless overflow of sensibility which has passed for fiction in recent years. But the point at present is that the failure to recognize *Ulysses* for what it is—perhaps the most objective work of fiction ever created, a work about which it is impossible to say that it is written in such and such a style, since it is written in as many styles as there are characters and situations to be rendered—is what is most responsible for the habit of ascribing to its author a psychology and point of view which really belong to one of his characters *at a certain stage in his development.*

This confusion has most recently reasserted itself in the concerted effort on the part of several American critics to bury Joyce, along with the other major writers of his generation, in the interests of a strictly contemporary view of the artist and his relation to the society of his time. According to these critics Joyce is no longer eligible as a "guide" for contemporary writers. Like Baudelaire, Henry James, Sarah Orne Jewett, Hermann Melville, Lewis Carroll, and almost every other writer of the last few centuries whose name comes to mind, Joyce declined to participate in the social and economic struggles of his age, preferring to express the personality which this age had molded in the terms of an obscure and aristocratic art. In Joyce's case the refusal to engage in action, or in that form of action which is called propaganda, was particularly obdurate in view of the unusual opportunities which his country offered. "How much have we lost because Stephen drew back from the revolution that attracted him?" we are asked to contemplate. How much have we lost because he indulged the trinity of personality vices which an analysis of his temperament reveals—"pride, contempt, ambition"? If we can no longer admire the artist whose work has been motivated by these essentially individualistic vices, it is because our whole notion of the artist's role in society has undergone a profound change. The tradition to which Joyce must be assigned is the nineteenth-century tradition, which believed not only that the artist was a privileged member of society, immune from all moral and social responsibility, but also that he was the high priest of a cult or religion—the religion of art. In rejecting this tradition we must reject Joyce—or at least we must reject him if we accept the picture that has just been given, which is the picture drawn for us by the ultra-Marxist wing of recent American criticism.

But it may be that we need not accept such a picture as a true picture of the author of *Ulysses*, although as a picture of Stephen Dedalus there is little in it to which we might object. What is not taken into account in such an analysis, of course, is the fact that the "morbid-minded aesthete and embryo philosopher" of the morning, afternoon, and evening of June 16, 1904, is not, and could not be, the author of the mature, harmonious, and extraordinarily robust work of art that is *Ulysses*. It takes no account of the important spiritual progression that has taken place in Stephen's consciousness on this momentous day—a progression which reaches its climax in one of the three great moments of inner dramatic crisis in the work.

For each of the three major characters there is such a moment of intense psychological crisis, marking the most extreme degree of anguish and confusion to which the gradually accumulated conflicts of each of them attain. If Stephen's crisis is the first that is presented to us, it is because his particular conflicts have been raging with intolerable force all day and because the structure requires that this crisis be over with before the theme can be advanced to its resolution. As everyone who has studied the work knows, Stephen's long agony reaches its climax at that moment in the celebrated scene in Bella Cohen's brothel (page 567 in the present edition * of the text) when he turns from the women around him, brushes away the persistent ghost of his mother, and screams out the single word "*Nothung!*"

> He lifts his ashplant high with both hands and smashes the chandelier. Time's livid final flame leaps and, in the following darkness, ruin of all space, shattered glass and toppling masonry.

This gesture that Stephen makes marks not only an end but a beginning. It symbolizes his exorcism of the past: the images in which the ideals of race, religion, and education have clothed themselves will never again appear to haunt him. Although he will never be altogether free from "history," history will no longer be the nightmare that it has been for him. Not only has his center of gravity been displaced, as he remarks a little while afterwards, but it will never be the same again. And for this reason we may say that at this moment Stephen Dedalus, as we have known him up to this scene, vanishes from existence, and the author of

* New York, Random House, 1934.

Ulysses is born. Or, if we persist in referring to them as one and the same person, we may say that whatever Stephen Dedalus produces thereafter must come out of a different world, a world of brighter and more tangible human substance, in which the tired ghosts of Aristotle and Aquinas will have to make room for Leopold and Molly Bloom.

For *Ulysses* does not end with that gesture with which Stephen seems to smash to earth not only the chandelier in a Dublin brothel but also the whole unsteady weight of Western European culture that has been bearing down on his brain. He has yet to have his encounter with Leopold Bloom, an encounter that is to lead to his attainment of a new and different state of grace from that he had enjoyed in the far-off days of the *Portrait*. He has yet to acquire that richness of perception and understanding which will enable him to write the last glowing pages of Molly Bloom's monologue, with which, finally, the book does come to its end. If we desire to seek the real meaning of Stephen's career, therefore, it is to these last pages that we must turn—not to those sections in which he has traced out his tortured and difficult evolution as an artist, but to his final magnificent reassertion, in the terms of the most objective art, of the ultimate triumph of reality over whatever ideas or systems of ideas the mind may attempt to impose on it.

The last word on the last page of this book of almost eight hundred pages is Molly's word "Yes," and because it is the last word in the book we may feel secure in believing that it is also Joyce's last word as a man and as an artist. To identify Joyce with the backward-moving direction in modern letters, to align him with the party of sterility and death, can only seem, therefore, a grievous blunder on the part of those interested in the creation of a society which will not perpetuate the conditions that caused Stephen Dedalus to live out his life in "silence, exile, and cunning." For out of his pride and contempt and ambition, Joyce has given us a work which leaves us, at the end, with a still passionate faith and trust in the reality which even societies must keep in mind if they are to survive.

Notes on *Finnegans Wake*

[*1939*]

Nothing could be less profitable than any attempt to offer a definitive analysis or evaluation of the new Joyce work * at the moment. It is true that sections of it have been available for fourteen years; we have had time to become accustomed to its difficult language and technique; and there have been a number of tentative exercises in exegesis and interpretation. (The best of these are still those to be found in the symposium issued by Shakespeare and Company in Paris ten years ago and recently republished in this country as *An Exagmination of James Joyce*). But the work in its entirety has been off the presses only a few weeks; it is over six hundred pages long; and it is written in an idiom that can very easily create that state of panic which the mind experiences when, to recall a phrase of Proust's, it feels itself passing beyond its own borders. This last statement is not intended to be derogatory. It means simply that the impact of the book is such as to cause an extraordinary strain on the normal equilibrium of our faculties of response. It is not altogether a joke when Joyce refers to his *"funferal"* as designed for "that ideal reader suffering from an ideal insomnia." And since few of us can answer to the requirement we must follow the admonition

---

* *Finnegans Wake*, New York, Viking, 1939.

to patience offered elsewhere in the text. What we must try to avoid is the facile and premature judgments that attended the publication of *Ulysses*, realizing that in the seventeen years that have elapsed since that event no single adequate interpretation of the central symbolism of the book has been written. Interpretation must precede evaluation; and, for several reasons that will become evident, the problems of interpretation in *Finnegans Wake* are beyond those presented by any other modern work. If we have enough confidence in the task on the basis of Joyce's other performances and of those sections of the present work that we have already learned to appreciate, we will be content to proceed for some time by what Yeats somewhere calls "little sedentary stitches."

The first and most obvious of the problems is, of course, that of communication. Here the most simple-minded explanation that can be offered is that Joyce is reducing language to "pure music." It is undoubtedly true that the musical effectiveness of the style is quite overwhelming; there is nothing like it in contemporary writing. To hear portions of the work read aloud, especially if it is by Joyce in the phonographic recording he has made, is to relax all too easily into the kind of swoon induced in untrained listeners by music. But this is a danger always inherent in really successful verse, and perhaps the first point that should be made is that, if the style here is not exactly that of verse, it is something intermediate between that of verse and that of prose. It depends for its movement pretty consistently on a recognizable unit of verse structure. This is the pattern of movement established by the three-syllable foot, dactylic or anapestic, with its possibility of almost infinite variation within the line through the substitution of other shorter feet. "Latin me that, my trinity scholar, out of eure sanscreed into oure eryan." This is a line capable of being analyzed as a quite acceptable example of the rare dactylic octometer—with a cæsura after "scholard." More often than not, Joyce begins with a regular metrical beat only to drop it suddenly for an effect of surprise: "Drop me the/sound of the/findhorn's/name, Mtu or Mti, sombogger was wisness."

The first two feet are perfect dactyls, the third a spondee, and then the line seems to dissolve into prose. The predominant foot throughout the work, however, is the more lilting, caressing anapest, because of its closer correspondence to theme and subject. As Samuel Beckett points out in the symposium already mentioned, the work is "not *about* something; *it is that something itself.*" And if the anapest is used so often, it is because it is the inevitable movement for rendering the babbling and the bubbling of the "gossipaceous" Anna Livia, that is, the river of Time: "with a beck, with a spring, all her rillringlets shaking, rocks drops in her tachie, tramtokens in her hair, all waived to a point and then all inuendation."

But this is still not to give justification to the charge that Joyce has reduced language to pure sound, which is to betray an unawareness of the functional interrelationship that always exists between sound and meaning in poetry. In music the individual unit of expression, the sound, is an abstraction; form and content are indistinguishable; the *meaning* of a piece of music resides in the total organization of its separate units. But in poetry, where the individual unit of expression is the word, sound is the *medium* or vehicle of meaning. Poetry, as has often been stated, is the more difficult because the more impure of the two arts. Yet this has been its principal glory: the maintenance of a proper harmony between the sound and the meaning of words, both taken separately and in their interpenetration, has constituted the art of poetry. And we may suggest that if the "pure music" fallacy crops up here again it is because of the now almost universal incapacity to make an adequate response to poetry. What is being offered to us more and more in the name of poetry is something hardly different from the matter-of-fact type of statement about a situation that used to be limited to prose. We have forgotten that the special function of poetry is not so much to describe or explain a situation as to express an ordered emotional attitude toward the situation. Music is involved in such expression because of the still unanalyzed and probably unanalyzable effect of music on our psychology—its power of rousing, sustaining, and ordering our emotional states. It is neither an accompaniment nor a decoration; it is an imponderable part of the poem, "the thing made." And this is to say that it is inextricable from the *meaning* of the poem as a whole. These are elementary considerations; but they perhaps cannot be repeated too often in an age given over so exclusively to the situation.

In the extraordinary richness and variety of musical effect in his writing, therefore, Joyce is simply pushing to a high degree of development qualities that we find in all authentic poetry. And the same can be said of his manipulation of the content-meanings of words. Here the principal point to be made is that the poet does not use words for their past history alone. This would be indistinguishable from the manner in which the mathematical scientist assigns one fixed and immutable meaning to his symbols. From the standpoint of poetry such symbols are inert, dead, and hence inoperative. Poetic symbols consist not only in all their past histories but in whatever special modification of their meanings are involved through their use in a present context. A word, in the terminology of modern physics, is a time-space event. It is not too much to say that for the poet no word in a language is ever used twice exactly in the same way. William Empson has written a stimulating book on the subject entitled *Seven Types of Ambiguity.* An ambiguity, according to Empson, is "any consequence of language, however slight, which adds some nuance to the direct statement of prose." Of course it is an implied joke that the possible "consequences" cannot be reduced to the mystic number seven; and I. A. Richards, in *The Philosophy of Rhetoric,* demonstrates even to himself the bankruptcy of the attempt to submit imaginative expression to the quantitative method. Poetry refuses to become a branch of behaviorist psychology. And Richards is finally brought to agreement with Coleridge that in poetry language is "everywhere at its goal": you cannot separate the leaves from the tree without doing violence to the whole. (Joyce uses the identical image to indicate the organic relationship between his subject and his style.) But it may be worthwhile to look at an instance of this determination of the full meaning of a word by its place in the context in the poetry of the past:

Ram thou thy fruitful tidings in my ears,
That long time have been barren.

This is from Act II, Scene V, of *Antony and Cleopatra*, and is addressed by Cleopatra to the messenger from Antony. Everything in the scene up to this point has served to bring out the mood of febrile desperation to which Cleopatra has been reduced as a result of Antony's long absence. Yet the eighteenth-century commentator George Steevens could not believe that Shakespeare would have had Cleopatra use such a word as "ram"; he proposes "rain" as a more sensible reading. Although he was quite right in believing that there should be some connection between the main verb and the image of "fruitfulness," he was too "sensible" to appreciate the Shakespearean fondness for ambiguity. For it is of course no accident that of all the possible verbs in English denoting "press" Cleopatra should have hit upon the one that is derived from the name of the animal which is a sacred symbol of fertility. As a matter of fact, it is possible to go further and relate the association to the play as a whole, in which Antony is continually being referred to as a god and Cleopatra compared to the earth goddess Isis. And in this way the word "ram" would take on its full significance only in relation to the play as a whole.

Is such a use of language what we usually describe as punning? Several of Joyce's reviewers have been content to leave the matter at that. But there are obviously puns and puns; we say that some are pointless, some make sense. Undoubtedly, Joyce allows a certain number of the pointless variety to creep into his book—if for no other reason than that pointlessness is one of the inherent capacities of the human mind. What shall we say, however, of those words which, like Cleopatra's "ram," begin to make sense only when we relate them to other things in the work. For exam-

ple, there is the line, "My cold cher's gone Ashley." It has probably been already pointed out that "cher" makes at least three
associations in the mind: it is the name of a river at Oxford, and
its sound suggests both the French word for "flesh" and the English word for a common article of furniture. Even within the
limited context of the "Anna Livia Plurabelle" episode it is possible to establish some connections. For "Cher," like Ashley in
the same passage, is simply one of the innumerable names of the
one river that is Time; flesh is identical with earth through which
Time passes as History; and "chair" may refer either to the bank-
side on which the washer-woman is sitting or to the earth as a
whole. It would seem, then, that if this is punning it is a very
special kind of punning. And for the kind of pun that accom-
plishes a meaningful fusion between disparate things we have
the term metaphor. The important difference between the ordinary or mechanical pun and the metaphor is that where the first
is content with the purely intellectual perception of the accidental
formal resemblances between words the second is concerned not
only with more essential resemblances but with putting these
together into a new whole. The first is the work of the abstract
intellect, the second of the imagination.

In classical rhetoric the device by which a part is used for the
whole or the whole for a part is called synecdoche. This is the
device we use in common speech when we refer to a workingman
as a "hand" or to spring as the "year." Synecdoche is only one of
the devices of rhetoric; metonymy is another; and the dictionary
defines metonymy as that figure of speech in which "not the literal word but one associated with it is used; as, the 'sword' for
war." But the distinction is a rather quibbling one, for "hands"
are associated with men just as much as the sword with war. In
fact, the more closely we study these metaphorical devices the
more they break down into the single device of synecdoche. All
metaphor would seem to be an expression of the inveterate human need of coordinating experience.

Is it possible that Joyce intends not only every word but the
book itself to be an example of synecdoche? Let us look for what

clues we may discover in the title. The identification of Tim Finnegan, the Irish hod carrier, with Finn MacCool, the Irish hero, and the suggestion of a pluralized form of "again" may be related to the main subject—the resurrection of the hero. "Wake" is one of those words that have undergone a radical transformation into their opposites in the course of their usage. Derived from an Anglo-Saxon root meaning "to be born," it seems to have acquired by association the meanings "to be awake" and, by further association, "to be watchful." From the last of these meanings it came to be applied to the watch over the dead. The additional sense as the trail left behind by a ship is of independent origin. Now all five of these senses are capable of being related to the main structure of the work: H. C. Earwicker, in whose sleeping brain is retraced the whole wake of history, will rise up again like Finnegan at his wake and be born again. "Life, he himself said once . . . is a wake, livit or krikit, and on the bunk of our bread-winning lies the cropse of our seedfather."

But this is merely another striking instance of the use of a part for the whole. Of what whole might the book itself be considered a part? Joyce describes the work in a number of passages in the text—practically the whole of the fifth episode of Part I is devoted to this purpose—and refers to it by various names and phrases. It is a "vicociclometer," a "collideoscope," a "proteiform graph," a "Jeeremyhead sindbook," and a "polyhedron of scripture." But perhaps the most revealing of these "kennings" is "Meanderthale." For as the Greek river Meander wound its circuitous course through so many valleys (German, *Thal*) of the earth to the sea, the tale will finally have its ending (Latin, *talis*) with Earwicker's dream of Anna Livia (the stream of History) returning again into the sea of Time. Moreover, like the river whose substance is the ever changing distillation of the ever unchangeable elements, its substance is the ever changing and unchangeable stuff of human history. It is, in brief, the verbal equivalent of the processes that are its subject and theme; the concrete realization of the identity of time and space. But since it does possess its own being, its own ontology, it may be said to stand in relation to time-space as a part to a whole—a synecdoche. Or, shall we say, it is a kind of *Logos* of the Einsteinian vision of the universe.

According to Vico, each of the three successive ages of history had its appropriate mode of communication: in the Theocratic period, it was the Hieroglyphic; in the Heroic, the Metaphorical; and in the Civilized, the Abstract. "The language of the gods was all dumb, and very little articulate; the language of heroes was composed of equal quantities of articulation and dumbshow; the language of men was all articulated, and very little in dumbshow." By the Hieroglyphic, Vico seems to mean that before primitive men could register in speech their reactions to Nature —the thundering of the Sky-god, for example—they made use of signs and gestures—an anticipation of the school of Paget in England today. And since the visual precedes the aural image, the first recorded language is the pictograph. Now one of the features of the Joycean method that we have left unmentioned is the importance of the visual aspect of the word, its "look" on the page. Although rarely if ever does a verbal effect depend on the eye to the exclusion of the ear, he does employ punctuation, space-divisions, capitals, and other visual equivalents for aural effects. Modern language, insofar as it is set down in print, is pictorial; and part of our response to the meaning of a word is our sense of its visual image. To this extent it also is hieroglyphic.

The point is worth making because Vico believed that in the period of "the barbarism of reflection" that marked the final stage in the historical cycle language returned once again to the hieroglyphic. This is not a clean-cut stage like the others but rather one of confused transition between decadence and the emergence of real barbarism. It is the moment when the rational and the prerational function side by side with mutual indifference. In this Alexandrian interlude the scholiasts, encyclopaediasts, and other "looters" of the knowledge that has just been accumulated function side by side with the prophets of the emergent barbarism. Since Joyce includes uproarious parodies of the first (the whole second episode of Part II) and examples of the hyperbole of the second (the sixth episode of Part I), we can conclude that the style of *Finnegans Wake* is compounded of the characteristic modes of expression of all three epochs of history.

The *form* of the work is, therefore, contained in each of its parts. "In fact, under the closed eyes of the inspectors the traits featuring the *chiaroscuro* coalesce," we are told on page 107, "their contrarieties eliminated, in one stable somebody . . ." The problem of interpretation is the detection and labelling of these traits—symbols, images, motifs—and the reordering of them according to some logic of the mind. And this is a problem that is rendered almost hopelessly difficult by the very nature of the narrative method that Joyce has adopted.

It is clear that the center of everything is the dreamer, H. C. Earwicker; but while this citizen of Dublin is an individual character, highly particularized in many respects, he is also an archetype of the race. This is to say that his dream is conducted simultaneously on the two planes of the personal and the universal; and one is by no means always able to determine the exact nature of their "coalescence." This may be illustrated by the treatment of the Fall-motif, which occupies the first episode. The Fall is rendered from every one of its possible aspects. There is first of all the fall of the earth from the original Chaos: the Humpty-Dumpty ballad harks back to the most ancient cosmological myths, like that of the Orphic conception of the universe as an egg upon the waters, whose breaking was responsible for the earth and other planets. Primitive man fell from the state of animal unconsciousness when he lifted his eyes in terror to the sky and inquired the source of the thunderbolt: *Finnegans Wake* may be said properly to begin with the polylingual word for thunder on page 1. Adam fell from the state of innocence and grace when he ate of the tree of the knowledge of good and evil; and Phoenix Park takes on much of the vegetation of the Garden of Eden throughout the episode. Then there are the innumerable falls of heroes and men, which would include those of Agamemnon and of Finnegan from his ladder. All these are to be identified with Earwicker's own fall from virtue through some unworthy act in Phoenix Park one spring morning. But the exact nature of his crime is made known to us only gradually and by the most tenuous references throughout the text. In other words, the chronological method, in which effect follows upon cause, has been abandoned for what might be called the method of *simultaneity*. And it is a consequence of this method that effects may precede causes whenever they like because all that is recorded is the order of "events" in the consciousness.

For the origin and development of this particular method we can discover three distinct influences: Vico's theory of the flux and reflux of history, Jung's conception of the collective unconscious, and Einstein's theory of relativity. Several summaries of the first have already been offered; and indeed we need not look outside the work itself, which abounds with passages like the following: "a good clap, a fore marriage, a bad wake, tell hell's well; such is manowife's lot of lose and win again." The mistake, as Samuel Beckett points out, is to make too "neat identifications"; for the Viconian account of history serves as hardly more than the loosest sort of formal framework. It is comparable to the various occult and mythological machinery by which Yeats— in poems like "The Second Coming" and "The Magi"—sought to express a similar intuition of the recurrent patterns of human culture. Moreover, Joyce does not adhere literally to the order of Vico but, as we have seen in the case of the language, telescopes all the different epochs into one at every point in the work. Also the notions of the "collective unconscious" or "the Great Memory," by means of which the individual is supposed to carry around in him the mythical formations of the whole racial experience, might have been appropriated by Joyce equally well from Yeats, A. E., and certain others in the generation that preceded him in Ireland. There is, it is true, in the latter part of the work, a close application of the Jungian description of the manner in which the individual is freed from the repressions of the social self through re-identification with the symbols of myth and religion. Nothing leads us to suppose, however, that Joyce shares Jung's view that these patterns have an hereditary physical foundation. As for the contribution of modern physics, everything in the book—language, form, and theme—may be related to the Einsteinian concept of the time-space event. We tour in a "no placelike, no timelike absolent." And the work is full of such passages as this: "some saying by their Orlog it was Sygstryggs to nine, more holding with the Ryan vogt it was Dane to pfife."

After the account of the Fall just mentioned, nothing less than the whole terrain of human history lies before us. Part I is a treatment of man in his first stage of heroic fatherhood; Earwicker has heard the thunderclap—the voice of authority that is here sometimes identified with the police—and settles down to the relatively more stable life of the hearth. He has fallen from the state of grace as a result of the infamous charges that have been made against him. These are hinted at in the blasphemous "Ballad of Persse O'Reilly." It is clear that Earwicker is one with all the heroes who have ever walked the earth; the different epithets by which he has been known are listed on pages 71–72. Because with the sense of sin men ceased to copulate in the open fields but hid their shame in the caves that were the first homes, the All-Father of the race must submit to marriage. Not until this event can we say that history begins; for the woman-principle is also the time-principle. Man, the idea of Man, is no more than an eternal abstraction, which would be condemned to sterility if it did not become united with time, which is history.

In the hilarious fifth episode there is much description of a book which is at once the book that we are reading, since Earwicker is actually writing it in his sleep, and also the book of the earth—a "claybook." It would seem, however, that the author of this book is not Earwicker but one Shem the Penman, who is vilified at length in a later episode and whose career bears remarkable points of resemblance to that of Joyce himself. This is a conundrum that begins to approach solution only when we apply some of the Cabalist-Gnostic symbolism which Joyce probably acquired from Blake and which figures so largely in *Ulysses*. For here Earwicker would seem to represent Adam-Caedmon, the original and perfect man, from whose dismembered body have come the multiple phenomena of the earth. Shem is that principle of reason which is responsible for the separation of the Many from the One. If he is reviled by the Father, it is because he has preferred the consciousness of existence to existence itself, knowledge to life. He is guilty of the primal impiety. Like his biblical prototype, who was punished for looking on his father's nakedness, he is branded as a "Pariah, cannibal Cain." Because of this betrayal and irreverence, the great mother—"the turfbrown mummy"—is surging down on both of them to take them in her embrace. Because of this destruction of his original unity the First Man must take on all the innumerable forms that history will impose on him, and the episode closes with the dancing footsteps and the trilling voice of Anna Livia—the mother of heroes and men.

With the famous Anna Livia Plurabelle episode, we come to the end of what in Vico is the Theocratic period, when men were engaged in making their gods out of their readings of the universe. All the symbols here are of the elemental forces. The two washerwomen on either bank of the Liffey represent organic and inorganic nature, life and death, wrangling between them over the flux of human history that rolls indifferently on toward its goal. At the end the one will be turned into an elm and the other into a stone. The Hill of Howth, overlooking Dublin bay, stands as the symbol of male permanence. As in Proust's "Overture," the episode includes nearly all the themes and motifs that will be elaborated in the succeeding parts; the river holds in precipitation, so to speak, all the figures and events that will rise to its surface with the passage of the generations.

Beyond this point these notes will not go very far. It is reasonable to suppose that the next two parts bear some kind of significant correspondence to the Viconian cycle. Part II opens with descriptions of the Ice Age and the Flood, which suggests that we are picking up the thread at a moment when mankind has so doomed itself that it has to start all over again. It concludes with the first full statement of the Tristan-Isolde theme, which is so prominent in the third part. The progression would seem to be

from boisterous heroic action through feudal romance to the combination of abstract and psychotic preoccupation with sex of the
modern civilized period. It is evident that Earwicker is reliving
his own youth through identification with his children, who become transformed into all the most cherished archetypes of
strength and beauty that rise up out of the racial tradition. We
will probably have to keep in mind Jung's description of the manner in which by this process we seek to work out for ourselves in
sleep a new equilibrium for our waking life. But, just to the extent
that the hero's actual experience rises to the surface and becomes
involved in the fantasy, the language seems to become more
blurred and evasive. One cannot always distinguish between the
sleeper and the figures of his dream; Earwicker melts into Shaun
and Shaun into Earwicker; their voices become confused in the
dusk of language.

This is illustrated in the last passage of all—the beautiful swan-
song with which the work ends. The final section is in the form
of a *coda*, which reassembles in a great pæan of resurrection all
the themes that have been developed. Earwicker wakes from his
long Saturday night's sleep and turns toward the morning light.
But it is a resurrection in more than this superficial and rather
comic sense: he has traversed the whole time-space world, and
this too has turned out to have a pattern like that of individual
human life—of waking and sleeping, of beginning and ending, of
being young and growing old. The effect of his dream has been
to reconcile him to his present stage of life, and this may be considered a new equilibrium. In the course of the process he is able
to realize also his wife's feelings about the old age that is over-
taking them both; he identifies himself with her to the extent of
thinking her thoughts and going over her memories. And by the
time we reach the threnody beginning "Soft morning, city!" the
identification is so complete that he is speaking in her voice—
which has now become also the voice of Anna Livia, returning to
her father the sea. In other words, Earwicker's resurrection consists in his sense that he too will soon become part of the record,
that he will breathe the air of the heroes in the common element

of history. "Mememormee" is one of the very last of the difficult words in this difficult book.

Is it possible that *Finnegans Wake* represents a final stage in that long process of transcendence which has characterized Joyce's work from the beginning? In A *Portrait of the Artist as a Young Man* Stephen Dedalus passes through what might be called an initiation rite to emerge as an artist dedicated to the creation of the "uncreated conscience" of his race. But this was not an adequate transcendence, in the sense either of primitive religion or of modern psychoanalysis, in which the individual always carries over elements of the old self into the new self that is restored to the world. Stephen had left behind all the old symbols of love and authority without discovering any new ones to take their place. The identification rather is with the *idea* of the role of the artist, which is simply one of the projections of what Freud calls the superego. *Ulysses* records in its opening episodes the insufficiency of the program of "silence, exile, and cunning." And the crisis to which his new spiritual isolation has brought him is not resolved until he is put into communication with Bloom, the representative of common humanity. Through his imaginative sympathy with Bloom he is restored to the state of grace which will make freedom of creation at last possible for him. Now the main difference between *Ulysses* and the present work is that, where humanity is represented in the first by a "coalescence" of universalized traits into a single figure existing in time and space, in the second these traits are diffused through time-space and coalesce finally only in the *pattern* of history. Humanity is impressive not in its actuality but in its immanence. And this becomes something comparable to the conception of the Divine Idea of the medieval theologians—that which is capable of taking on matter but is itself infinite in time and space.

Naturally the question is whether such an idea of humanity is "anterior, posterior, and superior" to the individual, whether it can be an adequate object for transcendence. Croce, in his work on Vico, stresses the latter's theory of knowledge—the basis of which is the formula that only that can be known which is created. Perfect knowledge is the province of God alone because God created the universe. Man cannot know even the world of nature because he did not create it; therefore, the Cartesian school of his time were moving up a blind alley in their attempts to chart nature with their geometry. But Vico did insist that there is one realm which man could know because he had created it— and that was his own history. Michelet sums up Vico's thought with the sentence: *humanity is its own creation*.

According to such a criterion of truth the symbols included in the myths and legends of the human past are just as capable of allegiance as the truths presented by the discursive intellect. The myth of man would be as true as the myth that has arisen through the separation of his reason from the rest of his nature at the Renaissance. But the pragmatic test of truth here as elsewhere would be the extent to which it could be made to function for the individual. And for the artist no truth may be said to exist that cannot find concrete expression in the order and unity to which he reduces his experience.

To raise these questions is not to guarantee their answers. But it may be pointed out that the most recent and hard-working school of Shakespearean criticism, with its concentration on themes and symbols rather than on ideas in the plays, may be helpful in enabling us to understand much that is difficult and forbidding in the literature of our time. The conclusion of this school is that in the later Shakespearean plays the world represented is no longer the world of contemporary Elizabethan actuality charted out by the Renaissance mind. *Othello, Hamlet,* and *Antony and Cleopatra* end up by taking us to a realm of human passion and feeling that can only be described as "transcendental." For this is a realm in which the images of human grandeur and suffering take on quasi-divine dimensions and significance. Piety to it is the act of commemoration: Hamlet's injunctions to Horatio that his story be told, Cleopatra's confidence that her love for Antony will live in the memory forever. By such an act of piety the imaginative artist in a period of cultural confusion still managed to preserve the forms and sentiments of a religious society without any of the theological obligations.

What is being suggested is that Joyce in this new work, like Yeats and Mann, seeks his salvation not in any escape from the present but in a transcendence of the present through the past. And the question of his seriousness, which has bothered some people, will be solved if we consider the piety that is involved in the energetic and still uncorrupted affirmation of life that is implicit in every movement of his writing. This is the seriousness of the greatest comedy, which always keeps in recollection the tragic knowledge that is at its base.

D. H. Lawrence as Hero

[1933]

D. H. Lawrence was a crank, a sex-ridden degenerate, a belated Rousseauist, a besotted Christ, and "a Jaeger poet" (Miss Edith Sitwell). Or else he was a seer, "a beautiful soul," a *divine* fool, a modern Prometheus, and a very great artist. Lawrence may be placed beneath one or the other of these two sets of labels, or he may be distributed by the cautious somewhere between them, but the fact becomes more and more evident that he is at present, almost three years after his death, easily the most *living* of contemporary English writers. Not only are his poems, novels, and essays more widely read than at any moment in his own lifetime, but there has also grown up around his name a body of popular biographical literature unique for any modern writer. And the wide public response to his recently published letters is serving to provide further evidence of the profound if still indeterminate influence he is exerting on the mind of our time.

There is a curious but significant contradiction to be found in Mr. Aldous Huxley's otherwise finely written introduction to the *Letters*. "It is impossible to write about Lawrence except as an artist," says Mr. Huxley, and then proceeds to show how impatient Lawrence was of the imposed discipline of the artistic process, his positive hatred of that discipline. "I'm doing a novel," Huxley quotes from one of the letters, "which I have never grasped. Damn its eyes, there I am at page 145, and I've no notion what it's about. I hate it. F. says it is good. But it's like a novel in a foreign language I don't know very well. I can only just make out what it is all about." Whatever else these may be they are not the words of the artist as we have come to think of him, the artist consumed by the passion of *making* and by the desire of achieving perfection in the *thing made*. "Lawrence was possessed by his creative genius," Mr. Huxley declares, but what is probably closer to the truth is that Lawrence was possessed by the *idea* of creative genius, for his genius went not so much into the creation of works of art as into the passionate intellectual search for a means of attaining to a truly creative attitude in life itself. The cultivation and perfection of his art was always subordinated to this search: it was a means toward the end of self-knowledge and ultimate fulfillment. It was therefore something pragmatically helpful to him, a kind of intellectual and hence psychological catharsis: "One sheds one's sicknesses in books—repeats and presents again one's emotions to be master of them." It follows that Lawrence seldom revised or corrected his works, never kept copies of certain of them, and was wholly indifferent to their fate once he had rid himself of their contents. Such a use of art by the individual is not unprecedented; "art for my sake" has always been a protest of a certain type of romantic; but it is a mistake to confuse this type of artist with the classic artist who uses art, if he may be said to "use" it at all, to express something already completed and perfected in his own mind or nature.

Because of his special attitude toward the art process Lawrence never succeeded in any of his many poems, novels, and plays in producing anything which possessed the order, harmony, and self-sufficiency of a work of art in the classic sense. What he turned out resembled, on a more imaginative and usually more objective plane, of course, the essays of Montaigne; his works were trials, experiments, attempts at finding himself and working out a solution to the great problem that obsessed him. Unlike the classic artist, he was not able to operate on some cohesive view of the universe fully absorbed and assimilated in the personality. His works can only be interpreted and judged as records of the successive steps taken by his mind in the effort to discover for himself some such view, which would take the place of all those he had rejected in the thought of Europe and of his own time. And if the search in his case was so prolonged and difficult it was because of the particular manner in which it was carried out—not along the wide-open avenues of the dialectic intellect but through the "dark tunnel" of the instincts and senses. "We can go wrong in our minds," he writes in an early letter. "But what our blood feels, and believes, and says, is always true." The books that gushed out, two or three a year toward the end, from the tremendous sources of energy in his personality were only milestones along the "savage pilgrimage" of his life, none of them complete in itself, either as providing a definitive intellectual conclusion or as a fully achieved work of art. To have provided either would have been for Lawrence a betrayal. "When I have a *finished* mental concept of a beloved, or a friend, then the love and friendship are dead. It falls to the level of an acquaintance." This is from *Fantasia of the Unconscious* in 1922, and the supplied italics are important. For it is apparent from this and other statements that Lawrence's real objection to a "finished" work of literature was that it implied a stopping-point in his development, that is, a conclusion arrived at by the intellect and hence invalid and without life. (It may be noted that here Lawrence paralleled an intuition that was arrived at separately by two other "searchers" in recent literature, Paul Valéry's Monsieur Teste and Thomas Mann's Hans Castorp.) In literary form, therefore, Lawrence could only see something sterile, dead, and to be avoided. What does this deep-rooted resistance to the very idea of crystallized expression suggest but that Lawrence is at the opposite pole from the artist considered as the poet or *maker*? If we attempt to explain him simply as a writer, as Mr. Huxley tries to do, we have to make most of the qualifications that we are forced to make in explaining certain other post-Renaissance writers whom Lawrence resembled in various respects—Blake, Dostoievski, the later Rimbaud, and Whitman. It is necessary to make the same qualification that must be made of any, even the greatest, novel by Tolstoy. Perhaps the closest actual parallel to the state of spiritual activity behind a novel of Lawrence's would be such a work as Rimbaud's *Saison en Enfer*. Here also what we get is not an ordered literary composition but a direct transcription of the consciousness in the process of rejecting an old world and reaching out for a new. In Lawrence's poems and novels we are presented with the crises of a sensibility that remained always in a state of flux, a sensibility that had to remain in a state of flux in order to remain alive, since the stopping point demanded of art would have resulted in the petrifaction of death.

(Of course this is not equivalent to denying the existence of any elements of artistic interest in the work of Lawrence. *Sons and Lovers*, for example, possesses at least as much organic form as any other English novel of its period. But one must at once make the observation that in comparison with his later novels the theme of this early work is quite limited and even elementary. It may almost be stated as a principle that as his theme grew larger and more ambitious the form of his novels became increasingly more unsatisfactory. Certainly this would seem to be true for *The Rainbow, Women in Love*, and *The Plumed Serpent*. At the end, in *Lady Chatterley's Lover*, when the theme again becomes too simplified, it is interesting to note that the form congeals into something as mechanical as a medieval morality play or a modern problem-drama. Form, as we have seen, was the one thing which Lawrence did not and could not strive to attain; but on the other hand he did happen to be remarkably talented in the use of certain important subordinate or incidental elements of his craft. His style and method of description, for example, were both highly developed and hardly surpassed by any of his contemporaries. For a close analysis of these the excellent little monograph of Stephen Potter is useful. Not enough credit has been allowed Lawrence for his superb handling of the *mise-en-scène*, which reflects a sense, surprising in so subjective a writer, of the objectively dramatic. Certain scenes in the novels and stories of the middle period, when his focus was directed sharply on the violent touch-and-go of sex antagonism, are as poignantly realized as anything in Dostoievski, of whom they most remind us. And the dialogue especially in these scenes is true, natural, and effective. But, unfortunately, even over those things in which he most excelled Lawrence was not always in control; the description is all too often diffused, the drama left unresolved, and the dialogue artificial. At the same time in any estimate of Lawrence as an artist it would be unfair and inaccurate to ignore the considerable incidental artistry to be found throughout the body of his work.)

The question of whether Lawrence was an artist or not is raised at all only because it may suggest the reason why these letters are so important, why they may even prove of more enduring interest than any single book he published in his lifetime. Because we do not expect them to conform to the necessities of art we are not disappointed or confused as we so often are in our response to the poems and the novels. Yet everything that was unique and valuable in his work is concentrated in them; all that is essential in the thirty-odd volumes he tossed out periodically to a bewildered public is here summed up in a form more absolute than that of any one of his books—the form of his own life. It is indeed because Lawrence was so imperfect an artist that his letters are so good: the excess of personality that marred his works becomes in the letters a virtue, the source of their greatest distinction. "In them," says Mr. Huxley, "Lawrence has written his life and painted his own portrait." Indeed, he has done these things and something more besides—he has left us his *chef d'oeuvre*.

The *Letters* are Lawrence's masterpiece because in them the great central problem of his personality is represented more completely and terribly than in any single one of his works. To read them is to get a concentrated impression of his life and thought (in his case so singularly identified) that could only otherwise be secured by a laborious burrowing through the whole of his writings. Another advantage of such an impression is that it prevents us from swallowing too easily any of the current "explanations" of him—that he was a sexual neurotic, for example, or as is more recently maintained that he was yet another victim of the class struggle—which are the result of generalizations based on the reading of sporadic passages from the works. There emerges, on the contrary, with unmistakable definiteness, what was from beginning to end the first great principle of his life and thinking—the metaphysical belief in the absolute and inviolate character of human individuality, what Lawrence in less abstract language defines in another place as *the principle of essential human loneliness*. This is the principle that is at the basis of everything Lawrence wrote as a writer, that explains everything he was as a man. And in the *Letters* more clearly than anywhere else we can see reflected the misery, torture, and final frustration that resulted from his continuous effort to reconcile it with the conditions of ordinary social living.

For the central conflict in Lawrence's personality to which we have referred was between this fierce intellectual pride in his own individuality and his quite human need to lose that individuality in someone or something outside himself. It may be pointed out that actually Lawrence possessed no more individuality than anyone else—which is true enough as far as it goes. The only point to be recognized in Lawrence's case is that his sense or intellectual awareness of the fact of individuality was developed to an unusual degree of intensity, beyond that perhaps of any other figure of his generation. And this characteristic of his mind or temperament had the effect of intensifying the normal difficulties involved in the adjustment of the individual to other individuals and to society as a whole. The strength of his self-pride was not as great as he pretended; it did not save him from the common desire and impulse of mankind to *merge*. (His contempt for the great "mergers" in American literature was really only an effort of his mind to conceal or quiet the same impulse in himself.) The difficulty was that the conflict seldom became clearly objectified in his own mind; and this is what is responsible for the obvious contradictions and frequent confusion in his pronouncements which have turned so many readers away from him.

This is also the dilemma which gives such a strong undercurrent of continuity to the *Letters* and is the secret source of that vitality which has for Mr. Huxley and will have for other readers "the attractiveness of beauty." It would be possible in a longer study to make an interesting correlation between the various sections of the letters and the corresponding periods in Lawrence's writing career. There were, if we may briefly review them, three different stages in the long-drawn-out attempt to resolve his conflict in his books. In the first stage, reflected in all his early novels up to *The Rainbow,* love is rejected as a possible or desirable means of self-abandonment; in the second, beginning with *Women in Love* and ending with *Kangaroo,* friendship between men, a Utopian community, and heroic leadership are each successively offered and rejected as a means to the same end; and in the third, the period of *The Plumed Serpent,* the story "Sun," and the posthumous *Apocalypse,* the individual is finally recommended to lose his identity by abandonment through one or another medium to the non-human sources of energy in the blood— "the dark gods." For obvious reasons, each of these stages is not reflected with the same fullness and emphasis in the *Letters.* We are given few letters, and those rather unimportant, of the period preceding the composition of *Sons and Lovers* in 1912. And toward the end, as Mr. Huxley explains, Lawrence's correspondence was slight and marked by an increasing weariness of tone, as if he were at last able to dispense with the need of human communication. ("The world is lovely if one avoids man—so why not avoid him! Why not! Why not! I am tired of humanity," he writes from Mallorca in May, 1929.) The greater number of the letters, and much the most interesting of them, correspond of course to the middle stage in his development, that is, the long period in which he chafed under his isolation and sought in every possible direction for some method of union with others.

The two motifs that run most persistently through the letters are the ideal of "friendship" and the dream of a Utopian community. It is perhaps even unnecessary to make any such distinction between them, because Lawrence's incorrigible hope, even in a personal relationship, was for a careful preservation of the separate identities of the two parties concerned. And this usually ended up by requiring a mutual subordination to some great "purposive" activity (the exact nature of which, of course, was left undefined to the end). "If we are going to remain a group of separate entities separately engaged," he writes to Lady Ottoline Morrell, "then there is no reason why we should be a group at all. We are just individualists. And individuals do not vitally concern me any more. Only a purpose vitally concerns me, not individuals —neither my own individual self nor any other." Such outbursts are frequent throughout—the occasion may be a biography of Van Gogh, a proposed lecture-series by Bertrand Russell, or the latest spiritual adultery of J. M. Murry. But it is all too apparent that this dream, this notion in Lawrence's head of a perfect human communion without loss of identity on either side was at bottom nothing more than a hoping against hope. In his actual relationships Lawrence seems to have been unwilling to accept the personality of others or to relinquish his own, and it is probable that he would not have been able to do either whatever the cause or the purpose. The whole tragicomedy of his relations with Murry, which has been so much vulgarized by Murry himself and others, was really based on his inability to accept them for what they were instead of trying to make of them a super-individualistic arrangement that seems to have been impossible for both men. And one is certain that the recurrent Utopia motif is to be explained in the same way, as a rationalization of Lawrence's understandable human need for some dependable company in a world which in his stronger moments he was able to reject in its entirety. (Perhaps the coolest letter in the whole volume, incidentally, is the one in which Lawrence draws himself away from the one English disciple who followed him to New Mexico.) Although Lawrence singles out the Brook Farm experiment for special ridicule in his essay on Hawthorne as being the supreme example of the American passion for "merging," what he was himself unconsciously seeking to do was not essentially different. The only difference was that his mind steadily refused to admit that he could not have his cake and eat it too.

At the end it is sad to observe how Lawrence is gradually

brought to recognize the insoluble nature of the contradiction which his great first principle involved. In an important letter to Dr. Trigant Burrow (also quoted by Mr. Huxley) he calls this recognition by its right name, "frustration"; frustration, specifically, of the "societal instinct."

Toward the very close, as we have seen, Lawrence returned to the drastic conclusion that he had stated much earlier in his career, during the war, in a letter to Lady Cynthia Asquith. "And it comes to this, that the oneness of mankind is destroyed in me. I am I, and you are you, and all heaven and hell lie in the chasm between." He returned to it after having discarded in his life and in the trial-and-error exercises that were his novels all the possible modes of adjustment that occurred to him on the merely human plane. In *The Plumed Serpent* and in *Apocalypse* he sought release by a union, a distinctly mystical kind of union, with that "otherness" of the early novels, now invoked as "the dark gods." This is not the place to enter into the whole host of questions immediately raised by the mention of the solution which he finally seemed to find for the problem that had obsessed him all his life. The *Letters*, as we have seen, are extremely reticent about this ultimate stage in his thought—or rather in his feeling. For, in the last analysis, Lawrence was not a thinker or a philosopher, any more than he was purely an artist, although he was more of an artist than he was a philosopher. He was, if he was anything that we may classify, a religious prophet, one of the few really sincere and impressive examples of the type in our time, and the final questions about him are not for the literary critic at all but for the metaphysician or the theologian.

As a prophet Lawrence has proved himself a great deal more compelling in his own métier than a great many better artists of our time in theirs, as the increasing dimensions of his myth would indicate. To interpret him as an artist, even as a certain kind of artist, as Mr. Huxley does, is to expose him to a too facile application of literary standards, ending perhaps with ultimate dismissal. The other error is to attempt to reconstruct the ideological structure of his works in strictly intellectual terms. "What a man has

got to say is never more than relatively important," Lawrence remarks in a letter to J. M. Murry. More significant than any single
idea he ever formulated, more imposing than any system of ideas
that might be erected out of his published works, is the *revelation*
of the personality that comes to us through those works and
through the letters.

> I do think that man is related to the universe in some "re-
> ligious" way, even prior to his relation to his fellow men. And
> I do think that the only way of true relationship between men
> is to meet in some common "belief"—if the belief is but physi-
> cal and not merely mental. . . . There is a *principle* in the
> universe, toward which man turns religiously—a life of the
> universe itself. And the hero is he who touches and transmits
> the life of the universe. The hero is good—your own effort is
> heroic—how else understand it.

This passage from a very long letter written by Lawrence a few
years before his death gives us, if we care to read enough between
the lines, a notion of the sort of role that he himself preferred
to think of himself as playing in the modern world. "Hero" is
the name he gives to the man who transmits and puts us in touch
with the universe; and "hero" is as good a word as prophet to
apply to Lawrence and probably as descriptive of the peculiar
quality of his genius.

The Lawrence Myth

[*1938*]

Of the many examples of the artist as "suffering hero" thrown
up by the nineteenth century and afterwards (Blake, Hölderlin,
Baudelaire, Wagner, Melville, Van Gogh, all belong to the tradition), D. H. Lawrence is perhaps the only one who took the next
logical step and identified himself overtly with a mystery god.
That this is not a conceit but actually what happened in Lawrence's case is apparent from even the most casual survey of his
career. The process was a gradual one, to be sure, and the special
aura that surrounds such early heroes as Birken in *Women in
Love* and Lilly in *Aaron's Rod* condenses only by degrees into the
unmistakable halo of *The Man Who Died*. But already in *The
Ladybird* (1921) Lawrence had given to one of the most auto-
biographical of his heroes the name of Dionysus himself. In his
poetry this is to be traced out through the change from the rather
conventional nature imagery of his early verse to the recondite
symbolism of *Last Poems*. The whole process may also be cor-
related, of course, with the shifting of his intellectual interests
from Freudian psychoanalysis to anthropology and comparative
religion, from one type of mythology to another and much older
one. For most people, however, the most striking evidence will
be the biographical: the persecutions and humiliations, the jour-
neys by water, the agonies in the wilderness, the betrayals and

final apotheosis at the hands of his disciples. Catharine Carswell, in her account of the burlesque Last Supper at the Café Royal, does not quite explain how Lawrence ever came to lend himself to such a disgusting performance; and if Lawrence is finally forced to advise the editor of the *Adelphi* to wipe away the "Judas slime," the casualness of the implied relationship is rather astounding. But nothing could be more revealing than those last paintings of himself and his family which the British censor was required to bar on the grounds of blasphemy. Because these belong so clearly to biography rather than to art, because they represent self-expression at its most naive and irresponsible, they leave no doubt as to the image of himself which Lawrence came to realize at the end. He had become, as he put it in a deathbed fragment, "like a Lord!" As for his posthumous reputation, a literary analogy is fortunately available and will suffice: the last scene in *Le Rouge et le Noir*, in which the lovely ladies, gathering at Julien's tomb at midnight, join forces in building up a little shrine.

Lawrence is, to a remarkable degree even among contemporaries, a "case," and he has received drastic treatment as such from all quarters. But it is really not helpful to be told by the psychoanalysts that he suffered from one or another malady, or by a theologian like T. S. Eliot that he was possessed of the Devil, or (what perhaps amounts to the same thing) that he was an unfortunate product of the capitalist system. All of these interpretations have their relevance; but none of them quite explains away the phenomenon which, in the first place, has compelled our attention. So much is true for any writer and for any phenomenon, of course, and even leaving aside the matter of special bias every critical approach is limited ultimately by the categories of the thinking mind itself. The problem is always to discover the approach that will do least violence to the object before us, that will reconcile the greatest number of the innumerable aspects that every object presents to the understanding. It merely happens that, in Lawrence's "case," criticism has been more than ordinarily handicapped by a certain difficulty in determining exactly what the object itself really is. Although Lawrence speculated in several fields of knowledge and contributed many valuable insights, he did not leave a systematic body of thought; yet some people base their approach to him almost exclusively on what they call his ideas. On the other hand, if he is treated as an artist, there is the hard fact to get around that all but a few of his poems and novels are lacking in some of the most prominent features usually associated with works of art. To add to the confusion, if his so-called art is as often as not admired or condemned for its thought, his so-called thought is either accepted or rejected because of the art through which it is expressed. It does not help to draw parallels with Whitman and Melville; for these figures too have been singularly viscous objects for criticism. Perhaps the biographers and memoir writers have been closest the mark, after all, in almost ignoring Lawrence the thinker and Lawrence the artist for Lawrence the man.

In any case, Lawrence's hold on the contemporary imagination seems to have been as much the effect of his reputation as of his accomplishments; and to say that it was based on the total image presented by his career is perhaps to take everything into account. This is not to dismiss his accomplishments but to put them in their proper relation to something else. "What a man has got to say is never more than relatively important," Lawrence remarks in the *Letters*; and, while this may not be true for everyone, it was true enough for him to suggest an approach that will undertake at least to describe what it was to which his confused mass of writings may be related. What is here suggested is a view of Lawrence based on the view that he finally came to take of himself, the view of himself as a kind of contemporary reincarnation of the dying god.

Such an approach may seem far-fetched; but no other enables us to reconcile so much of what is admirable and silly, sincere and false, profitable and dangerous in the Lawrence "case." For example, the formlessness of his writings, to which the purely esthetic critic invariably turns his attention, is immediately seen as not so much a technical deficiency as a function of his role.

"They want me to have form," he complained, "that means, they want me to have *their* pernicious, ossiferous, skin-and-grief form." Or, as he put it in *Fantasia of the Unconscious*, "As soon as I have a finished mental conception, *a full idea even of myself*, then dynamically I am dead." How such a dynamic view of the self is to be related to the practice of an objective art is of course the question; and the answer that Lawrence gives elsewhere is unsatisfactory: "One sheds one's sicknesses in books—repeats and presents again one's emotions to be master of them." But as an artist one successfully masters one's emotions only by giving them esthetic form, and Lawrence has already had his say about form. In his handling of the allegory, perhaps, he most clearly reveals his predicament; for, if this is the inevitable vehicle for revelation, it also requires the most deliberate manipulation of concepts. But since Lawrence will have nothing of concepts, most of his novels, from *The Rainbow* to *Kangaroo* are allegories, whose morals are either confused or postponed. In *Lady Chatterley's Lover* he does for once keep to a simple and consistent pattern and the result is significantly the deadest writing of his career. He is at his best when he is most faithful to his rôle—in the apocalyptic passages of the novels, in the "Osiris-cries" of his successive resurrections, in his sermons on the mount. In *The Man Who Died* he wrote a moving and terrible story because he turned from allegory to myth—to the one and only myth to which he had been conforming all along. All of his formal vicissitudes are traceable to the intellectual difficulties in the way of being at once a functioning divinity and a practitioner of the arts. He was not a religious poet, as someone has said, but a self-induced earth god who sometimes wrote verse.

Both in his life and in his works Lawrence illustrates what Nietzsche, in his well-known analysis of the Dionysus myth, calls "the agony of individuation." This will have an unpleasantly metaphysical sound to modern ears; but it must be recalled that to the generation to which Lawrence belonged life still presented itself in terms of metaphysical problems. To these problems any serious discussion of Gide, Proust, Mann, and Joyce must likewise sooner or later be conducted. No matter into what unpopularity metaphysics has fallen, it is the only relevant approach to these writers. So much seems necessary before offering the following interpretation of Nietzsche's phrase: Nature (the undifferentiated flux of phenomena) takes on form; every form involves limitations; and as a result every individual must exist in a state of perpetual inner strife which can be terminated only through dissolution into his original substance. We need not ask what these limitations are, whether there is any less drastic mode of solution, or even whether this is in fact an accurate statement of the problem of being. It will have to be enough to suggest that Lawrence's career was like a ritualistic exhaustion of the paradoxical ambition to enjoy nature, in the sense defined above, and to preserve the character of his individuality at one and the same time.

Nature in Lawrence is commonly supposed to be identified *tout court* with sex; but there are innumerable passages in which it is carefully explained that sex is but the medium or agency of a power still greater than itself. For this reason he is so hard on those who, like Benjamin Franklin, profane it in terms of hygienic "use." Nor is it a pastime for a jaded epoch: "Buy a king-cobra and try playing with that." Contrary to the general belief, Lawrence is more truly moral on the subject of sex than on any other subject. Also it is made clear that sex is not to be considered an end in itself, a solution to the individual problem; this is the thesis of *The Rainbow* and *Women in Love*. What the power that it represents actually is, Lawrence attempts to reveal through a variety of means. In his best poems and novels this power is rendered for us through an interfusion of characterization and description: the early poem "Fireflies" and the scene by the pool in *Women in Love* are examples. Lawrence's specialty as a novelist, it may be noted, is in the recording of such "vibrations." This power is also personified in the familiar little dark man who remains so identical throughout the long roll call of the novels. But it is perhaps most clearly indicated through the metaphorical light-dark antithesis. By contrast with the world that he rejects Lawrence gives us the sharpest impression of the world that he

would put in its place. If the light symbolizes the over-spiritual-
ized, over-intellectualized, and wholly devitalized "white consciousness" of our time, which it should not be difficult for most
readers to recognize, the dark can only stand for its opposite—the
unspiritual, unintellectual, and wholly vital world of nature. The
darkness materializes into "the dark gods" and finally "the dark
god"; it invests itself in the innumerable forms of dragons, birds,
insects, and little black men. But what it really amounts to
throughout is something that no church father would have any
difficulty in calling by its right name.

"My great religion," Lawrence wrote, "is a belief in the blood,
the flesh, as being wiser than the intellect." This sums up so completely his attitude toward nature that we can pass to his actual
handling of the problem of individuality. None of the so-called
individualistic writers of recent generations, it may be said, projected the problem with the same deliberation and insistence.
"Insofar as he [man] is a single individual soul, he *is* alone—ipso
facto. Insofar as I am I, and only I am I, and I am only I, insofar
I am inevitably and eternally alone, and it is my last blessedness
to know it, and to accept it, and to live with this as the core of
my self-knowledge." This is typical of any number of pronouncements on the subject. In the brilliant *Studies in Classic American
Literature* the attack is consistently directed against what Lawrence believed to be mankind's reprehensible passion for "merging." All of the novels, as a matter of fact, are object lessons in
the consequences of losing self-identity. In *Sons and Lovers* spiritual love, in most of the other early novels up to *The Rainbow*
sexual love, and in *Women in Love* and *Aaron's Rod* friendship
between men are successively examined and rejected as a possible
means of individual fulfillment. Beginning with *Kangaroo*, however, we get a new and more positive note.

For if Lawrence through his heroes is so jealously defensive of
what he calls his "life-form" he exhibits all along an equally
strong counter-impulse toward just that sort of "merging" which
he condemns in others. The character Aaron replies to the statement in the above paragraph: "But—I can't stand by myself in

the middle of the world and in the middle of people and know I
am quite by myself, and nowhere to go, and nothing to hold on
to. I can for a day or two. But then it becomes unbearable as
well." This dialogue between Aaron and Lilly, who represent the
two poles of Lawrence's nature, objectifies the conflict by which
he was tormented from beginning to end and which was the real
source of his astonishing energy. The other side of his eccentric
individualism is seen in the febrile quality of his personal relationships and in his numerous projects for a model colony—in Flor-
ida, Cornwall, Sicily, Mexico, and again in England. It is interesting that the latter desire seems to have been more powerful than
his judgment, for he had been annihilating in his ridicule of the
Brook Farm experiment in the book on American literature. Lawrence's social need was so intense that it is not only the main
theme of his *Letters* but the motive power behind them—the
reason that he is one of the great English letter writers. But
nothing could be franker than the following confession to Dr.
Trigant Burrow: "What ails me is the absolute frustration of my
primeval societal instinct. . . . I think societal instinct much
deeper than sex instinct—and societal repression much more
devastating. There is no repression of the sexual individual comparable to the repression of the societal man in me, by the individual ego, my own and everybody else's. I am weary even of
my own individuality, and simply nauseated by other people's."

Apparently "fulfillment" involves the satisfaction of other
needs of man's nature than his purely private sense of communion
with the darkness. In the posthumous *Apocalypse* Lawrence begins to make a distinction between the personal and the collective
man, but this soon evaporates in a blast of red dragon's breath.
Lawrence never really faced the question, for it would have taken
him right out of the realm in which the assurances of the blood
are sufficient. It would have required intellectual evaluation and
moral choice. But we may consider the general solution that he
came to offer for the relationships involved in sex, society, and
politics. This may be indicated through an inaccurate analogy
with the medieval doctrine of grace. Through sex the separate

individuals in any relationship are restored to an organic union with the processes of nature; and through this experience they are strengthened, in the best religious sense, both in themselves and in their relations with others. At least this is the only meaning that emerges through the banal conversations and tirades of *Lady Chatterley's Lover*, which belongs late in the Lawrence canon.

Politically, of course, such a doctrine leads straight into the very dark burrow of fascism. But it may be worth while to trace out Lawrence's political development, if it may be called such, a little more carefully. As a coal miner's son, as a suffering artist, and as an intelligent observer of contemporary life, he could never have been very sympathetic to the ideal of modern bourgeois democracy. All of his work is an implicit, and much of it an explicit, criticism of mass production in ideas, emotions, and men. He was a revolutionist, therefore, in the sense that every Bohemian artist under the bourgeois regime has been a revolutionist. But it does not follow that he could have turned to the Fabian socialism of prewar England or, later, to Soviet communism. What he objected to in communism was its failure to provide any ideal better than the one to which he had been opposed all along: "The dead materialism of Marx socialism and soviets seems to me no better than what we've got." In *Apocalypse* communism is defined as a power-driven movement in which the proletariat is motivated entirely by the desire for *revenge* on the ruling class. It is "the old will of the Christian community to destroy human worldly power, and to substitute the *negative* power of the mass. . . . In Russia, the triumph over worldly power was accomplished, and the reign of saints set in, with Lenin as chief saint." To Lawrence, power, the only real power, is to be achieved, as we have seen, through identification with nature; he is against the intellectual will expressing itself in any sort of active dogma. But this power would seem to be considerably variable between individual and individual. In such a situation the inferior men must bow down in homage before their acknowledged lords and masters; only in this way will a continuous "stream of life" be maintained. In other words, it is the old medieval hierarchy, with grace (sex) once again thrown in as a safeguard. In *Kangaroo* the fascist labor leader wins the support of his followers only to renounce it because he is still not on good enough terms with "the dark gods." The same notion is repeated in the diffuse and hysterical *Plumed Serpent*. Led into confirmation of a political religion with whose only practical expression he would have been the first to quarrel, Lawrence illustrates the dangerous foolishness of his logic once it is applied.

Only by courtesy of course is it to be called logic at all; here surely it is the blood and not the intellect that is doing the thinking. For sex is not the equivalent of medieval grace, in the sense of being a mode of communication between two absolute orders of being, but something common to both man and nature. Grace was invented by the theologians because it was necessary to establish some bridge between the human and the divine by which man could receive some assistance in controlling the forces of his nature; but in Lawrence sex is indistinguishable from these forces themselves. To attempt to improve human relationships through sex is therefore like attempting to improve nature by lifting it on its own bootstraps. It is an attempt for which Lawrence could have found a discouraging precedent in a much earlier representative of the tortured Anglo-Saxon Protestant mind, who sought "the perfection of nature" only to end his days with a Yahoo babble in his brain. Swift belied human nature by projecting it too purely on its Houyhnhnm side, Lawrence by giving too much scope to its Yahoo side; but both pictures equalize in their common injustice to the reality.

In his remarkable essay on Poe, Lawrence demonstrates how the Western will, become converted into the "will-to-know," turns in on itself and becomes an instrument that ends by destroying its own object, as the hero of "Ligeia" wills the death of his beautiful young wife. It never seems to have occurred to him that his own version of the Schopenhauerian "will-to-live," despite its up-to-date anthropological trappings, could also turn in on itself and blight the very sources of its energy. Yet in a story like "The Ladybird" there is an odd ambiguity in the manner in

which the hero, Count Dionys Psanek, vacillates between being
a sympathetic avatar of his mythological namesake and a somewhat sinister emissary of Avernus. In fact, there is something
rather sinister about all the little black heroes, and Dionys is
selected only because he is the blackest and smallest and most
obviously sinister of the lot. A German army officer imprisoned
in England, he renews his friendship with a childhood acquaintance, the pale and virginal Lady Daphne, whose husband is away
at the war. Through a series of distinctly cruel conversations he
manages to persuade her that she is a "whited sepulchre" and
that her husband is probably no better. Upon the latter's return,
he induces her, through the spell of his singing, to come to his
room at night. There he is "seated in flame, in flame unconscious,
like an Egyptian King-god in the statues." At first he hesitates
but then decides: "Take her into the underworld. Take her into
the dark Hades with him, like Francesca and Paolo. And in hell
hold her fast, queen of the underworld, himself master of the
underworld." He informs her, "In the dark you are mine. And
when you die you are mine. But in the day you are not mine,
because I have no power in the day. In the night, in the dark, and
in death, you are mine."

This talk of intermingled love and night and death—we have
heard it all before. Nineteenth century romanticism had been a
deathward movement, as Mann shows in his Wagner essay, and
through the Nietzsche influence it is simple enough to relate
Lawrence back to the sources of Poe, Wagner, Baudelaire, and
the other great celebrants of the tomb. Despite the superficial
exaltation of birds and beasts and flowers, despite the eloquent
stressing of the natural beauty and power in man, Lawrence's life
and work are rooted in an irrepressible yearning for the grave.
For to what can this extinction of the daylight world, this abandonment of reason, lead but a surrender of the finite human self
to the infinite nothingness of the flux? For the romantic there is
always the moment when Life, with a capital L, must be equated
with death; it is the moment when the expanding sense of nature
in him causes him to break irrevocably the limitations which

alone guarantee his identity. "Rich, florid loosener of the stric-
ture-knot called life," cries Whitman. "Sweet, peaceful, welcome
Death." If this loosening was indeed what had been desired all
along, it was of course foolish to talk so big on the subject of life.
For if life, human life, is a knot, reason is one of the two controlling cords. To discard reason is to throw over the only thing
that can give life definition. Lawrence's program is, in the last
analysis, a program for a mystery god—but hardly for a man. And
Dionysus in every age can terminate his agony only by dissolving
into his native element.

These considerations are so obvious that they would not be
raised if they had not been ignored by Lawrence right up to the
end. Toward the last the strain is quite evident in the paintings,
poems, and tales, so that as the affirmative note became more
emphatic the underlying despair rose more and more to the surface. Like Melville's whale, "life dies sunwards full of faith."
Sometimes the longing comes through as clearly as this:

> Life is for kissing and for horrid strife,
> The angels and the Sunderers,
> And perhaps in unknown Death we perhaps shall know
> Oneness and poised immunity.*

But Lawrence's importance is that of a cult leader, a kind of
latter-day mystery god, as we have said, and to disinfect his ideas
is not to reduce the objective importance of his myth as a whole.
It is perhaps an empty characterization to say that he was, in
any case, one of the great personalities of his generation. For the
isolated qualities of honesty, courage, and intensity there was
perhaps not a man in England worthy to touch the hem of his
much battered garments. To say that he possessed integrity is to
strain the meaning of that term; but we can say that he kept to
his rôle with an irreproachable consistency. Even as an artist his
least successful organ notes proved more penetrating than the
tinny whistles of the Shaws, the Wellses, and the Huxleys. He

* From "Kissing and Horrid Strife," in *The Complete Poems of D. H. Law-*
rence, New York, Viking, 1964, II, 709.

was a necessary antidote, for the parched young of two conti-
nents, to the salty fare of a superior artist like T. S. Eliot both in
the latter's wasteland and holy water phases. "Man seeks perfection of the life or of the work," as Yeats has said, and Lawrence's
life was very nearly perfect of its kind. It was a perfect example
of what it is to be a mystery god in our time.

What then is the value of the Lawrence myth to a generation
that is now perhaps far enough removed from it not to fall into
the danger of a facile self-identification? It is the value, in the
first place, of *any* myth: the vicarious exhaustion of possibilities
that are inherent in the human being in every time and place.
Lawrence overplayed one impulse of human nature on a scale
and in a fashion to stand as a highly moral experience to anyone
willing to follow him through to the end. Although he never
achieved real tragedy in any of his works, he was himself a tragic
figure in a drama that lacks a chorus. To appreciate him, we must
try to supply this chorus and the proper language for it. In the
second place, his story includes elements that should contribute
to a deeper realization both of ourselves and our surrounding
world. If we distinguish between its positive and its negative
aspects, we must admit that the latter constitute an impression
of the contemporary world which no honest and sensitive person
can fail to recognize. As a reflection of the formal and qualitative
disintegration of human life at present, it is more compelling
than the jeremiads of the reformers, the analyses of the psychologists, or the charts of the economists. Lawrence was not primarily
a social critic, as some people have insistently maintained, but his
epos is a damning criticism not only of our socio-economic organization but of our whole culture to its roots. This is not to say
that he was a mere product of this culture; the psychoanalysts
can make an equally convincing case along quite different lines.
After all, the pattern to which he conformed was something
much older even than our culture. It is necessary to make this
point very clear, because the conclusion must not be, as Lawrence
himself insisted, that we can solve everything by an immediate
fiat of the intellectual will. Finally, the meaning of his myth is

that whatever rational program we do undertake to alter the external situation must take sufficient account of that side of life to which he gave such fanatical allegiance.

In his last years Lawrence was much fascinated by a conception which, if he had lived long enough to develop it, might have led to a different solution to his many problems. It is the notion of the Greek "gods of limits," the Dioscuri, or Heavenly Twins, who divided all things between them—earth and sky, Heaven and Hades, the upper and lower regions of consciousness. In *Apocalypse* Lawrence tells us a great deal more about them: they were "witnesses," for example, to Adonai, the lord of life. They were "rivals, dividers, separators, for good as well as for evil: balancers." But, characteristically enough, Lawrence is more impressed by their negative aspect as sunderers or destroyers than as balancers between opposites. To him they seem to appear at successive moments of time rather than simultaneously. They tend to cancel each other out rather than to define the unity of whatever is the organism in which they are present. But to the Greek mind, to which they were above all witnesses to something, their principal function must have been that of definition. From such a brief summary it may or may not be evident how such a notion may be related to the dialectic or process type of thinking, which, in its various expressions, is perhaps the characteristic type of thinking of our time. With little difficulty "the gods of limits" can be appropriated to the needs of much modern philosophy, psychology, politics, and science.

For the present discussion they are useful as another restatement of the nature-reason antithesis that has been suggested as the real problem behind the Lawrence myth. If human life is a process that is in turn defined by these two processes, if it is divided between them, it is something that can be supported only if we can imagine at least temporary states of comparative stability. This solution has points of resemblance both to the Whiteheadian "event" in physics and to Dewey's "equilibrium" in psychology. But the question is always to what extent such a resolution involves a virtual capitulation of one or the other of the contending parties. Lawrence was someone who spent his entire career combatting what he believed was an undue balance in the structure of human life at the expense of the animal nature in man. In his reaction against the scientific rationalism of the later nineteenth century he undoubtedly plunged himself into the most abject nature-mysticism. But the reaction against Lawrence in turn need not be anything so simple as a renewed assertion of pure scientific rationalism. For scientific rationalism, in any of its current forms or derivatives, does not really provide a resolution of the conflict of which Lawrence's career was the rather sensational rehearsal. Insofar as it is applied to the kind of problems with which he was concerned, it can only lead to an unequivocal victory of the one side of man's nature over the other. It can only lead to a further building up of precisely those structures under which the individual has been buried for centuries. The only real resolution would be a redefinition, in terms of what both man's reason and his nature are at present, of man himself. It may be that such a redefinition may be accomplished within one or another of the available contemporary programs; or it may be that none of these quite avoids falling over into one of the two extremes. But what is certain is that no definition will be satisfactory that does not take into important account all those values to whose defensive assertion Lawrence felt obliged to devote his career.

A Note on Gertrude Stein

[1933]

There have always been only two questions about Gertrude Stein: What, precisely, has she been trying to do these many years? What, if any, is the value of what she has done? The first, which has never been satisfactorily answered, is a question that has to do not only with her method, style, and processes of composition but also with her view or "vision" of experience. The second, which cannot very well be answered before the first, is a question involving all the questions of evaluation involved in discussing any artistic work. Most of the confusion in regard to Miss Stein's work has come from the attempt to answer the second question without adequately recognizing the difficulties of the first. For Miss Stein, who happens to possess at once a highly-trained metaphysical mind and an extremely refined esthetic sensibility, offers unusual difficulties to the critic—more perhaps than any other creative writer of our time. Before disposing of her work with any real comfort it is necessary to know a great deal not only about William James and Bergson and Whitehead but also about Cézanne and Picasso and Juan Gris. Her so-called naive and primitive writing, moreover, represents such a complex synthesis of these influences that the most painstaking analysis is required to reveal them with any degree of clarity. In the end, it is much easier to turn to a "difficult" writer like Mrs. Virginia Woolf. All that will be pointed out here is that, in the general character of her mind and in its central orientation, Gertrude Stein is not nearly so isolated and eccentric a figure in American letters as is often believed.

Before Gertrude Stein went to Paris in 1903 she had been a favorite student of James's at Radcliffe, she had published a paper in the *Harvard Psychological Review*, and she had spent four years at Johns Hopkins, where her researches had been praised by Halstead and Osler. She did not take her degree there because, as she says, medicine bored her. In Paris she immediately met Matisse, Picasso, Braque, and other young painters who were busily overthrowing the "literary" painting of the previous generation in favor of an ever more abstract practice of their art. Under their inspiration she appears to have done her first literary work; "Three Lives" was written, literally, under the shadow of Cézanne. The effect of this worship of abstraction on a mind already trained in metaphysical speculation was to alienate its owner even farther from the concrete life of her own time and country. In the rue de Fleurus Miss Stein settled down to the creation of a form of writing which in style attempted to reproduce the movements of consciousness, as described by James and Bergson, in form and diction to conform to the ideal of austere simplification followed by the new school of plastic artists. Like them, she hated "literature" and sought "the destruction of associational emotion in poetry and prose." Like them also, she was indifferent to the qualitative aspects of subject; she merely "rendered" people, landscapes, and events. And because her passion for "elemental abstraction" appealed to a generation that had just been through the concrete discomforts of a world war, she became in time a kind of High Priestess. Although a follower like Hemingway, remaining "nine-tenths bourgeois," never got away from the "museum smell," her non-associational prose became one of the greatest single influences on the prose of her time.

In her detachment, her asceticism, and her eclecticism, Miss Stein can only remind us of another American author who lived in Europe and devoted himself more and more exclusively to the abstract. The principal difference between Henry James (whom Miss Stein reads more and more these days) and Gertrude Stein is that the former still kept within the human realm by treating moral problems. (Miss Stein has a more absolute esthetic ideal: "the *intellectual* passion for exactitude in the description of inner and outer reality.") Moreover, what Miss Stein has in common with James she has in common with Poe, Hawthorne, Melville, and several other important and characteristic American writers: an orientation from experience toward the abstract, an orientation that has been so continuous as to constitute a tradition, if not actually *the* American tradition. Of this tradition it is possible to see in Miss Stein's writing not only a development but the pure culmination. She has pushed abstraction farther than James or even Poe would ever have dared—to the terms of literary communication itself, "Words and Sentences." The final divorce between experience and art, which they threatened, is accomplished. Not only life but the traditional means of communication in life are "simplified" to suit the patterns which she offers in substitute.

F. Scott Fitzgerald

I *The Perfect Life*

[1935]

Although it is one of the most obvious statements that can be
made of any novelist, it has never exactly been pointed out about
Scott Fitzgerald that what he is principally concerned with in
all his novels and tales is character. "She was a fine girl—one of
the best," remarks the hero of one of the stories in *Taps at Rev-
eille* of the wife who has abandoned him to follow her own career.
"She had character." All the important personages in the book
have character, or are trying to have character, or have irretrievably lost their character. Whether the emphasis is on achievement or struggle or failure the theme is one and the same. Whatever may be their age or sex or background, all of them are sooner
or later confronted, like the adolescent Basil Lee, with the vision
of "the perfect life." This rambunctious Middle Western school-
boy, whose inner gyrations occupy the first story in the volume,
is the father of the chastened hero of "Babylon Revisited," which
is the last. Of course neither Basil nor his feminine counterpart,
the precociously scandalous Josephine, is presented in any ear-
nestly moralistic fashion; their adolescent crises are more often a
source of amusement than of edification; but what gives to their
histories a direction and finally a meaning is their common effort
at some sort of personal regeneration. In the other stories, which
deal with people adult at least in years, the theme is naturally

treated with a more becoming gravity. "Babylon Revisited," one of the best of them, deals with the not quite successful attempt of a reformed survivor of the Paris pleasure front of the twenties to wrest custody of his child from skeptical relatives. "The Last of the Belles," as the title may suggest, is the record of a young Northerner's gradual recovery from the narcotic influences of the romantic South. In the somewhat melodramatic "Family in the Wind," a middle-aged country doctor emerges triumphantly from a long season with the bottle. The gin-colored twilight of Hollywood film-colony receptions supplies the atmosphere for another such drama of self-conquest in "Crazy Sunday." In the strangest of all the tales, "A Short Trip Home," Mr. Fitzgerald's obsession drives him to the frankly allegorical: the sinister Joe Varland, hanger-on of poolrooms and tracker of women, is the almost abstract embodiment of evil. Indeed, the only exception to the generalization that has been made is the slight and ineffective "Night of Chancellorsville," which would seem to prove that Mr. Fitzgerald is interesting only when he is at grips with the problem of character.

Now the problem of character, which is first and last the moral problem, is not popular with many of the writers and readers of contemporary fiction; it has been relegated to that class of quaint antiquities which includes Malthusianism and the Boston rocker. The reasons for this are obvious enough and need not be rehearsed; but the consequences for fiction have become increasingly more overwhelming during the past two book seasons. For the area of moral conflict, the area which most of the older novelists chose as their terrain, has been substituted the vast, the unchartable, the uncontrollable ocean of the sensibilities. As the tide rises the flood threatens to carry all before it—readers along with writers. The inheritors of the Joycean dispensation, unencumbered by the self-wrought bonds of esthetic discipline which restrained the master, are intent on submerging the universe. What used to be called character has dissolved in the confused welter of uncoordinated actions, sensations, impressions, and physico-chemical reactions which currently passes for the art of fiction.

Mr. Fitzgerald, in his persistent concentration on "those fine moral decisions that people make in books," is fundamentally, therefore, a rather old-fashioned sort of storyteller. He has more in common, let us say, with George Eliot, Henry James, and Joseph Conrad than with any of the more prominent members of his own generation. One should not be misled by the strong sense of the *Zeitgeist* reflected in his choice of subjects and characters. Although the experience is as contemporary as that of Faulkner or of Hemingway, the focus on the experience is very different, and the technique that is the result of this focus is different. It is not experience *qua* experience that is important but the ordering of experience, the arrangement of experience according to some scheme of developing moral action. This is the reason why Mr. Fitzgerald in even his worst lapses, such as the story called "Majesty," is always able to sustain a certain interest, to provide the kind of interest that we are accustomed to receive from prose narrative.

The observation that Mr. Fitzgerald is one of the few American writers still occupied with character, and that this is responsible for the distinction of form and technique in his writing, is not equivalent to a definitive evaluation of that writing as a whole. It is of course a temptation to say that stories like "The Last of the Belles" and "Babylon Revisited" are worth a half dozen novels of more pretentious length and substance published this season. It is the same sort of temptation that has caused certain critics, grateful that anything possessing so many of the features of a great work of fiction could be written in America, to speak of *The Great Gatsby* as if it were *Madame Bovary* or *War and Peace*. But while Mr. Fitzgerald is excellent in tracing the vacillating curve of character in his works, his standard or criterion of character itself is not always easily to be determined. Sometimes it would seem to be the manliness of a Yale football captain, sometimes the innocence of a Middle Western debutante, some-

times no more than the ability to conform to the mores of respectable middle-class society. Especially from "A Short Trip
Home" does one derive the impression that evil is always to be
found in poverty-stricken back alleys downtown, and goodness
always in the warmly opulent mansions of Summit Avenue. The
vision of evil is that of the adolescent suddenly frightened by the
glimpse of the great impersonal continent outside the frosted
windowpanes of the Twentieth Century Limited. The moral interest in all these stories is acute, but the moral vision is vague
and immature. If Mr. Fitzgerald could enlarge his vision to correspond to his interest, he would do much both for his own reputation and for the amelioration of current American fiction writing.

II   The Authority of Failure

[1945]

Of course, in any absolute sense, Scott Fitzgerald was not a failure
at all; he has left one short novel, passages in several others, and
a handful of short stories, which stand as much chance of survival
as anything of their kind produced in this country during the
same period. If the tag is so often attached to his name, it has
been largely his own fault. It is true that he was the victim, among
a great number of other influences in American life, of that para-
lyzing high pressure by which the conscientious American writer
is hastened to premature extinction as artist or as man. Upon the
appearance of *The Crack-Up*, a selection by Edmund Wilson of
Fitzgerald's letters, notebooks, and fugitive pieces, it was notable
that all the emptiest and most venal elements in New York journalism united to crow amiably about his literary corpse to this
same tune of insufficient production. Actually their reproaches
betrayed more of their own failure to estimate what was good
and enduring in his writing than his acknowledgeable limitations
as an artist. If Fitzgerald had turned out as much as X or Y or Z,
he would have been a different kind of writer—undoubtedly more
admirable from the standpoint of the quasi-moral American ethos

of production at any cost, but possibly less worth talking about five years after his death. And it might be said that Fitzgerald never hovered so close to real failure as when he listened from time to time, with too willing an ear, to these same reproaches.

But Fitzgerald brought most of it on himself by daring to make failure the consistent theme of his work from first to last. (Similarly Virginia Woolf used to be accused by the reviewers of being a sterile writer because she made sterility her principal theme.) It is perhaps only adumbrated in *This Side of Paradise;* for the discovery of its hero, Amory Blaine, that the world is not altogether his oyster is hardly the stuff of high tragedy. The book is interesting today as a document of the early twenties; nobody who would know what it was like to be young and privileged and self-centered in that bizarre epoch can afford to neglect it. But it can also be read as a preliminary study in the kind of tortured narcissism that was to plague its author to the end of his days. (See the article called "Early Success" in the Wilson collection.) *The Beautiful and the Damned* is a more frayed and pretentious museum piece and the muddiest in conception of all the longer books. It is not so much a study in failure as in the *atmosphere* of failure—that is to say, of a world in which no moral decisions can be made because there are no values in terms of which they may be measured. Hardly is it a world suited to the purposes of the novelist, and the characters float around in it as in some aquamarine region comfortably shot through with the soft colors of self-pity and romantic irony. Not until *The Great Gatsby* did Fitzgerald hit upon something like Mr. Eliot's "objective correlative" for the intermingled feeling of personal insufficiency and disillusionment with the world out of which he had unsuccessfully tried to write a novel.

Here is a remarkable instance of the manner in which adoption of a special form or technique can profoundly modify and define a writer's whole attitude toward his world. In the earlier books author and hero tended to melt into one because there was no internal principle of differentiation by which they might be separated; they respired in the same climate, emotional and moral;

they were tarred with the same brush. But in *Gatsby* is achieved a dissociation, by which Fitzgerald was able to isolate one part of himself, the spectatorial or esthetic, and also the more intelligent and responsible, in the person of the ordinary but quite sensible narrator, from another part of himself, the dream-ridden romantic adolescent from St. Paul and Princeton in the person of the legendary Jay Gatsby. It is this which makes the latter one of the few truly mythological creations in our recent literature—for what is mythology but this same process of projected wish fulfillment carried out on a larger scale and by the whole consciousness of a race? Indeed, before we are quite through with him, Gatsby becomes much more than a mere exorcizing of whatever false elements of the American dream Fitzgerald felt within himself: he becomes a symbol of America itself, dedicated to "the service of a vast, vulgar and meretricious beauty."

Not mythology, however, but a technical device which had been brought to high development by James and Conrad before him made this dissociation possible for Fitzgerald. The device of the intelligent but sympathetic observer situated at the center of the tale, as James never ceases to demonstrate in the Prefaces, makes for some of the most priceless values in fiction—economy, suspense, intensity. And these values *The Great Gatsby* possesses to a rare degree. But the same device imposes on the novelist the necessity of tracing through in the observer or narrator himself some sort of growth in general moral perception, which will constitute in effect *his* story. Here, for example, insofar as the book is Gatsby's story it is a story of failure—the prolongation of the adolescent incapacity to distinguish between dream and reality, between the terms demanded of life and the terms offered. But insofar as it is the narrator's story it is a successful transcendence of a particularly bitter and harrowing set of experiences, localized in the sinister, distorted, El Greco-like, Long Island atmosphere of the later twenties, into a world of restored sanity and calm, symbolized by the bracing winter nights of the Middle Western prairies. "Conduct may be founded on the hard rock or the wet marshes," he writes, "but after a certain point I don't care what it's founded on. When I came back from the East last autumn I felt that I wanted the world to be in uniform and at a sort of moral attention forever; I wanted no more riotous excursions with privileged glimpses into the human heart ever recurring." By reason of its enforced perspective the book takes on the pattern and the meaning of a Grail romance—or of the initiation ritual on which it is based. Perhaps this will seem a farfetched suggestion to make about a work so obviously modern in every respect; and it is unlikely that Fitzgerald had any such model in mind. But like *Billy Budd*, *The Red Badge of Courage*, or *A Lost Lady* —to mention only a few American stories of similar length with which it may be compared—it is a record of the strenuous passage from deluded youth to maturity.

Never again was Fitzgerald to repeat the performance. *Tender Is the Night* promises much in the way of scope but it soon turns out to be a backsliding into the old ambiguities. Love and money, fame and youth, youth and money—however one shuffles the antitheses they have a habit of melting into each other like the blue Mediterranean sky and sea of the opening background. To Dick Diver, with a mere change of pronoun, may be applied Flaubert's analysis of Emma Bovary: "Elle confondait, dans son désir, les sensualités du luxe avec les joies du coeur, l'élégance des habitudes et les délicatesses du sentiment." And it is this Bovaryism on the part of the hero, who as a psychiatrist should conceivably know more about himself, that in rendering his character so suspect prevents his meticulously graded deterioration from assuming any real significance. Moreover, there is an ambiguous treatment of the problem of guilt. We are never certain whether Diver's predicament is the result of his own weak judgment or of the behavior of his neurotic wife. At the end we are strangely unmoved by his downfall because it has been less a tragedy of will than of circumstance.

Of *The Last Tycoon* we have only the unrevised hundred and thirty-three pages supported by a loose collection of notes and synopses. In an unguarded admission Fitzgerald describes the book as "an escape into a lavish, romantic past that perhaps will not come again into our time." Its hero, suggested by a well-known Hollywood prodigy of a few years ago, is another one of those poor boys betrayed by "a heightened sensitivity to the promises of life." When we first meet him he is already a sick and disillusioned man, clutching for survival at what is advertised in the notes as "an immediate, dynamic, unusual, physical love affair." This is nothing less than "the meat of the book." But as much of it as is rendered includes some of the most unfortunate writing which Fitzgerald has left; he had never been at his best in the approach to the physical. Nor is it clear in what way the affair is related to the other last febrile gesture of Stahr—his championship of the Hollywood underdog in a struggle with the racketeers and big producers. Fortuitously the sense of social guilt of the mid-thirties creeps into the fugue, although in truth this had been a strong undertone in early short stories like "May Day" and "The Rich Boy." It is evident that Stahr is supposed to be some kind of symbol—but of what it would be hard to determine. From the synopses he is more like a receptacle for all the more familiar contradictions of his author's own sensibility—his arrogance and generosity, his fondness for money and his need for integrity, his attraction toward the fabulous in American life and his repulsion by its waste and terror. "Stahr is miserable and embittered toward the end," Fitzgerald writes, in one of his own last notes for the book. "Before death, thoughts from *Crack-Up*." Apparently it was all to end in a flare-up of sensational and not too meaningful irony: Stahr, on his way to New York to call off a murder which he had ordered for the best of motives, is himself killed in an airplane crash, and his possessions are rifled by a group of school-children on a mountain. If there is anything symbolic in this situation, could it be the image of the modern Icarus soaring to disaster in that "universe of ineffable gaudiness" which was Fitzgerald's vision of the America of his time?

Inquiry into what was the real basis of Fitzgerald's long pre-occupation with failure will not be helped too much by the auto-biographical sketches in *The Crack-Up*. The reasons there offered are at once too simple and too complicated. No psychologist is

likely to take very seriously the two early frustrations described—
inability to make a Princeton football team and to go overseas in
the last war. In the etiology of the Fitzgerald case, as the psychologists would say, the roots run much deeper, and nobody cares to
disturb them at this early date. His unconscionable good looks
were indeed a public phenomenon, and their effect on his total
personality was something which he himself would not decline to
admit. The *imago* of the physical self had a way of eclipsing at
times the more important *imago* of the artist. But even this is a
delicate enough matter. Besides, there were at work elements of
a quite different order—racial and religious. For some reason he
could never accept the large and positive influence of his Celtic
inheritance, especially in his feeling for language, and his hark-
ing back to the South has a little too nostalgic a ring to be convincing. Closely related to this was the never resolved attitude
toward money and social position in relation to individual worth.
But least explored of all by his critics were the permanent effects
of his early exposure to Catholicism, which are no less potent because rarely on the surface of his work. (The great exception is
"Absolution," perhaps the finest of the short stories.) Indeed, it
may have been the old habit of the confession which drove him,
pathetically, at the end, to the public *examen de conscience* in
the garish pages of *Esquire* magazine.

To add to his sense of failure there was also his awareness of
distinct intellectual limitations, which he shared with the major-
ity of American novelists of his time. "I had done very little
thinking," he admits, "save within the problems of my craft."
Whatever he received at Princeton was scarcely to be called an
education; in later years he read little, shrank from abstract ideas,
and was hardly conscious of the historical events that were shap-
ing up around him. Perhaps it is not well for the novelist to en-
cumber himself with too much knowledge, although one cannot
help recalling the vast cultural apparatus of a Tolstoy or a Joyce,
or the dialectical intrepidity of a Dostoievski or a Mann. And recalling these Europeans, none of whom foundered on the way,
one wonders whether a certain coyness toward the things of the

mind is not one reason for the lack of development in most American writers. Art is not intellect alone; but without intellect art is not likely to emerge beyond the plane of perpetual immaturity.

Lastly, there was Fitzgerald's exasperation with the *multiplicity* of modern human existence—especially in his own country. "It's under you, over you, and all around you," he protested, in the hearing of the present writer, to a young woman who had connived at the slow progress of his work. "And the problem is to get hold of it somehow." It was exasperating because for the writer, whose business is to extract the unique quality of his time, what Baudelaire calls the quality of *modernité*, there was too much to be sensed, to be discarded, to be reconciled into some kind of order. Yet for the writer this was the first of obligations; without it he was nothing—"Our passion is our task, and our task is our passion." What was the common problem of the American novelist was intensified for him by his unusually high sense of vocation.

In the last analysis, if Fitzgerald failed, it was because the only standard which he could recognize, like the Platonic conception of himself forged by young Jay Gatsby in the shabby bedroom in North Dakota, was too much for him to realize. His failure was the defect of his virtues. And this is perhaps the greatest meaning of his career to the younger generation of writers.

"I talk with the authority of failure," he writes in the notebooks, "Ernest with the authority of success. We could never sit across the same table again." It is a great phrase. And the statement as a whole is one neither of abject self-abasement nor of false humility. What Fitzgerald implies is that the stakes for which he played were of a kind more difficult and more unattainable than "Ernest" or any of his contemporaries could even have imagined. And his only strength is in the consciousness of this fact.

III CONTINENTAL LITERATURE

Stendhal: In Quest of Henri Beyle

Whoever is gifted with alert and daring senses, curious to the point of cynicism, logical almost from disgust, a solver of enigmas, friend of the sphinx like every well-born European—he will be compelled to go after him.—FRIEDRICH NIETZSCHE

[1942]

On a fine morning in October, 1832, on the Janiculum at Rome, there might have been observed a pudgy middle-aged Frenchman expensively attired in tight-fitting white trousers of an English material. (The latter are important because later to be concealed in their cuff was the sentence, written in English and jumbled "so that it should not be understood," *Imgo ingt obefif ty*.) Who was this personage and of what was he thinking among so many interesting reminders of the human past? The first of these questions is by no means easy to answer. According to one estimate the number of his pseudonyms was one hundred and sixty, and his disguises, which included those of a Cistercian monk and a woman of quality, were more than thirty. It is a mere accident of literary history that of the many names attached to his published writings one in particular should be associated with his reputation. Less accidental perhaps, but of some significance, is the fact that he should be remembered only as a writer; for he was in his time a lieutenant of Dragoons, a grocer, a commissar in Napoleon's army, a suspected police spy, a consul, and, through all, the self-styled Lovelace of his age. In the arts his interests included music and painting as well as literature—with a passion for *opera bouffe* perhaps lending a certain unity; and his works represent not only all the known genres but also some that cannot be too easily placed. Indeed, the difficulty of "placing" the figure on the hilltop is no greater for us than it seems to have been for Henri Beyle himself—to use the convention of labelling an individual by his baptismal name. The moment is memorable, because for some unexplained reason—the blended influence of autumn sunlight and Roman ruins and the prospect of his fiftieth birthday?—it determined him to write his autobiography. "I shall soon be fifty," he writes in *The Journal of Henri Brulard,* "it is high time that I got to know myself. What I have been, what I am, I should really find it hard to say." This autobiography would be composed "without lying . . . but with pleasure, like a letter to a friend," for its purpose was to be no less than to discover *"what manner of man I have been."* As to his hero Lucien Leuwen, the occasion had finally come for the secret and heart-rending interrogation, "Who am I?"

Like Beyle himself, nearly all the good critics in his own language have focussed his problem quite squarely, and rightly so, on the metaphysical problem of identity. To the excellent studies of Fernandez, Valéry, and Seillière there is perhaps not a great deal to be added along this line. But today we are so much impressed by the manner in which metaphysical considerations are bound up with psychological considerations and both with the general cultural situation that the time is appropriate for the sort of comprehensive stocktaking that Beyle himself seems to have had in mind. For example, a little further on in *Henri Brulard,* the memory projects the following very interesting little *spontanée:*

> It was two months ago . . . while I was musing upon writing these memoirs . . . that I wrote in the dust, like Zadig, these initials:
>
>   a   d   i l   ine pg de   r
>   V. A. A. M. M. A. A. A. M. C. G. A.
>   1   2   3   4   5   6

The initials turn out to be those of the various women that he has loved in the course of his life. What the whole incident reveals is some sort of mysterious identification in Beyle's mind between the impulse to discover the truth about himself and the delight in setting down this cryptogram of his amours. It illustrates the manner in which everything in his life and work—his writings, his theoretical speculations, his political attitudes—takes on a complex and imponderable character. More particularly, it provides us with the clue that somehow involved in his case is some disturbance or at least malaise of the emotions. And for such a condition it is pretty inevitable for us nowadays to look for an explanation in the genetic history of the individual.

Behind the boldest and most annihilating protestations of the *Moi* in Stendhal (to distinguish now between the man and the writer) there is indeed always the recollection of those long, abandoned hours—with his Rousseau, his memoirs of Napoleon, and his caged thrush—in the dank little room on the Place Grenette in Grenoble. Not less at work are the remembered buffetings of the temperament that was so formed in its collision with a society that was to undergo three revolutions in forty years. For a proper understanding of the man in the white trousers we are compelled, therefore, to put his public utterances in their right place, which is a relative one, and consider them both in relation to the personality from which they emerge and the society to which they were one kind of reaction. Perhaps through such an effort the celebrated enigma of Stendhal will prove less mysterious if not less remarkable.

The childhood of Stendhal is a Freudian classic even for the *grand siècle* of the Oedipus complex. "My mother, Madame Henriette Gagnon, was a charming woman, and I was in love with her," he announces in *Henri Brulard*. And, lest there be any doubt in the matter, he continues, "I wanted to cover my mother with kisses, and for her to have no clothes on. She loved me passionately and often kissed me; I returned her kisses with such ardor that she was often obliged to go away. I abhorred my father when he came and interrupted our kisses." But this is perhaps more than enough—except to note that hatred of the father prevents him from referring to his mother except by her maiden name. It is demonstrated by any number of gloating recollections of infantile sadism. When his tame thrush disappears, for example, he insinuates that his father has killed it out of spite, and the latter, hurt at the suspicion, alludes to it one day in roundabout terms. "I was sublime; I blushed up to the roots of my hair, but I did not open my lips. He pressed me for an answer, the same silence met him; but my eyes, which were very expressive at that age, must have spoken for me." Thus was he avenged against the "tyrant," and for more than a month was proud of his vengeance—a laudable trait, we are told, in a child. Here we see, among other things, the beginning of that talent for *mystification*—a talent he shared with his contemporaries Poe and Baudelaire—which he was later to put to such a variety of uses. And in another quarrel with his father, a bourgeois with vague Royalist leanings, we have what is perhaps the key to his whole attitude toward any kind of authority. Instead of sympathizing with his father, who is on a list of suspects during the Revolution, he ponders, "My father glories in execrating 'the new order of things' (a term then fashionable among the aristocrats); what right have they to get angry?" This indignation not so much at injustice as at lack of logic, indicated by the peculiar emphasis on the word *right*, was to lead Stendhal to the rejection of much besides paternal authority. It had already led to a complete and final rejection of religion. At his mother's early death his main feeling is one of astonishment—perhaps that such a thing could happen to him. "I began to speak evil of God," he says simply. It was not "right" that the warm circle of his mother's affection should be intruded upon by the stupid fact of death.

But it is wholly unnecessary to prod further into what is the open scandal of *Henri Brulard* and the *Souvenirs of Egotism*. It will be enough to point to the more objective consequences. Turning to his first attempt at narrative, the tenuous but rather charming and too little read *Armance*, we find that the hero is a sensitive and gifted young aristocrat—the precursor of Villiers' Axel, Huysmans' Des Esseintes, and the early Proustian characters—suffering from a malady whose precise source is clear neither to himself nor the reader. Octave's "sole pleasure consists in living isolated and with nobody in the world having the right to address him a word." Exception is made for his mother—the only person in the world that he can love. Despite his avowed detestation of society he is persuaded to put in an appearance at certain of the great houses of the Faubourg, and in time becomes gradually involved in a curious sort of intimacy with a young woman of his own class. To call this a love affair is inaccurate; it is one of the vaguest relationships in all fiction. The girl is hardly more than a substitute for the mother as an audience for the hero's endless self-revelations and articulated *horror vitae*. Finally he admits to her that he cannot love either her or anyone else—because of a terrible secret that sets him apart from all living men. This secret turns out to be that he is a man altogether "without conscience." What is of course puzzling is the complete lack of any overt wickedness in his behavior and the reader is left wondering as to the particular nature of his crime. Yet other characters hint at sinister elements in his personality. His mother remarks, "This singular taste [for solitude] is the effect of your disturbing passion for the sciences; your studies make me tremble; you will end like Goethe's Faust." What is soon evident, however, is that Stendhal is having supreme difficulty writing a novel about a young man motivated by "the obligation not to love." There is nothing to do but have him hurl himself into the sea and send the girl to a convent.

Armance is a slight work, with neither the scope nor insights of the later novels, but its very simplicity throws into relief what was to be their remarkably uniform pattern. All of them are about superior young men who hover about the great bonfire of love without ever wishing to approach near enough to get burned. All of them are built on an essential pattern of frustration. In every case the hero, like Fabrizio in the *Charterhouse of Parma*, although "in love with love," is blocked by some overwhelming obstacle either in himself or in external circumstances. To establish this obstacle Stendhal at times is reduced to far-fetched and improbable dodges. In *Lucien Leuwen*, for example, the hero, after trying through several hundred pages to make up his mind, is saved by the false information that the very virtuous heroine is having a child by another man. This relieves Lucien of the necessity of declaring his love but it prevents Stendhal from finishing the book. The relationship between Fabrizio and his aunt Madame de Sanseverina in the *Charterhouse* is kept pure through an implied antipathy for incest. That there may have been other reasons, however, is suggested in certain passages. "I was in love with love," Fabrizio tells the Duchess. "I have done everything in the world to acquire knowledge of it; but it appears that nature has refused me a heart to love, and to be melancholy." And perhaps nowhere is the dread of taking on the responsibilities of physical love better symbolized than in the closing scenes of the same work, in which Fabrizio carries on a liaison with the jail-keeper's daughter from behind the bars of his cell by means of a sign language. During this period he is at last completely happy; and when Sanseverina and the others plot for his escape he announces that he prefers to remain in jail. Here the iron bars provide an "obstacle" as irrefutable as it is substantial.

But it is of course in *The Red and the Black* that we find the most elaborate as well as most comprehensive treatment of the love theme in Stendhal. And here the first of the two obstacles in the way of the hero is one that loomed quite large at times for Beyle himself—poverty. To consider Julien's relations with the two women in the novel without taking account of his origins is to miss much that explains their peculiar character and development. Julien, alone of these agitated young men, is of lowly birth —the son of a carpenter, who knocks him about brutally and sells him to the local representative of the rising *haute bourgeoisie*, M. de Renal. Apparently he has also been knocked about by his many older brothers and has never known the protection of maternal love. At the moment we meet him he is steeped in Napoleon's memoirs and Rousseau's *Confessions*. And the physical description is revealing enough to be quoted in full:

His cheeks were flushed, his eyes downcast. He was a slim youth of eighteen or nineteen, weak in appearance, with irregular but delicate features and an aquiline nose. His large dark eyes, which, in moments of calm, suggested a reflective, fiery spirit, were animated at this instant with an expression of the most ferocious hatred. Hair of a dark chestnut, growing very low, gave him a narrow brow, and in moments of anger a wicked air. Among the innumerable varieties of the human countenance, there is perhaps none that is more strikingly characteristic. A slim and shapely figure betokened suppleness rather than strength. In his childhood, his extremely pensive air and marked pallor had given his father the idea that he would not live, or would live only to be a burden upon his family. An object of contempt to the rest of the household, he hated his brothers and father; in the games on Sunday, on the public square, he was invariably beaten.

Of what this countenance is actually characteristic, Stendhal does not mention; but it is easy to detect in it the compounded lineaments of the Man of Feeling—the "delicate features," the "marked pallor," and the "pensive air"—and the Satanic hero—the fiery dark eyes, the wicked dark hair, and even the aquiline nose. By 1830 the process of assimilation between them had been completed; and in Julien we can see unmistakably how the hypertrophied sensibility of the former merges into the neo-Machiavellian diabolism of the latter.

In the de Renal household Julien is motivated neither by a thirst for experience nor by simple material ambition but by what may be called a sense of duty. The briskly conceived campaign by which he seduces Madame de Renal is an affair not so much of the heart as of the will. It is his "duty" to make love to this virtuous and naive woman in order to prove to himself that he is the equal of the class to which she belongs. "It would be cowardly on my part not to carry out an action which may be of use to me, and diminish the scorn which this fine lady probably feels for a poor workman, only just taken from the sawbench." And again, "The ruthless warfare which his sense of duty was waging with his natural timidity was too exhausting for him to be in a condition to observe anything outside himself." This condition is not relieved until the first great climactic scene, in which Madame de Renal permits him to hold her hand. "His heart was flooded with joy, not because he loved Madame de Renal, but because a fearful torment was now at an end." The next morning he is filled with joy that *"He had done his duty, and a heroic duty."*

Duty toward what or toward whom? Fortunately, Stendhal provides an explanation: "Instead of paying attention to the transports that he excited, and to the remorse that increased their vivacity, the idea of *duty* was continually before his eyes. He feared a terrible remorse, and undying ridicule, should he depart from the ideal plan that he had set himself to follow. In a word, what made Julien a superior being was precisely what prevented him from enjoying the happiness that sprang up at his feet." Discussion of this "ideal plan" belongs to a later section of this paper. But it must now be pointed out that realization of his duty is for Julien never more than a momentary source of self-satisfaction. The primary struggle is not with Madame de Renal or with society but in himself, between the unacknowledged promptings of the heart and the dictates of the intellectual will. His confusion is betrayed in the paradoxical antithesis: "I ought to be stirred by her beauty; I owe it to myself to be her lover." The whole pathos of his situation is summed up in Stendhal's comment on the incident of the hand-holding: "The idea of a duty to be performed, and of making himself ridiculous, or rather being left with a sense of inferiority if he did not succeed in performing it, at once took all the pleasure from his heart."

What constitutes the source of Julien's ordeal may be more apparent if one recalls what has been said of Henri Beyle's childhood. It is not without significance to Julien that Madame de Renal is many years older than himself—and a mother. The encounters between them are unlike those of adult lovers: Madame de Renal is too shocked by the impact on her innocent nature of her first experience of real love to maintain any strong sense of reality; and Julien is too dominated by his will to recognize the extent and quality of his attraction toward her. It is very nearly as "pure" a relationship as that between Fabrizio and the Sanseverina; descriptions of its physical side are suspiciously vague and uncircumstantial. For the most part Julien behaves like a spoiled child engaged in an intrigue with his mother. Only at rare moments of collapse, such as the one in which he is rebuked for breaking into Madame de Renal's bedroom at night, is the real basis of his trouble, the *natural* Julien revealed:

> "Wretch!" she cried. There was some confusion. Julien forgot his futile plans and returned to his own natural character. Not to please so charming a woman seemed to him the greatest disaster possible. His only answer to her reproaches was to fling himself at her feet, clasping her round the knees. As she spoke to him with extreme harshness, he burst into tears.

Different in kind and development, however, is the relationship with Mathilde de la Mole. Like the heroine of the fragmentary *Lamiel*, this character is a feminine counterpart for the desperate and amoral heroes. To Julien the obstacle that she presents is of course that of social rank; she is at the very top of that ladder that he must ascend to guarantee his victory. From her standpoint she is fascinated by the idea that there is something "daring and audacious" in loving one so far beneath her. If Julien had been merely another suitor of her own class, the affair would lack that element which characterizes great passion: "the immensity of the difficulties to be overcome and the dark uncertainty of the issue." At times she is the transparent little sadist: "She had infinite cleverness, and this cleverness triumphed in the art of torturing the self-esteem of others and inflicting cruel wounds upon them." The meeting of these two can only be sterile and mutually destructive; it has the character of moral or spiritual incest—a merging of identities in the flux. As incapable of love as her husband, she seeks to escape the ennui of her class and her position by a kind of perpetual titillation of the soul. At the top of one of the chapters Stendhal quotes from some forgotten book of memoirs: "*The need of anxiety*, such was the character of the beautiful Marguerite de Valois. . . . The need of playing at a game formed the whole secret of the character of this amiable princess." And in nothing more than in this "need of anxiety" and "need of playing a game" does Mathilde resemble her lover and husband. What helps us explain these traits in him should serve also to explain them in her.

It is not too much to say that *The Red and the Black* is the first full-length treatment of the "split personality" in nineteenth-century literature. Of course this had been the secret basis of all the troubles of the heroes of the Gothic novel and of Byron; it was also being allegorically rendered in Hoffman's *Elixire des Teufels* and *Doppelgänger* as well as in Poe's "William Wilson." In Julien's case, however, the situation is presented almost as a problem or a demonstration (Beyle had had an early passion for mathematics): What would happen if someone really attempted to separate the intellectual will from the impulses of the simple heart? Stendhal, a kind of naturalist of the heart, puts his hero through the paces as a scientist his guinea pig through a maze. Actually, the analogy is as unsound as it is trite; for the paces happen to be the still incompletely unravelled interplay of human thought and feeling, and the maze is the whole organic complex of human relationships. Nor is the observer nearly so detached as he pretends. But Stendhal brings to the problem the kind of patient and exhaustive analysis of its elements that we like to think of as modern; through his influence on Nietzsche and possibly also on von Hartmann he may be considered as one of those responsible for the modern movement of psychoanalysis. In Julien what was to be the predicament of nearly all the major heroes of later nineteenth-century literature—those of Dostoievski, Melville, Proust, and Kafka—is forecast with the bareness of a penny horoscope.

We say everything perhaps when we state the cause of this predicament as a dislocation for the individual of his normal or traditional objects of love. But this is to be quite general, to be confronted immediately with the unlimited range of possible operations open to the human organism. Before attempting to describe further what seems to be happening in the typical Stendhalian hero, therefore, it will be necessary to do what in the case of a writer of more complete or self-sustaining works would be less legitimate—to turn back again for a moment to the life. For Stendhal must be classed with an important type of modern writer in whom the life and the work are so mutually indispensable that the latter does not yield up its real interest or significance when taken alone. Together they constitute what may be called a phenomenon—not only within literature but within their culture as a whole. Certainly Poe, Rimbaud, Nietzsche, and even Melville are more interesting when considered in this way rather than in relation solely to their incomplete and variously confused productions. Less obviously apocalyptic in style than any of these perhaps, Stendhal's writing has the same quality of being the casual outpouring of someone who is essentially more the prophet than the artist.

In a preface to the perplexing and inconclusive *Armance*, André Gide, who has an excellent nose in such matters, advances the theory that the only possible meaning to be extracted from the book is that the hero is impotent. Gide proceeds to suggest that it is a study in the superiority of spiritual love over physical—impotence having a merely symbolic value. Even if this is untrue for this particular work we cannot help being tempted to apply the clue to the other Stendhal novels. In going over the roll call we have seen that at least two of his heroes, Octave and Lucien, appear to have gone to their graves in a virginal state. Fabrizio admits equivocally to not having been born to know "the taste of love," and we have noted the rather suspect quality of Julien's passion for the two women in his life. (In fact, he finally says of Mathilde, "She is my wife, but she is not my mistress.") Moreover, the notion that Octave's "lack of conscience" was a euphemism for another kind of lack cannot but direct us to certain avowals of the author of *Armance* himself. In that same scene in his autobiography in which he writes the initials in the dust, he adds, "The fact is that I have possessed only six of the women whom I have loved." And later, "With all of these, and with several others, I have always been a child." Recalling his early years in Milan, he complains, "Nobody took pity on me or aided me with some charitable advice. I therefore spent the two or three years in which my temperament was most active *woman-less.*" (The italics are his own.) Moreover, from an obscene remark in a letter to Merimée there is evidence to be drawn that his much recollected life in Marseilles with the little actress Melanie Louasan was of the more innocent sort. This is also one interpretation to be placed on a passage in a letter written by her after his abandonment of her—in any case, one of the most pathetic documents in literary biography:

> I assure you again of my loyal devotion and genuine tenderness; I have already given you sufficient proofs of both, and you have replied only with vague letters, saying that you love me, that you still love me, and that I will realize it two weeks from now when I see you again. All of that means only that when we meet you will make love to me a great deal, and swear you adore me, and that you live again now that you are with me, and all that sort of thing. That may seem like a great deal to you, but I am afraid it has very little real meaning to me, especially when I consider your conduct as a whole, and your character as a whole; it cannot prove to me that you love me as I wish you to and as I must be loved if I am ever to be happy and at peace. And that is why I beg you to be frank with me.

Of course it cannot be proved definitely that Henri Beyle suffered from a real or psychopathic impotence. Nor is it to be supposed that even if such proof were available it would adequately explain everything in his life and work. But if the value of any hypothesis is to be tested by the number of things that it allows us to put together we have here an extremely fertile hypothesis. Not only does it suggest the reason for the obsessive repetition of the frustration pattern in the novels and the peculiar opacity of his treatment of love but also for his attitudes toward many other unrelated subjects. For the dislocation of the love object, which here may now possibly be more closely defined as an enforced separation of sentiment from its appropriate object, is not a single aspect of an individual; it affects every aspect of his being.

Very generally, it determines what may be called the dominant personality tone—in Stendhal's case, the sense of self-humiliation. Like Lucien Leuwen, who compels a beautiful and virtuous woman to fall in love with him simply because she has once seen him fall off a horse, his sole impulse is to *prove* himself to himself by some objective and incontrovertible gesture. But since this cannot be accomplished in any direct and sincere fashion he resorts to two extreme stratagems—deception and violence. It is clearly the first that explains the fondness for intrigue, masquerade, and pseudonymity already indicated. And most of the characters have the same secretive cunning about them: Octave has his "terrible secret" from the world; Julien confides only in the mountains and the skies the extent of his Napoleonic campaign against society. But deception actually turns out to be self-deception, and, as we have seen, all of them come to a bad end. The Machiavellian will does not easily displace the wounded sensibility of which it is the inverted expression. But since it is through his celebration of the other mode of self-assertion, the mode of violence, that Stendhal has probably had his most concrete influence, we must look at the manner in which this is represented in his work.

Violence in the crude sense finds its symbol in the familiar figure of the outlaw or criminal. Ferrante Palla, the nationalist revolutionary poet in the *Charterhouse*, is rendered with such *brio* as to emerge the only truly heroic character in that novel. At the end Julien succeeds in becoming what he has subconsciously desired to be all along—an enemy of society in deed as well as in thought. In the notes for *Lamiel* we are told that the hero was to be an arch-criminal named Valbayre, who would declare, "I am waging war on society, which is waging war on me." Symbolically enough, the heroine was to avenge his death by burning down the Palace of Justice, in the ashes of which her own bones were to be found. Even mild-tempered Fabrizio seems to be delighted when referred to as the "great culprit." Undoubtedly, there is a survival here of the Noble Brigand tradition of Schiller and Byron—a popular literary tradition. And Stendhal was among the first to introduce that nostalgic glorification of the exploits and misdeeds of the Italian city princes of the Renaissance which was to be carried so far by Burckhardt. But what is important is the manner in which these outside influences are modified to suit the necessities of a particular sort of temperament at a particular moment of time.

The criminal type is no longer the confused and sometimes philanthropically motivated rebel of the romantic period; he is more cerebral; he has taken on a Latin sharpness and lucidity of mind. There has also intervened the grand example of Napoleon —the criminal among the nations. He now knows that what he is against is not a class but the whole of society—even the *idea* of society. Of all the men at a ball, Mathilde de la Mole is interested only in a picturesque Spanish conspirator who is under sentence of death. "I can see nothing but a sentence of death that distinguishes a man," she remarks, "it is the only thing that cannot be bought." In such an epigram Stendhal says as much about the particular society of his time as Balzac in the whole of *César Birotteau* or *Lost Illusions*. But this disgust is ultimately translated into an intellectual contempt for the world in general. Of Octave it is remarked, "No suspicion of personal interest came to attack the purity of his diabolism." And we have already seen how Julien is equally "detached" toward all the social classes to which he is exposed—the peasant, the bourgeois, the clerical, and the aristocratic. There is nothing but the stripped ego against the world—the whole personality canalized in the intellectual will. At least this is the self-conscious ideal that these characters set before themselves; and action, instead of being the expression of some material or idealistic motive, becomes more and more an end in itself. Action, that is to say, is something spontaneous and essentially irrational—to use a word that Gide has made well-known, *gratuitous*. It has no meaning except as an objectification of the "pure will" of the doer.

But if the ideal of a Napoleon operating on society through other means than the sword dominates the mind, there linger in the sensibility the still unquieted echoes of J. J. Rousseau. And, at the end, as a Freudian critic would put it, the assertions of the superego are successfully drowned out by the protests of the id.

When Julien makes his attack on the life of his former mistress, it is not out of the assumed necessity of justifying himself by such an act—as with Raskolnikov's murder of the two women in *Crime and Punishment*. It is far from being a "gratuitous" act. It is rather the act of an exasperated child—a means of relieving the too great tension created by the contradictory nature of his feelings toward her. Afterwards, just before his execution, he confesses, "And why be a hypocrite still, when I am cursing hypocrisy? It is not death, nor the cell, nor the damp air, it is the absence of Madame de Renal that is crushing me."

The consequences of this ordeal are strikingly reflected in the formal bankruptcy of the Stendhalian novel. Because his heroes are incapable of action in the classic sense Stendhal is forced to rely almost exclusively upon analysis. Of course one admits that the analytical is the modern habit of mind; *Hamlet*, as Monsignor Kolbe has pointed out, is fundamentally a play *about* analysis. But in Stendhal the analysis is a vast and endless improvisation, without center and without limits—a medley of conflicting themes and motifs that can never be resolved because they are never really grasped. Distinctions, comparisons, and qualifications of the most tenuous sort must be made for every movement of the mind or sensibility. It would not be hard to discover in this mania for analysis a symptom of what we today call paranoia. In *Lucien Leuwen* at least it is carried to the point of absurdity if not of madness; and it is no wonder that the book is uncompleted. Indeed, of all Stendhal's novels only *Armance* may be considered complete, and that simply terminates with the unexplained suicide of the hero.

Yet even the briefest résumé of any one of them reveals that there *is* action—a kind of action. But this is neither the rapid and vigorous melodrama of Balzac nor the mechanical Punch-and-Judy show of Flaubert and the naturalists. Rather, the web of analysis is punctured at intervals by unprepared and frequently meaningless outbursts of ferocity—like the end of *The Red and the Black*. Because the conflict cannot be resolved it is elaborated and repeated; and there are lacking all those qualities of movement and design that we expect of the novel form. If we compare the work just mentioned with another on which it had a direct influence, *Crime and Punishment*, we see the difference between a work that renders only the *agon* and *pathos* of the hero, to use the terms of classical tragedy, and one that includes within it something like an *epiphaneia*. The value or feasibility of the latter in Dostoievski may be questioned; but, from the esthetic point of view, it gives finality and completeness. Stendhal cannot be numbered among those few great novelists who were also artists; his works have been interesting for other things than their style and form. And to discuss these things is to turn from such action as we find in his novels to some of their theoretical aspects —to what is sometimes called his "philosophy."

For Stendhal had no philosophy of a systematic kind, nor were his major ideas and opinions even very original for his time. His metaphysic of the Will was a common heritage from German idealism; it is present in Balzac and it will be a little later in Schopenhauer. (We know also that Stendhal read and was rather impressed by Fichte.) This famous Will was destined to take two directions in the later course of the century—according to whether emphasis was placed on the individual or the race. From Fichte, Gobineau, and Nietzsche was to come the cult of racism that has been translated into action in our own time. The cult of egoism, reaching its peak in the eighties, found its spokesman in Germany in the now forgotten Max Stirner and in France and elsewhere in Stendhal. Of a common philosophical origin, however, both are subject to the identical philosophical objections.

Beylism is indeed as good as any other label to cover the moral and intellectual anarchy of the undefined individualism of the modern world. For actually the romantic will, as we have seen it at work, is nothing but instinct parading as Machiavellian reason. The cult of the *Moi* becomes a cult of self-destruction the moment the individual realizes the interdependence between the sense of his own being and society. The notion of an altogether free and irresponsible individuality becomes a metaphysical conundrum if one inquires how a human individual could exist without a social environment to which he may offer the resistance by which he can be measured and defined. And it may be shown that when the individual makes his instinct the sole measure not only of himself but also of the universe, as did Stendhal and many other writers of his century, he runs the risk of becoming indistinguishable from the universe—which may provide certain satisfactions but certainly destroys the possibility of individuality. In fact, he achieves a state that is indistinguishable from the state of death.

The same objection is to be made to the implied ethics of the passage on Julien's "ideal plan" quoted earlier. According to this plan the individual would seem to project a sort of ideal version of himself—once again the superego at work—by which he must be governed in all his judgments and actions. But we have seen that what creation of this ideal self involves is a drastic separation of will and feeling that results in a total disruption of the personality. What it amounts to is a particularly hazardous mode of self-hallucination. "I am isolated here in this cell," Julien tells himself, "but I have not *lived in isolation* on this earth; I had always the compelling idea of *duty*. The duty that I had laid down for myself, rightly or wrongly, was like the trunk of a strong tree against which I leaned during the storm; I tottered, I was shaken. After all, I was only a man. . . ." At the last Julien does seem to have learned that the individual man has never been able successfully to lift himself by his own bootstraps.

In the political realm Stendhal reveals the same confusion; to reduce to logic his innumerable utterances on the political events and ideas of his time is impossible. In childhood his sympathies were republican, and he was seized with an acute sensation of joy upon the execution of Louis XVI. But it is clear that this is but one more expression of the revolt against his father— like his anti-clericalism. Denunciation of the class that the Revolution actually pushed into power abounds everywhere in his writings—for example, the treatment of the de Renals and the diatribes against "middle-class meanness." And of the people he has this to say, "I abhor the mob (that is, any contact with them) while at the same time, under the name of 'the people,' I have a passionate desire for their happiness." Nothing better states the contradiction between the snob who boasts of his liaisons with duchesses and the child who exults in the death of kings. In the novels, as we have seen, cynicism and abuse are distributed almost equally among all classes of society and all shades of political opinion. Stendhal is much interested in politics; *The Charterhouse* and *Lucien Leuwen* are novels with political backgrounds; but he was interested in politics and life as in "a game of chess." The truth is that he could not remain faithful to any political party or even program for the reason that he was incapable of any kind of allegiance. The refusal to accept any responsibility in his relations with society is of a piece with his attitude toward his father and toward women. His politics, like his ethics, end up in a completely naive anarchy.

Certainly French society of the thirties and forties—with the old guard scheming to hold power even at the expense of selling France to the Prussians and the liberals barricaded behind their meretricious press—was not such as to elicit much faith in man as a social animal. And the Church, somewhat dazed by events, but also struggling for power, offered few securities of a moral or spiritual variety. But there were other possible modes of adjustment; Balzac, Baudelaire, and even Flaubert, each in his way and to a greater or less extent, achieved some sort of private solution in spite of the public chaos. What is noteworthy in Stendhal is the manner in which the private history and the public history are identified, in which the moody and recalcitrant child of the Place Grenette grows up into the avowed enemy of the whole social order. This is to say that he is to be explained neither by a glib invocation of the Oedipus complex nor by a description of the now quite familiar socio-economic contradictions of bourgeois society. It is rather that the whole soil of Western European culture in his time was such as to bring to monstrous flowering those talents for confusion and self-destruction which his early experience enabled him to contribute to it. It was such as to give special scope—in his case, largely intellectual, although in the next century such scope was to be active as well—to the potentiality for pure evil that exists in the race in every time and place. And the reciprocal nature of the whole process should prove as much as anything to what extent even in the negative sense the individual is involuntarily tied up with his society and committed to its destiny. But to pursue the point further is really to return to the question raised at the beginning of this paper.

Who, in the last analysis, is the *person* that emerges from behind the slily constructed barrage of subterfuge and deceit that was the career of Henri Beyle? Or, at least we may ask, what *kind* of person? In attempting an answer we have depended much less on his own explicit statements about himself than on the monotonously consistent pattern underlying his life and work. This pattern we have seen as the hackneyed modern one of frustration —the brisk progress to death and destruction of some unusually gifted and equally handicapped individual. Even when it has not been too apparent on the surface of the works we have insinuated that the basis of this handicap was some secret sense of sexual inferiority. Also noted has been the process by which what was originally a rejection of the father symbol is translated into a rejection of all existent religious and social symbols. And the whole operation has been seen as one made possible only by the particular situation of early nineteenth-century culture. But for a fuller identification of the type we must now consider him from the perspective of a much broader and also more traditional framework of human thought and values.

From the beginning one cannot but be struck by the sacrificial and even hieratic air that surrounds most of Stendhal's characters. "At times I find something superhuman about him," Octave's own mother remarks. And his uncle exclaims, "I conclude that if you aren't the Messiah awaited by the Hebrews, you are Lucifer in person, returning to this world expressly to addle my brains." It is harder perhaps to detect the sacrificial in Fabrizio, although he is if anything the *victim*—of his family, of the Milanese police, of Parma, and, most of all, of his own indefinite sensibility. He is, in any case, allotted an early death. Lucien Leuwen too is martyrized largely through his own incapacity to feel strongly enough to make a choice in any situation. But in *The Red and the Black* the note is sounded in the first description of Julien's treatment at the hands of his brothers: "The jealousy of these rough laborers had been so quickened by the sight of their brother's handsome black coat, and air of extreme gentility, as well as by the sincere contempt which he felt for them, that they had proceeded to thrash him, leaving him there unconscious and bleeding freely. Madame de Renal . . . saw Julien lying on the ground and thought him dead." There can be no doubt that what we witness here is the "superior being" at the mercy of the gross and uncomprehending social group—Joseph and the brethren. And what is the whole narrative up to the last explosion into febrile and pointless action, as has already been suggested, but the *pathos* of ritual and tragedy—the representation of the suffering that the hero brings upon himself through the excessive assertion of his will? As a modern, it is true, Julien's suffering comes before rather than after the action; it is the malady of the split will itself that constitutes the real suffering; and overt action is no more than a temporary and unsuccessful anodyne. Pathos on the physical plane is mutilation or dismemberment; and lest we think that Stendhal has limited himself only to moral and psychological dismemberment we need only recall the last scene of all, in which Mathilde places Julien's head upon a marble table and kisses it. "A great number of priests escorted the coffin and, unknown to all, alone in her draped carriage, she carried upon her knees the head of the man whom she had so dearly loved." Like Oedipus and Hippolytus, he will have a grotto erected in his honor and presumably become a local cult among the people.

How much of all this is deliberate in Stendhal and how much the unconscious symbolization of his own old and deep-seated sense of martyrdom is not the kind of question to be easily answered. It is significant, however, that for his finest and most enduring novel he should find his "objective correlative" (to use T. S. Eliot's phrase) in an account in the *Grenoble Gazette* of the guillotining of a handsome young man for a *crime passionel*.

Entirely by chance life threw up for him what elsewhere his imagination failed to accomplish—a design that gave an illusion of unity to all the elements in his long internecine warfare with society. By his choice of symbols is Henri Beyle finally found out; and in identifying himself with the criminal who pays to society the debt for which it does not deserve recompense, he becomes identifiable in our eyes as the familiar and immemorial scapegoat hero. The romantic outlaw of the Gothic tradition is apotheosized into the sacred criminal. To such an extent does the aureole gather round Julien's head that the old Abbé is obliged to protest, "This Julien is a strange creature, his action is inexplicable. . . . Perhaps it will be possible to make a martyr out of him." And let there be no mistake about it: Julien himself, in his last agony of self-communion, accepts his fate with the pride and also the fullest consciousness of his rôle: "The accuser whom society sets at my heels has been made rich by a scandalous injustice. . . . I have committed a murderous assault, and I am rightly condemned, but, short of murder only, the Valenod who condemned me is a hundred times more injurious to society."

In the classic manner the Stendhalian hero rehearses in the cycle of his own rise and fall the pattern of his culture as a whole. He takes on himself the guilt that is the result, in individuals and societies alike, of the disequilibrium between the principle of conservation, expressed in the limitations set by tradition and the moral code, and the principle of expansion, expressed in the interests and motives of the will. As a prefiguration of the destiny of that culture, his career has perhaps more meaning and a more terrifying reality for us today than when it was recorded. Prophecy has become a *fait accompli*. Not only does it throw into boldest relief the most obsessive problem of our time, the problem of justice, but it also demonstrates to what extent this problem is ultimately dependent for its solution on the problem of love. And this in turn is the problem of what is to become of the individual in a culture which, by reason of its structure and fundamental naiveté in regard to the human individual and his needs, is incapable of providing him with adequate objects of transcendence.

The lonely and somewhat grotesque figure of Henri Beyle gazing down upon the ruins of the Holy City is a symbol of a society without love—a society which has so far forgotten the meaning and importance of love as to be doomed to pay the consequences.

On Rereading Balzac:
The Artist as Scapegoat

[1940]

Balzac is little read nowadays; he is remembered as one of the more unkempt geniuses of an unkempt century. As a psychologist he is not to be compared with his contemporary Stendhal, nor as a craftsman with his successor Flaubert. He is rather to be held up to the young as a monumental example of the consequences of indiscipline. The highest compliment likely to be paid him is that he was one of the first and most "strenuous" critics of bourgeois society. Karl Marx admitted to having learned much of his knowledge and his theory of that society from the *Comédie Humaine*. This is in a straight line with Brunetière's judgment, in his famous Centenary Address at Tours in 1899, that Balzac would gain in value and importance with the passage of the years because his works were essentially "scientific documents."

Yet an open-minded rereading of Balzac can only leave us with the feeling that none of these judgments does justice to the real quality and nature of his achievement. True, his psychological analysis lacks the concentrated brilliance of Stendhal at his best. But, then, it comes out of an incomparably broader grasp of the complexities of the situation. Balzac is continually trying to get more into the picture than Stendhal was capable even of imagining. (His own criticism of the author of *Le Rouge et le Noir* is that he was completely lacking in the moral sense.) And the same defense may be made in any comparison with his two immediate successors: his obsession with fact did not cause his emotions to seek relief either in the sulphurous pessimism of Flaubert on the one hand or in the blowsy optimism of Zola on the other. The view of life on which he operated was equally realistic with theirs; but it was a realism that had more in common with that of the Church than with that of nineteenth-century science. If we look at all closely into the view of life on which he was most of the time working we must decide that it was the tragic: the human will, taken either in the individual or in society as a whole, is the principle of evil. It is a force for destruction that it is the better part of wisdom to recognize from the beginning.

To refer to Balzac as if he were a tragic poet is of course to throw a certain amount of confusion into those who have become accustomed to Brunetière's estimate of the work. But it is to keep well in mind Balzac's own plan of the *Comédie Humaine*, according to which the first part, the *Études de Moeurs*, was to be devoted to a comprehensive treatment of every one of the social *effects* of French national life in the early nineteenth century, while the second part, the *Études Philosophiques*, was to deal with its more abstract and generalized *causes*. A third part, the *Études Analytiques*, which was to deal with its *principles*, was never completed. "Then, after I have made the poesy, the demonstration of a whole system," he writes, "I will write the Science of it in an 'Essay on Human Forces.'" Although a word like "demonstration" has a rather bad sound here, it is clear that he is making a sharp distinction between "poesy" and "Science"; that the *Comédie* is to be taken as a vast symbolical edifice, rising in tiers from the twenty-four volumes of the first part to the fifteen of the second and the nine of the proposed third. Not only is this "poesy," but it is "poesy" on a Dantesque scale; and we hardly need the title to suggest that he was attempting nothing less than a parallel for his time of the synthesis repre-

sented in the *Divina Commedia*. And here also we may see how
he intended science to enter the work.

It is evident that Balzac hoped to reconcile both the method
and the discoveries of the science of his time with poetry. The
building of effects by the massing of factual detail is the application to narrative of the quantitative method of science. The Balzacian world is on the surface an interlocking system of atoms
separately collected and put together by the synthetic will. Part
of our response to his work—as with painters like Meissonier and
Delacroix—is expected to be an awareness of the amount of sheer
labor that has gone into the execution. And in this sense its
quantitative aspect may be said to be imponderably bound up
with the total esthetic effect. For Balzac's generation the immense
world of fact opened up by science had something like the awe-
inspiring fascination of Nature for the primitive mind; it made
possible once again a poetry of size. But there is the more important sense in which all this elaborate and painstaking documentation is after all no more than the *vehicle* of what is an essentially
imaginative reading of life. The celebrated description of the
Pension Vauquer, for example, is as itemized as a bailiff's inven-
tory. At the same time there is scarcely an article of furniture that
is not symbolical of the theme and subject as a whole. Quasi-
scientific documentation is simply an expansion of what is the
"literal" level of communication in a poet like Dante. The great
difference between Dante and Balzac, of course, is that where
the first had his meanings already embodied and ordered in a set
of traditional symbols the second had laboriously to reassemble
into wholes meanings that had been fractured through the analytical exploits of the previous two centuries.

So much for method. More interesting to consider perhaps
would be the ambitious attempt to identify the laws of science
with the moral and metaphysical concepts of the older religious
or poetic synthesis. To Louis Lambert, "Will" and "Thought"
were "living forces" capable of being measured and charted.
Raphael, in *The Magic Skin*, refers to the human will as "a nat-

ural force, like steam." "The boldest physiologists," Balzac writes in *César Birotteau*, "are frightened by the physical results of this moral phenomenon, which is, nevertheless, an inward blasting, and, like all electrical effects, capricious and strange in its methods." Is it too much to see here what would be the promise of a harmonization of the most advanced biochemistry, like that of Dr. Carrel, with the most advanced modern physics? The human "field of forces" is elsewhere defined: "Our brain is the matrix into which we transport all that our diverse organizations can absorb of ethereal matter—the common basis of several substances known under the improper names of electricity, heat, light, galvanic and magnetic fluid, etc.—and from which it issues in the form of thought." Like Poe in "Eureka," it is clear that Balzac had the dream of a fusion of all the branches of human knowledge. Instead of submitting to the scientific absolutism of his epoch like the naturalists or of retreating from it like the romantic sentimentalists, he sought to absorb the scientific worldview into the larger vision of the mystic.

But these notes must confine themselves to the single consideration of what more than anything else reveals the fundamentally poetic pattern that lies beneath the vast farraginous mass of the *Comédie Humaine*. If Balzac possessed the tragic vision, as has been suggested, we should expect to find it expressed nowhere more forcibly than in the treatment of his hero. And here also we may see how sharply he is to be distinguished in depth and breadth of imagination from any of the members of the two important schools of fiction that grew out of his work in France.

Balzac identifies himself with two quite different types of hero, corresponding to a division between his intellectual will and his imagination. Vautrin is the supreme example of the first type— a lineal descendant of Macheath through the Noble Brigand of German romantic drama and the Fatal Man of the Gothic novel. The other type is the Man of Sensibility of the eighteenth century now appearing under his true light as the artist himself suffering at the hands of a vulgar and immoral society. In Lucien de Rubempré and Raphael de Valentin, Balzac has drawn this type so fully that one wonders why so many writers throughout the remainder of the century felt impelled to repeat the pattern. Although we have stated that the two types are distinct, they have a common historical origin, and even in Balzac they are continually melting into each other. For the Fatal Man was in the beginning a sensitive and even radiant soul. Feeling lies at the root of his rebellion against authority; and the intellectual will of a Satan, a Faust, or a Manfred can easily enough be interpreted in modern psychological terms as inverted love. The Fatal Man —with his aspect of fallen angel of light, his harrowed countenance, and his addiction to sadism—was an expression of the violent revenge that Feeling began to inflict upon Reason by the end of the eighteenth century. He was the personification of an exasperated sentimentalism. If the man of refined moral and emotional impulses fared so badly in a world given over to a cynical skepticism in thought and an uninhibited selfishness in action, one solution for the superior individual was to outwit this world at its own game. The victim of life can always make the world his victim. Vautrin has not less feeling than Lucien or Raphael; his homosexual attachment to the young murderer whom he saves from the gallows is evidence of his capacity for suffering. It is simply that feeling in his case has been diverted into a monomaniac, anti-social passion.

In Vautrin, Balzac exhausts imaginatively that contempt for the hypocrisy and corruption of Restoration society which might very easily, in a man of his extraordinary vigor and detachment, have been converted into action. There is a sense, of course, in which all the personages of the *Comédie* are autobiographical. Every one of them, from pathetic little Birotteau to the rapacious de Nucingens, is a projection of the same terrific will that their creator is working off in his writing. When one of them looks down from the Butte Montmartre and swears to bring the whole city to his feet, it is Balzac himself supplying another image of his own determination to submit the whole of French life to his pen. But Vautrin is the will-to-power as pure reason; he is motivated not so much by material interests as by simple pride of intellect. And this is the unpardonable sin—the sin of Lucifer. When we first encounter him, in *Père Goriot*, he is the evil mentor of Rastignac, whom he is assisting in plotting a match with a rich society woman. The plot fails, and he is unmasked as the notorious Jacques Collin, former galley slave, long wanted by the police. In *Splendor and Misery of Courtesans* he appears in the robes of an important Spanish ecclesiastic whom he has murdered, and whose credentials, which he has stolen, will open to him all the doors of the Court and the Government. On the road to Paris he picks up poor Lucien de Rubempré, and the thought occurs to him to make him his creature. In the Machiavellian oration that he delivers on the vices and follies of high society, on how much the young poet must sacrifice if he would be a success in it, it is the very voice of Balzac himself that we seem to hear; it is like the plot of one of his novels. And it is then that we are made aware of the parallel between the artist and the criminal, between the "detached" observer of society and its detached enemy. Not only are both outside the pale but both are professionally given to the spinning of enormous plots. Vautrin is simply the artist functioning in the realm of action, the Fatal Man transported from the pages of fiction into actual life.

In *The Last Transformation of Vautrin*, which was probably the first gangster novel ever written, there is hardly any difference between the viewpoint of the author and his hero. Now we are introduced right inside the prison yard of St. Lazare and into the secret of that vast organization which Vautrin has built up and over which he rules like a dictator. Later, upon his escape, this organization will enable him to pass through the police nets of Paris as through a sieve. For this underworld confederation is represented not as a section or portion, a specific area of infection, of the body of society as a whole. It is rather a counter-society, with its own laws, customs, and loyalties, and with what may be described as only a *functional* relationship to "good" or official society. It exists by virtue of the failure of the latter to maintain at all times a proper equilibrium between its practical interests and its avowed moral or ethical attitudes. The rôle of a Vautrin, the man of superior intellect unimpeded by such self-deceptions, is to serve as a constant threat and menace to the universal fiction, to keep the writing on the wall always fresh and terrifying. For this reason the attitude of society toward the criminal is always ambivalent—divided between fear and respect: fear, lest its own motives be brought into the light through open prosecution; respect, in that he realizes with a brutal finality instincts which it can express only through the impure medium of its ritual. This is demonstrated in the altogether cynical manner in which Vautrin's long-drawn-out feud with society is brought to a close. His system of espionage and counterespionage has reduced so many of its best elements to his mercy that there is no solution but to make him chief of the secret police of Paris.

Vautrin corresponds, as has been said, to what must have been in Balzac the temptation of the intellectual will. Confronted with the teeming world of Restoration society, with a world altogether without values of any kind, Balzac must have found that temptation great indeed. Out of the mentality reflected in Vautrin and in that other great master of masquerade, Stendhal, was to develop the whole movement of thought that culminates in Stirner and Nietzsche. And out of these power philosophers in turn were to be spawned in the twentieth century those exponents of power politics whose success in "calling the bluff" of the more genteel *quartiers* of Europe is one of the most remarkable phenomena of the moment. But Balzac preferred art to action; he sought power elsewhere than in the Tuileries or in St. Lazare. And while he admits the perennial threat, even necessity at certain times, of a Vautrin, he discovers his fullest image in his other type of hero —the victim not so much of society as of life.

The simplest interpretation of the de Rubempré cycle is to discover in it another study of the manner in which bourgeois society treats the artist. In *Lost Illusions* Lucien is the poet as unspoiled child of nature, an innocent sentimentalist composing bad imitations of De Musset and Lamartine for the local bluestockings. But already his head is turned by flattery and he is willing to cast aside the image of idyllic domestic life presented by his friend and brother-in-law Séchard. A *Great Man of the Provinces in Paris* takes him to the capital in the equipage of Madame de Langeais, who soon abandons him, through a brief period of self-imposed asceticism in the Latin Quarter, to a rapid ascent and even more rapid descent in the vast ant-hill of Parisian journalism. No more devastating picture of the perennial corruption of the newspaper and publishing world has ever been drawn than in this section. And there is no depravity of this world that Lucien is not made to taste before he loses his fortune, his reputation, and his mistress. The section closes with two agonizing scenes: one in which he is forced to write a rollicking drinking song to pay the expenses of his mistress' funeral; another in which he has to accept from her maid money that she has earned through prostitution. His first great assault on the city has ended in a descent into the abyss—as did Joseph's in the land of Egypt. The second is made possible only by a complete sacrifice of what remains of his soul to the devil. When Vautrin picks him up on the road to Paris he has just succeeded in ruining his brother-in-law; he has suffered the mockery of being fêted by his fellow townsmen; and he is altogether penniless. Nothing remains but absolute capitulation to the forces that have already twice betrayed him. Throughout the first part of *Splendor and Misery of Courtesans* he seems relatively happy in the luxurious establishment that Vautrin has set up for him and his new mistress, the fabulous Esther Gobseck, in an obscure corner of Paris. But he is soon caught like a fly in the ever more complicated web of intrigue that his protector has spun in his feud with society. In the end the de Nucingens triumph; and this most Arabian of all Balzac's modern Arabian Nights Tales closes with Esther's murder, Vautrin's return to prison, and Lucien's suicide.

Such a long summary is offered to make clear the point that guilt is not shifted from the artist to society—as in the treatment of the subject by the Naturalists, for example. Lucien is betrayed by the weakness of his own nature. Essentially a noble soul in the most sentimental tradition, he has been undone by his need for fame, luxury, and social position. For these things he has sacrificed love, whose symbols are his family, the friends of the Latin Quarter period, and poetry. Society is involved in the drama, however, in one very important respect and in a manner quite different from the way in which it is ordinarily involved in tragedy. Even in *Antigone*, in which the claims of society are held in uncertain balance with more ancient pieties, society stands for order—an objective and authoritative norm by which individual conduct may be measured. But the society that Balzac describes is itself given over to the unregenerate expression of "Will"; it is simply an aggregation of predatory individuals. It is in no sense better than the individual. This is to admit that society is to blame for Lucien's situation to the extent that it offered him no values other than its own value of success at any price. It is no more than his own career written large—without, as yet, the tragic culmination. Or, to reverse this description, Lucien rehearses in his career the immemorial struggle between will and reason, matter and form, of which his society is unconscious because it has not yet been brought to tragic knowledge. He is the scapegoat of his society. He is the scapegoat not only in the degenerated modern sense of the term but in the original religious sense of someone who takes on himself the guilt of existence, who undergoes the agony of matter whenever it assumes form.

But before developing this idea it may be well to look at an even more transparent rendition of the same theme. The Rubempré cycle belongs to the *Études de Moeurs*; the symbolical pattern must be reconstructed out of the welter of detail into which it is analyzed. In *The Magic Skin*, which belongs to the *Études Philosophiques*, the symbols are reduced to the brittle abstractions of allegory. Raphael is another young provincial writer (he has actually composed a "Treatise on the Will") who has come to Paris only to make the classic gesture by the Seine. On the way to self-destruction he stops in at an old antiquarian's shop, where history heaped up in the floor upon floor of *objets d'art* is made to seem to him "like a witches' sabbath worthy of the Brocken and Doctor Faust." "He saw the conquest of Alexander on a cameo, the massacres of Pizarro in a matchlock arquebuse

. . ." The effect is to alter his mood from despair to an intense yearning for life, and he accepts the offer of the Magic Skin. Possession of it guarantees the immediate realization of every desire—with the terrible proviso that thereby so much is cut off from the term of life. At once Raphael is surrounded by wealth, fame, and admiring friends. But soon the sense that, like the Skin, his life is shrinking with the gratification of every wish makes him live in a state of desperate anguish. Previously he had laid unsuccessful siege to a very beautiful but strangely "cold and disinterested" society woman named Fédora. But now he experiences no feeling at the sight of her in an opera box. For a while there is promise of salvation through his marriage with the poor hotelkeeper's daughter who had befriended him in his worst poverty. But his love for Pauline is not the "true love" that she bears for him; it is still too much infected with lust; and the Skin shrinks to the size of an oak leaf. Resort to science does not help him, for his malady is "on the dividing-line between word and deed, matter and spirit." And at the end of two months he dies in Pauline's arms.

This fable scarcely needs interpretation: the Skin is of course the substance of its being which Balzac's society, like Raphael, was using up through the "material explosions" of the will. The beautiful and sterile Fédora is finally personified as "Society." Balzac is working out what we have seen was his abiding obsession—the identity of material and spiritual forces in both the individual and the social organism. As one of the physicians in the book sums it up, "The fraction of the great All which by some higher will works within us the phenomenon called *life*, is formulated in a distinct manner in each human being, making him apparently a finite being, but at one point co-existent with the Infinite."

This may also be taken as a statement of the manner in which the sensitive artist type is related to society and both to the universe: each is a repetition of the same tension between the drive out toward expansion and destruction and the drive inward toward conservation and order. Insofar as they are the concrete representations of this tension both Lucien and Raphael may be said to fulfill, as has been suggested, the rôle that in more primitive and more religious societies is assigned to the scapegoat. For it is the function of the scapegoat to hold up to the group a vivid and incontrovertible image of its own inner conflict—which is between what we have called its "interests" and its "pretensions" —and by the relief that is provided to make possible a new equilibrium. It is a device by which the Many are restored to the One through a temporary dissolution of the One. And if the artist type is selected by Balzac to enact this rôle it is because no other type, in a society given over to the uninhibited expression of the individual will, retained as much sense of the moral and ethical values that had attached to the older religious poetic synthesis. The Rastignacs, the de Nucingens, and the rest of their crew lacked even the consciousness of guilt; they were simply the mechanical products of will; and they could not, therefore, qualify as tragic characters. It is their capacity for suffering that make Lucien and Raphael eligible for the rôle. "Whoever suffers in body or soul, or lacks power and money, is a Pariah in society," Raphael concludes. And it is, finally, because he is made to suffer most of all in soul—that is, as a man—that the artist type in Balzac appears to us as the nearest equivalent we have for the dismembered god or hero of more unified cultures. He is the nearest we have to a symbol of unity.

Balzac's view is, in the last analysis, the religious—despite the fact that his defense of the Catholic religion is pragmatic and insincere. It is religious not only in the sense of being profoundly and at all times moral—which distinguishes him from almost everyone else in his age except Baudelaire—but in plunging us back to the most fundamental problems in metaphysics. And since the religious view must always come to rest in its treatment of love, the reconciliation of the Many with the One, the great sprawling mass of the *Comédie Humaine* may be said to seek its center in the idea of a perfect and disinterested love. The Skin does not shrink when Raphael wishes to be loved by Pauline; for the difference between the desire for love, which is a state of pure being, and the possession of the object of love, which is an act, is absolute. Love in Balzac is that state of contemplation in which the individual is temporarily relieved of the solicitations of the will and therefore put into communication with the order of the universe. It is the mystic vision of the Whole. Like Blake, whom he so closely resembles, Balzac was forced to invent his own mythology—out of the materials of history, however, rather than out of hallucination. And, as is the case with Blake, the strain is so great that we cannot be sure he is in perfect control. In *Louis Lambert*, the most philosophical of his narratives, the hero's successful attempt to synthesize all knowledge is accompanied by a perfect love affair and marriage. But the vision has apparently been too much for him; he lapses into a condition of inarticulate madness. There is an ambiguity in this tale which can only raise questions regarding the degree of faith that Balzac actually did manage to summon in the possibility of mystical experience in his age. But these are questions that would carry us far outside the scope of this paper.

Postscript

[1955]

This piece was written in July, 1939, on the eve of a world conflict largely precipitated by two specimens of the artist manqué turned man of action, whose methods in undermining the whole European political structure were essentially those of Vautrin in his feud with the Paris police system. Both Hitler and Mussolini in their beginnings also wallowed in the same morbid sense of victimage that Balzac traces in his more sympathetic character, Lucien de Rubempré. Shortly after the publication of this essay there appeared in France a brilliant monograph by Albert Béguin significantly entitled *Balzac Visionnaire*, which develops more fully the view here presented of Balzac as seer and mystic.

Proust's Last Will and Testament

[1931]

Because of the numerous points of departure for a comprehensive approach to Proust made possible by the appearance of the final volume, *Time Regained*,* in English, I should announce that it is my intention to consider this section only in its relation to the whole and to examine the validity of the positive ideas expressed in its closing pages. For it must be taken more definitely than in the case of most great writers as being nothing less than a last will and testament.

If it has been apparent all along that the total design of Proust's work would finally emerge as something like the curve which Time has inscribed in the narrator's consciousness, it may be said that in this last section the curve is completed in a novel and satisfying manner. The novelty inheres in the fact that the experiences recorded have a value and significance which are different for writer and reader, relative to the different positions which each of them occupies in Time. From the viewpoint of the writer, existing in his own order of time in the work, these experiences are important because they are the origin and the stimulus of a work which he is planning to write in the future. From the viewpoint of the reader, on the other hand, they are a

* Translated by Stephen Hudson, Chatto and Windus, London, 1931.

part of that same work, which he has been reading all along in *his* time. It is as if the order of Time, which we assume to be constant for reader and writer, may be reversed on occasion; or as if here again there are those different and parallel series in Time which Proust remarked about in discussing "the intermittences of the heart." This switching of time-order, which has disturbed a number of critics, is actually a brilliant application to the structure of the general notions about Time stated throughout the work. It is by means of it that Proust is able to reveal that form "which, normally, is invisible, the form of Time" (p. 429).

In the first two hundred pages the narrator emerges from his sanatorium, from what has actually been a retreat in time as well as space, to visit Gilberte de Saint-Loup at Tansonville, to observe the effects of wartime psychology on Paris and to assist at the later stages of the moral and physical dissolution of the Baron de Charlus. The object of this portion is to serve as a transition, a kaleidoscopic vision of a handful of years in terms of the changes that have occurred to the principal personages of the story. But while all the important motifs of the work are brought up to date in these pages none of them is resolved in any absolute sense: the effect desired and achieved is of a "perpetual becoming." This is best illustrated in the case of Charlus, who does not die like Robert de Saint-Loup but lives on with what seems an infinite capacity for degeneration. The continued breach between the two sides of his nature is emphasized by the contrast between the two impressions of him we receive—at Jupien's *maison de passe* and in the course of his conversations about the war. It is clear that his verbose Germanophilism is intended to represent another sort of degeneration, a kind of elephantiasis of the mind. Charlus is an example of the application of the theme insofar as it relates to individual character and personality, as the party at the Guermantes in the pages which follow shows its application to a whole society.

This last "afternoon" of the Princesse de Guermantes has a symbolical relationship to each and all of the many gatherings held by both the Guermantes and the Verdurins in the course of the work. It is a "reunion" which is also in a sense a union of all the hitherto unreconciled elements in the work. Because of Mme. Verdurin's marriage with the Prince the two classes or factions which have been treated separately throughout are at last able to be studied as one—and by means of her party at one time and in one place. The drawing room of the Guermantes becomes the arena in which time and place, after a long struggle with each other, have come to terms. Not until this afternoon, which is the unforeseen consequence of all those other teas, evenings, and afternoons reported by the narrator, is the theme fully and absolutely identified with the subject. For the theme, which is the destructive action of Time on men and societies, is incommunicable except in terms of place, which supplies the position from which Time may be measured; and the subject is the description of those specific changes which have occurred to particular men and societies in their passage through Time. This necessity of fixing Time at successive points in space if it is ever to be measured and regained is one of the most clearly formulated of Proust's metaphysical ideas (p. 413); and the method of "spatialization" by the constant re-grouping of characters at social functions over an extended period is a good example of the manner in which his ideas are adapted to a traditional device from the novels and memoirs of the past (Saint-Simon, Balzac, Tolstoy). Perhaps no single sentence in the work is more vivid and terrible than this in which Time is contracted by means of an image taken from the realm of space: "A Punch and Judy show of puppets bathed in the immaterial colours of years, of puppets which exteriorized Time, Time usually invisible, which to attain visibility seeks and fastens on bodies to exhibit wherever it can, with its magic lantern" (pp. 282–83).

Moreover, the afternoon at the Guermantes is important from the standpoint of the genesis of the work for providing the material occasion and circumstances of the total vision of life that is realized in the narrator's consciousness: "an afternoon party such as this was something more than a vision of the past for it offered me something better than the successive pictures of the past separating itself from the present, namely, the relationship between the present and the past" (p. 284). The pure vision is almost instantly succeeded by the desire to re-create it in art; and for this task a technique has already suggested itself through a series of three experiences which have just occurred to the narrator on his way to the party. These have followed each other in rapid succession and are identical in nature and effect. To their analysis and interpretation are devoted some sixty-three pages of the text, undoubtedly the most important in the work for an abstract comprehension of the whole. Formally this soliloquy of the rational mind corresponds to the "Overture" which precedes *Swann's Way.* But in substance it develops, elaborates, and finally completes the reflections on memory presented in that section.

If the madeleine dipped in the cup of tea opened up the whole of the narrator's past life in Combray, his experiences today are elevated by his intelligence to a significance which amounts to nothing less than a complete emancipation of his spirit (p. 275). Perhaps it will be enough to retrace only the first and simplest of these experiences. Entering the courtyard of the Guermantes in a discouraged frame of mind, the narrator stumbles against some unevenly laid paving-stones, and in the effort to recover himself his foot steps on a flagstone lower than the one next it. In that instant his discouragement vanishes; he is possessed by a feeling of exquisite felicity, comparable only to the sensations produced in him at certain other moments of his life by the view of the trees round Balbec, the sight of the belfries of Martinville, the savor of the madeleine dipped in tea. This time he makes a conscious effort to discover why the effect of sensations of this order has always been a dissipation of his intellectual doubts and anxieties about the future, a forgetfulness even of death itself. The images which attach to the present sensation are "a deep azure," "a feeling of freshness and of dazzling light" (p. 210). Suddenly there returns to his recollection a sensation he had felt many years before on noting two uneven slabs in the Baptistry of St. Mark's in Venice. As the taste of the madeleine brought back Combray, his sensation now brings with it the whole periphery of associations surrounding the original sensation in Venice. It is not a moment of the past that is recalled; but something that is common to the past and the present, and more *essential* than both.

> But let a sound, a scent already heard and breathed in the past be heard and breathed anew, simultaneously in the present and in the past, real without being actual, ideal without being abstract, then instantly the permanent and characteristic essence hidden in things is freed and our true being which has for long seemed dead but was not so in other ways awakes and revives . . . (p. 218).

If it is the liberation of "essences" through the mechanism of the involuntary memory that is stressed in this passage it is the liberation of man from the order of Time that is important in the following:

> Of a truth, the being within me which sensed this impression, sensed what it had in common in former days and now, sensed its extra-temporal character, a being which only appeared when through the medium of the identity of present and past, it found itself in the only setting in which it could exist and enjoy the essence of things, that is, *outside Time* (p. 216).

Because we are thus enabled by the involuntary memory to recover our identity at moments by grasping "a fraction of Time in its pure essence," Proust asserts that the happiness which comes to us at such moments is the only fruitful and authentic one. It is authentic because its materials are our own past imprisoned in our own selves: "I had too clearly proved the impossibility of expecting from reality that which was within myself" (p. 223). The only real beauty is to be found in the past, the only real paradises are those we have lost. Moreover, the very fortuitousness of our recollections is the seal of their truth, for they rise up out of that darkness within us which the intellect can never penetrate with its logical truth, its possible truth. It is this "book of unknown signs" within us, this book which we do not create but which pre-exists in us, that is the only book worth reading. For reading or deciphering it is equivalent to writing it, the true act of creation. Art is a revelation of the impressions which life has made on us; it "recomposes" life; and it is therefore "the most real thing, the most austere school in life and the true last judgment" (p. 226). Through creation alone we are able to celebrate our release from Time, to assert our essential identity and to enjoy that happiness which is our sense of laying hold of the truth of things.

Such a résumé hardly indicates the richness of concrete reference and illustration with which Proust's thought in this passage is elaborated. But it is enough to make clear the emphasis placed on the extratemporal character of those sensations which for Proust had the effect of making him think life worth living (p. 415). It is enough to throw into sharp relief the doubts which are born in us when he refers to his discovery as "a lesson in idealism" (p. 265) and when some of his admirers perceive in it an adequate and positive statement of faith.*

When we say of a work of art that its implications are positive we usually mean that those of its elements which have been negative are pretty well cancelled out at the end. In Proust's work, certainly, there have been negative elements enough; its projection of men, societies, and civilizations has been affected by a metaphysical view of the darkest cast. In a word, its negation has consisted of a persistent questioning of the identity and continuity of the individual personality. Proust has illustrated his solicitude in a hundred different forms; he has exhibited love, friendship, human nobility in all its manifestations as no more than modes of the implacable law of change; he has dissolved even our ideas of these things. And what, at the end, does he offer us in their place? He confirms our intuition of existence only to destroy it in the next breath with the reservation that it is not always in

* "Pour tout dire d'un mot, l'œuvre négative de Proust s'y change en une œuvre positive." Benjamin Crémieux (*Nouvelle Revue Française*, January 1928).

our possession, that our awareness of it is a sporadic and involuntary affair, subject to the obscure laws of the memory and beyond the control of the will. He asks us to be content with what may be called a contrapuntal view of reality, a vision made up of occasional unrelated glimpses into a past which seems to have no other significance than that it has been lived. He places all value in the acquisition of that past, all exercise of the will in the reconstruction of its fragments.

Whether or not one may call adequate a program which leaves so little place for the moral will is another question which will have to be answered by those who believe we may discover philosophical consolation in the work of Proust. What M. Ramon Fernandez pointed out several years ago is even more apparent in the light of this last volume: there is no progress in Proust but the progress of the intelligence. The sole orientation of the will is in the direction of an object situated on the plane of pure knowledge. For moral action, with its orientation toward the future, is substituted "wisdom," a passive, self-sufficient knowledge having no end outside itself. The zone to which Proust retreats is outside moral necessity as it is outside Time. For this reason Proust must be distinguished from such an "immoralist" as Gide: his attitude toward values is one of indifference, not of reform. As a philosophical ideal M. Crémieux has been able to find analogies for it in the Stoic *ataraxia* and the Christian renunciation. But it is an error to press these comparisons too far. What Proust's ideal has in common with Latin mysticism, for example, is only its intensity, detachment, and abstention; neither its motives nor its objects are the same. For Proust his objects are immured in his own sensibility, the knowledge of them is an adequate end—"the supreme truth in life is in art" (p. 255).

A further difficulty is that the solution proposed by Proust is possible of acceptance only to those few who are specially endowed and trained for artistic creation. Reflecting on that "extra-temporal delight" caused by the taste of the madeleine, he asks himself:

> Was this the happiness suggested by the little phrase of the
> Sonata, which Swann was deceived into identifying with the
> pleasure of love and was not endowed to find in artistic creation
> . . . having died like so many others, before the truth, meant
> for them, had been revealed? (p. 224).

He is forced to conclude that even if the phrase had symbolized
an appeal to Swann it would have done him no good, since it
would not have created the force which would have made of him
a writer.

Finally, even for the fortunate artist himself, the happiness of
creation appears to be brief, relative, and unenduring. It would
seem as if it owed most of its quality to the relief and escape
which it affords, for the period of its duration, from the unhappiness of actual existence. "Our passions shape our books, repose
writes them *in the intervals*" (p. 261). At best the happiness
which comes through the act of creation seems like a brief and
transitory respite from the vicissitudes of Time. Toward the end
a remarkable and unexpected confession shatters whatever hope
has been built up in the dependability of art as a technique of
salvation. The narrator has just missed having a serious accident
descending the stairs in a friend's house. The shock has resulted
in a temporary loss of memory and thought, a complete apathy
of his powers, which has been like a prelude to death.

> Since the day on the staircase, nothing in the world, no hap-
> piness, whether it came from friendships, from the progress of
> my work or from hope of fame, reached me except as pale sun-
> light that had lost its power to warm me, to give me life or any
> desire whatever and yet was too brilliant in its paleness for my
> weary eyes which closed as I turned toward the wall (p. 426).

The purpose of dwelling on these defects and contradictions in
Proust's exposition has not been to disparage in the least degree
the absolute merits of his work as a work of art. It is disappoint-
ing, of course, to find that his ideas of life and art taken as a
whole do not coalesce into a unified and positive system of
thought. But it is now pretty generally recognized that it is too

much to expect of an artist in our time that he shall construct an adequate system, that he shall operate on any more universal set of ideas than is necessary for the expression of his personal vision. The mistake we should guard against making about Proust is the very easy one of taking him for the prophet he is not. The rewards of reading his work lie neither in prophecy nor consolation but, in his own words, in the revelation, through literary means, "of the qualitative difference there is in the way in which we look at the world" (p. 247).

The view of literature taken by Proust, which is first and last the subjective view, is the narrower of the two views that may be taken, but as it seems to be the only one which writers in our time are capable of adopting with sincerity we must judge his work according to its own standards. It will then be recognized that its force and beauty derive from nothing else but the absoluteness with which Proust has adhered to these standards, from the intensity and completeness with which he has worked out his limited personal vision within the conditions of his perspective.

Three Novels by André Malraux

I   Return to Tragedy

[1934]

For some readers the greatest significance of *Man's Fate*, which is significant in so many different ways, will be found in the fact that it restores to modern literature something which has been absent from it for a long time and to the complete disappearance of which one had become too easily reconciled. Tragedy, as it was more than once eloquently demonstrated during the last decade, disappeared from the modern world when Western man ceased to make any serious effort to relate his will to any conviction of his place and importance in the universe. Pathos, self-pity, morbid confusion, and simple undifferentiated gloom we have had in plenty, and modern writing on the whole has been anything but cheerful. But tragedy in the classical sense, which is still the only sense that matters, requires a more perfect synthesis of intellect and will, a cleaner definition of values, and a more developed capacity for action than were ever present at one and the same time in any of the heroes of the last literary generation. The most typical heroes of its fiction—the Edouards, the Birkins, the Hans Castorps—were seekers rather than actors. What they sought, of course, was something to which they might eventually give the full expression of their wills, which might enable them to become candidates for tragedy. But the will to discover is not the same as the will to act on what one fully and completely believes: the arena of tragedy is life and not the mind.

Unlike Lawrence, Gide, Mann, and most of the other important novelists of the last generation, Malraux does not need to spend his energy as an artist in the conscious search for values on which to construct the dramatic pattern of his work. The real importance of *Man's Fate* is that it marks the beginning of a new period of literary creation in which the artist, in order to give strength and beauty to his work, need only observe, understand, and record the operation in character and conduct of values already present in experience. Now that the will has again been released, tragedy is once more possible: the old curve may be retraced, the immemorial emotion evoked. Malraux has not been the only recent writer to use the proletarian revolution as a theme; but he is the only one to recognize that for the artist what counts in such a revolution is the fact that it supplies a new value, a new source for tragedy.

As Leon Trotsky points out in the interesting letter on the jacket, the background of the Shanghai revolution of 1927 in this novel is *only* a background and not the subject. It is a little dangerous to state, as the translator does in his foreword, that the book is a "revolutionary document," even if one qualifies this immediately by saying that it is also a work of art. Undoubtedly one can learn a great deal about the Chinese revolution in particular and about revolutionary tactics in general from this work, but it is not so much a record or a manual of revolution that Malraux has written as a profound study of universal human psychology under the pressure of a particular set of conditions. It is essentially a novel about individuals, about a group of the most widely diversified and sharply accentuated individuals, to whom the revolution, as Trotsky puts it, imparts "a breaking-point force." As a result of the upheaval the power-mad French capitalist loses his prestige and his mistress, the underdog little shopkeeper is freed from the bondage of wife and family, the young Chinese terrorist realizes his mystical union with death, the mountebank Clappique merges his mythomania with reality, and the philosophical Gisors is able to accomplish his complete retreat from life.

The novel is tragic because we participate in destinies which have been determined by the most conscious exercise of the will over circumstances or fate. Fate, however, is neither external nor remote; it is man's own state or condition, the human lot itself, which provides at once the challenge and the disaster: "the essence of man is anguish, the consciousness of his own fatality, from which all fears are born, even the fear of death." This is the voice of the elderly Gisors, the French intellectual abandoned to the opium dream of the Orient. And it is his voice again which murmurs, "It is very rare for a man to be able to endure—how shall I say it?—his condition, his fate as a man." The answer to this is supplied by his son, the Communist agitator, in whose blood East and West are united: "all that men are willing to die for, beyond self-interest, tends more or less obscurely to justify that fate by giving it a foundation in dignity: Christianity for the slave, the nation for the citizen, communism for the worker." Dignity is the name given to the value for which Kyo and his generation in China are fighting, and dignity is the word that comes to his lips shortly before he is condemned to death. It is not a new value, perhaps it is only a new restatement of an old one, but what gives such extraordinary power to Malraux's novel is the concentrated intensity with which it is worked out in the tragic pattern of his story.

The detached and melancholy Gisors stands in the way of our reaching any truly final conclusion as to the author's own attitude toward the particular temporal conditions presented in his book. For Gisors the world and reality are a dream, and, since the revolution is a reality, that too is a dream, even though it takes from him his son. It is undoubtedly to this character that Trotsky refers when he describes Malraux as an individualist and a pessimist. But it cannot be so easily demonstrated that this individualism or pessimism finally triumphs over itself, as Trotsky declares. Gisors preserves his inviolability to the end, like the leader in a

Greek chorus. To say that Malraux may be completely identified with Gisors is, in the last analysis, as inaccurate as to say that he is an active propagandist for revolution. As an artist Malraux turns to those materials and to that theme which represent the most vital interest in the mind of the contemporary man aware of his own time. But, also as an artist, he maintains toward them that detachment which alone makes them possible for art.

II *Canopy of Death*

[*1935*]

For readers of *The Conquerors* and *Man's Fate*, *The Royal Way* is likely to prove something of a disappointment. Yet placed in a proper time-relation to the two novels having a revolutionary theme it takes on great interest for the light it throws on the development of one of the most brilliant and mature of living fiction writers. If the assumption can be made that it was composed before *The Conquerors*, although first published two years afterward (and everything in the book, form and style as well as subject, gives strength to such an assumption), *The Royal Road* represents an exhaustion through the imagination, a kind of vicarious purging of the mood which was the legacy of the last generation of European writers to the present.

Most of the book consists of a dialogue between its two principal characters: Claude, the young French archaeologist who seeks an escape from the tedium of respectable bourgeois society in a ransacking of the past in the form of forbidden art treasures in the jungle-covered temples of Siam; Perken, the Danish adventurer, who is driven on by the interpenetrated symbols of ambition and lust. The subject of the dialogue is death. In both men the idea of death has become an obsession strong enough to unite them in a common enterprise of plunder and conquest. For both death is not so much a culmination as a process—the gradual decline of a man's life, the death-in-life which triumphs if one submits to one's destiny "like a dog in its kennel." "But, living, to endure the vanity of life gnawing him like a cancer; all his life long to feel the sweat of death lie clammy on his palm." Their only protection against this sense of "death's austere dominion" is found in adventure, which is described not as an evasion but as a quest. For the life of directed action is an attempt to turn the raw materials of one's existence to some account; a protest against what Perken, anticipating the title of a later book by Malraux, calls "the human lot," man's sense of limitations, especially his humiliation at the hands of Time. For Perken, as for the revolutionary adventurer in *The Conquerors*, any line of action—provided it is sufficiently dangerous, of course, and opposed to the established order—is its own justification because it is a defiance of death. To stake everything on one's last moment is also, in a sense, to choose one's death, which, as the character Claude remarks, nearly everyone bungles, in one way or another.

But the truth gradually emerges through all these dark speeches that what these two desperate fugitives from middle-class Europe really feel toward death is not enmity but infatuation. It is not to conquer but to surrender that they beat their way through the dense Asiatic forest. The sweetness of death, the wild elation which comes to Perken at the end, is really based on the sudden glimpse of the absurdity of life that it brings, the satisfaction that life is being annihilated.

> Nothing would ever give a meaning to his life—not even this sudden ecstasy that merged him in the sunlight. Men walked the earth, men who believed in their passions, their sorrows, their own existence—insects under the leaves, a teeming multitude beneath the far-flung canopy of death.

In the last analysis, the book is another expression of that mood of escape into the consoling embrace of death, whether through the avenue of introspection or of action, which runs through most of the fiction of the last generation. It will remind the reader in turn of Proust, of the early Mann, of the Conrad of *Victory* and *Heart of Darkness*, and of Hemingway. And in its peculiar emphasis on the vanity of life, the nullity of existence, and the rest, it may be easily enough identified with a literary period that now belongs quite definitely to the past. In *Man's Fate* Malraux has distributed Perken's character between the young Chinese terrorist Ch'en, with his longing for annihilation, and the elderly Gisors, with his habit of soliloquizing on the emptiness of life. But in Kyo, May, Katov, and the several young revolutionists in that novel he has created a new and quite different type of character, for whom action is not an aphrodisiac in the long tryst with death but a means to a definitely conceived and highly desired end. And because for this reason their lives mean very much to these characters their deaths take on a significance that is tragic rather than pathetic. The difference between *The Royal Road* and *Man's Fate* is more profound than a difference between an early and a late book by the same author; it measures exactly the change that has taken place in Malraux's whole view of life and character, a change that is certain to have great influence on the future course of fiction in his own country and elsewhere.

It is a duty to mention the superb translation that Stuart Gilbert has made of the lushly rhetorical style which Malraux adopted in this book.

III *Soliloquy in the Dark*

[1936]

After reintroducing Western literature to the pattern of classical tragedy in *Man's Fate*, Malraux returns in *Days of Wrath* to that fragmentary or at least subordinate form to which it has become almost resigned in the last few centuries—the soliloquy. Through all but a few pages at the beginning and at the end we are at the center of a conflict that is waged exclusively within the individual consciousness. The antagonists, in Malraux's own words, are the hero and his "sense of life." For this struggle the central situation, the imprisonment of a German Communist agitator in a Nazi concentration camp, is a symbolical framework: the walls of the prison cell represent the impenetrable barriers set up between the individual and his fellow men by the conditions of the modern world. Symbolical of the imminent breaking down of these barriers is the scene in which Kassner, at a particularly anguished moment, deciphers the tapping of a prisoner in a neighboring cell as the laborious spelling out of the German word for "comrade." For the most part, however, there is not even this much communication; the Nazi captors themselves are no more than the agents of a grimly automatic historical destiny. Inside there is a mind in dizzy pursuit of images that will sustain its life; outside, it is "the time of contempt," the temporary historical cancellation of those images. For unlike the heroes of *Man's Fate*, whose integration was a previously accomplished fact making possible an instantaneous participation in action, Kassner is forced by his predicament into a weighing and reweighing of those ideals on which he has staked his existence. A feverish *examen de conscience* replaces the brilliant drama of the earlier book; action is stilled by introspection. It is as if Malraux had replied to the charge that action is no more than an anodyne or showy form of escape for his heroes by submitting one of them to the full pressure of circumstances that will bring his faith to the test. Kassner is therefore comparable to the early Christian martyr, except that in every sense the arena is a private one. The physical torture inflicted by his enemies is less harrowing than the internal clash of the twin demons of faith and despair. What is required is not a public demonstration of faith but the more difficult proof of his faith to himself in a situation in which every hope is a mockery. And, finally, his triumph, when it is marked by his departing sane from the eleven days' confinement, is not salvation but the mere preservation of his belief in the possibility of salvation.

The soliloquy, both as an incidental and as a separate form, is a renowned vehicle for rhetoric; for in this form the individual is commonly engaged in opposing to his real or actual self an imaginative reconstruction of himself based on some system of moral or philosophical idealism. In Shakespeare the rhetoric derives from the hero's recognition, at the end, of his failure to measure up to his ideal; in the romantics, on the other hand, it is produced by an identification or perhaps confusion of the hero's limitations with his ideals. But in both cases the attempt at self-understanding involves a celebration of those things on which the individual believes his true identity can be based. For Malraux the only hope of integration for the modern individual lies in the creation of a society in which man himself will be restored as a value. That salvation for the race is a prerequisite to salvation for the individual is the first principle both of his ethics and of his psychology. It is the conviction which, operating actively in the conduct of Kyo and others in *Man's Fate*, becomes rhetorically explicit in the present work. The climax is not a decision, that is, a spontaneous act of will, but an experience, the moment in which Kassner assembles the scattered fragments of his personality by identifying a strain of music heard through the walls of his cell with the struggle of his comrades throughout the world in the same cause.

It was the call of those who, at this very hour, were painting the red emblem and the call to vengeance on the houses of their murdered comrades, of those who were replacing the names on street signs with names of their tortured fellow-workers, of those in Essen who had been beaten down with bludgeons, and who, as they lay there, limp like strangled men, their faces gory with the blood that streamed from their mouths and noses, because the S. A. men wanted them to sing the "Internationale," had shouted the song with such fierce hope ringing in their voices that the noncommissioned officer had drawn his revolver and fired. Kassner, shaken by the song, felt himself reeling like a broken skeleton. These voices called forth relentlessly the memory of revolutionary songs rising from a hundred thousand throats . . . their tunes scattered and then picked up again by the crowds like the rippling gusts of wind over fields of wheat stretched out to the far horizon. But already the imperious gravity of a new song seemed once more to absorb everything into an immense slumber; and in this calm, the music at last rose above its own heroic call as it rises above everything with its intertwined flames that soothe as they consume; night fell on the universe, night in which men feel their kinship on the march or in the vast silence, the drifting night, full of stars and friendship . . .

This is rhetorical writing of a very high order, and of a general type that has perhaps not appeared in France since the romantic movement. It is language infected by positive vision until, like that of Marlowe and the early Elizabethans, it takes on vigorous new rhythms and a fresh accretion of imagery. But it is also subject to all the objections that we commonly raise against rhetoric. It is the reflection of ideas and values which have not yet been wholly assimilated by the sensibility, so that at times Kassner seems to be resolving his conflicts by a kind of verbal self-hypnosis. From the standpoint of its author's work as a whole, *Days of Wrath* is almost certain to be regarded as a momentary lapse from that full conviction about his theme which made possible the highly disciplined art of *Man's Fate*. Its excitement resides too much in a certain use of language and too little in the ordering of materials.

Paul Valéry and the Poetic Universe

[1947]

Distinctions between poetry and prose have usually been of two kinds—those based on conventional form and those based on content. To Aristotle must be credited the belief, inherited in our day by both the Poetry Society of America and the man on the street, that the essential characteristic of poetry is its use of formal meter. As a definition it has indeed the supreme virtue of tangibility. But it is needless to describe the snarls involved in any effort to take proper care of such things as poetic prose or prosaic poetry (verse). This has been an especially trying problem today with the pretty general abandonment or at least relaxation of formal meter and the increasing tendency toward lyricism in the novel. And there is the closely related question of what is poetic diction. The profound faith in the existence in every language of a limited body of words which are hopelessly and inviolably poetic undoubtedly reached its peak in the Victorian period, although it has not entirely disappeared. Identification of poetry with a type of diction mutually agreed upon to be "beautiful," however, is less common in an age which is more and more uncertain of what it means by beauty or anything else. Likewise is this the case with the exponents of the content-theory of poetry; those who believe that as between the beautiful and ugly subjects which exist in the world poetry always chooses the former. Again one is confronted not only with the usual embarrassments of definition but with the historical fact that much of the best contemporary poetry is marked by a more intensified depiction of the ugliness of life—in its choice of subject, imagery, and even diction—than is the prose.

Paul Valéry was not the first to endeavor to base the great distinction on less superficial grounds. Long before, Coleridge had foundered heroically in the attempt; and Poe, although he did end up with talking about the science of verse and about the death of a beautiful woman as the most perfect subject for a poem, struggled for a while. In our time a number of enterprising critics—Eliot, Richards, Empson, Ransom, to mention only a few of them—have made serious and invaluable efforts at clarification. But no one has quite equalled Valéry in the philosophical *éclat* with which he went about the matter. Quite apart from the accident that he happened to know rather intimately what he was talking about, he possessed just the kind of metaphysical agility requisite for the task. Moreover, responsive as he was to the intellectual malaise of the modern world, he sought to relieve it somewhat by pointing to a mode of knowledge and existence which might offer some consolation—the poetic.

If Valéry left no cohesive system of esthetics, there are enough hints in both his verse and his prose to suggest to us what it would have been like. The purpose of these notes is no more than to lay the foundations for what might be a more complete glossary of certain remarks which he made in his preface to Gustave Cohen's admirable exegesis of *Le Cimetière Marin.**

> The poet, according to my view, gets to know himself through his idols and his privileges, which are not those of the majority. Poetry is distinguished from prose in having neither the same obstacles nor the same licences. The essence of prose is to perish—that is to say, to be "understood," which is to say to be dissolved, destroyed without hope of return, entirely re-

* All the extended quotations are translated by the writer from Paul Valéry's preface to *Explication du Cimetière Marin*, by Gustave Cohen.

placed by the image or the impulse which it signifies in linguistic terms. For prose always presupposes the universe of experience and action, a universe in which (or thanks to which) our perceptions and our actions or emotions must finally correspond or respond to each other in a single fashion—uniformly. The practical universe is reducible to an ensemble of ends. Such and such an end attained, the word expires. This universe excludes ambiguity, eliminates it; it demands that one move forward by the shortest routes, and it smothers as soon as possible the harmonics of every event which is made to occur in the mind.

Quite clearly Valéry intends to phrase the whole question in terms of *function*. What are the ends of poetry and prose? (The bludgeoning statement about the moribundity of prose is simply an exhibition of critical shock-tactics.) Poetry is as yet undefined except by elimination. But prose is defined—teleologically. The inner purpose of prose is to enable us to make an adequate adjustment to the world of concrete action and experience. To be adequate such an adjustment must be instantaneous, rapid, and represent a consistent parallel between what we think we see and how we feel and act. (This will recall of course St. Thomas' much more elaborate treatment of the "adequation" of the subject and the object in the *Summa*.) Moreover, Valéry seems to imply slyly that what we call the physical world is really only a kind of projection of ourselves—an objectified ensemble of ends which pre-exist in us as our own needs and desires. In this manner he somewhat dizzily identifies the teleology of the individual, taken as a willing and active being, with cosmology. The world is no more than an image of our minds—the idea which is, of course, the dominating theme of his own verse from *La Jeune Parque* to the *Fragments du Narcisse*. What we receive here is the metaphysical statement of the idea. For Valéry is close enough to Bergson to insinuate that our so-called physical universe is an abstract fabrication compounded of will and desire. Later he speaks of the extreme difference existing between the "constructive moments of prose and the creative moments of poetry."

What then are some of the logical attributes of prose? In the first place, the words point always to things outside themselves; they are a means to an end; in philosophical terms, they have no ontological value. And as a result their behavior follows a definitely negative pattern. Prose cannot allow itself to indulge in the rich ambiguities of a language not determined by the ideal of economy: it must take the shortest cut to its goal. It must "eliminate" instantly everything that stands in its way. Not for prose are those "harmonics," as Valéry unmistakably implies, which do actually occur when an event, in all its fullness, is produced in the mind.

To return now to the bold declaration with which the passage opens, a declaration which has the impact of a value judgment, we see why it is that prose is doomed by its essence to become extinct. It dies the moment that it is "comprehended"—in the original Latin sense of being absorbed or swallowed up by the conscious mind. For the reader of prose no longer has any use for this language after it has done its appropriate work. Paragraph by paragraph, sentence by sentence, it gives up the ghost. Its being is dissolved into whatever it is *about*, destroyed beyond recall, replaced by the image or action in whose service it is employed.*

Needless to say, this analysis is capable of starting up metaphysical fireworks of every sort. There is, for example, the time element. When we read a novel, a logical discourse, or a scientific description, we are counting off moments of time, each of which cancels out, in value and interest, the previous one. (In its original meaning, the Latin *narrare* is to count; in German, the word is *zahlen*.) Prose of any kind is unfolding history, the present always yielding to the past, and, therefore, moribund. And how does it stand in relation to space? Valéry, following Bergson, would probably reply that the practical universe, since it refers ultimately

---

* Ezra Pound, in *Make It New*, says much the same thing in a slightly different way: "Most good prose arises, perhaps, from an instinct of negation: in the detailed, convincing analysis of something detestable; of something which one wants to eliminate. Poetry is the assertion of a positive, i.e. of desire, and endures for a longer period."

to the realm of space, is subject to the limitations which belong to all things that exist in space. It is finite. And every action performed in it is finite, doomed sooner or later, as we are accustomed to say, to become spent. If we admit that prose is the verbal equivalent of these actions, we have another way of explaining its tragic destiny.

Of course, Valéry refers always to an *ideal* prose; in fact, his whole effort is to establish dialectically, once and for all, the irreducible essence of prose. He would undoubtedly recognize modes of expression intermediate between poetry and prose. But perhaps the greatest value of his definition is that it helps us understand the sense of discomfiture which most of us experience in the presence of works belonging to these modes—whether it is the poetic philosophizing of a Renan or a Santayana or the poetic narration of the early Melville and Virginia Woolf. We feel that, functionally speaking, this sort of writing is working at cross-purposes.

> But poetry insists upon or suggests a quite different "Universe": a universe of reciprocal relations, analogous to the universe of sounds in which musical thought has its birth and movement. In this poetic universe resonance gets the better of causality, and the "form," far from vanishing into its effect, is ordered back by it. The Idea reclaims its voice.

At first glance this may seem indistinguishable from the formula *de la musique avant toute chose*—another surrender to that "musicalization of literature" which Valéry's brilliant contemporary Julien Benda assailed in *Belphégor*. But Valéry is only making use of an analogy, declaring that, like music, poetry constitutes a whole and self-contained "universe" within which there can occur a multitude of possible relations. As a corollary, poetry, which is sufficient unto itself, is not subservient to any extraneous ends. But we can have no doubt that he means us to understand that the "resonance" of this universe which takes the place of the casual order of prose involves a much more complex blending of elements than does music. We know this the moment he introduces the concept of the Idea—for in music there is no such differentiation between the idea and the form. In poetry there is the ever troublesome consideration that its vehicle, language, happens also to be that of prose. The great question is how it is able to maintain its autonomy in view of this fact.

For Valéry, as we have seen, the question presents itself in terms not so much of language as of metaphysics; that is to say, he is not concerned with those problems of meaning which occupy I. A. Richards and his school. For example, Valéry takes almost for granted the important distinctions between the prose statement and the poetic statement made by Richards, whose approach is pretty consistently psychological. The latter has always been too little concerned with the musical values of language as a whole, although he recognizes that sound has something to do with the full value of a word. Valéry brings both his sensibility as a poet and his virtuosity as a thinker to determining precisely the relationship between "meaning" in poetry (its burden of detachable intellectual reference) and its music. But we must first take a look at some later passages in the same preface:

> The poetic universe which I was speaking about makes itself known to us by the number, or rather the density, of the images, figures of speech, internal relationships, by the interweaving of phrases and rhythms—the essential thing being to avoid constantly whatever would lead back to prose, whether out of a sense of regret, or in an exclusive pursuit of the idea.

While poetry is constituted of imagery and various musical devices, while these are what first impinge upon the mind's eye and ear, Valéry seems to say, there is something else at work, something which invites temptation and danger. It is this which expresses itself either as a feeling of uncertainty and guilt or as a desire to turn back altogether to prose, to the mode of the purely rational and abstract. And by way of demonstration he tells us what happens when we attempt to translate poetry into prose:

Lastly, the more a poem conforms to Poetry the less it can be thought out in prose without perishing. Briefly, to put a poem into prose is quite simply to misunderstand the essence of an art. By its very nature poetry is inseparable from its form taken as a whole; and the thoughts articulated or suggested by the text of a poem are not at all the sole and most important purpose of what is being said. But they are the means, competing equally with the sounds, the cadences, the meter, and other adornments, by which there is provoked and sustained in us a certain tension and exaltation, by which there is engendered in us a "world"—or a "mode of existence"—altogether harmonious.

These are not only the most richly suggestive and original sentences in the whole preface but they provide a reconciliation of all its "danger definitions," which amounts to a kind of religion of poetry. To begin with, there is a resolution of the great antithesis between prose content and musical effect. The process of the resolution is sharply dialectical: the two are engaged in an intense conflict with each other, on an equal plane, to produce the poem. Or rather this conflict itself is the poem—*la forme sensible*. (Much depends on our acceptance of the meaning of the adjective *sensible* to include everything which we take in with our mind as well as with our senses.) It will be noted that there is no real priority between the intellectual substance and the musical effect. Nor is either in itself the sole object of the poem. In fact, they are of relative importance in relation to the final result, for they exist only to make possible in us an experience which transcends either of them. Through the tension which they establish we are translated into the "poetic universe," in which we respire in such a superior atmosphere of harmony that it can even be said that we enjoy a special mode of existence. For it is neither the world of prose, in which we have our normal mode of existence, nor that of pure poetry, which would perhaps be insufferable if it were possible. It is a world that comes into being only through art, in which alone can be achieved a harmonization of the sensory and the rational demands of our being.

Also, needless to say, it takes us to a region which is beyond time and space.

In this way, then, Valéry comes round to his definition of poetry in terms of its end or *telos*. The end is nothing so simple as the Aristotelian "to give pleasure and instruction." If it is pleasure, it is pleasure of such an exalted kind that the word is scarcely adequate. For the end is the production in us of a state of experience which is indistinguishable from that of ecstasy—in the most literal sense. And this is immediately of course to suggest the mystical and the religious. But one must guard against identifying Valéry too closely with others who have concluded by elevating poetry to the status of a religion. He does not do so, for example, in the manner of Matthew Arnold, who, as T. S. Eliot complained, tried to force poetry to undertake the ethical responsibilities of a systematic religion. For better or worse, there is no allowance for either individual or social ethics in the Valérian scheme of things. Nor is it to be confused with that of Proust, who secures his relief from the discords of time and space by quite different boulevards and alleys. There is actually no quarter given to the claims of the intellect in the Proustian epiphany. If Valéry calls to mind any mystical writer of the past, it is, extraordinarily enough, Thomas Aquinas, providing only that we recall how that most learned of the saints was supposed to have had a vision in which all his philosophy and all his spiritual passion were combined in an irrecoverable harmony. But of course the state to which Valéry directs us is entirely secular and attained by secular means. It is attained through the imagination, which is available to us all. And if it is paralleled in the work of any more recent poets it is in a single stanza of that one of them who alone might be considered his peer:

> Labour is blossoming or dancing where
> The body is not bruised to pleasure soul,
> Nor beauty born out of its own despair,
> Nor blear-eyed wisdom out of midnight oil.

O chestnut tree, great rooted blossomer,
Are you the leaf, the blossom or the bole?
O body swayed to music, O brightening glance,
How can we know the dancer from the dance? *

* From "Among School Children," *Variorum Edition of the Poems of* W. B.
Yeats, New York, Macmillan, 1957, lines 57–64.

Myth as Progress

[1935]

Perhaps the most common of the objections raised in this country against the two volumes of Thomas Mann's trilogy that have so far appeared is the familiar one that here again a very distinguished modern writer has turned his back on his own time and sought refuge from its vicissitudes in the depiction of a remote and semi-mythical past. Mann has been denounced as an "escapist"; he has been advised by journalists to be more journalistic in his choice of materials. The implication is that any novelist who does not serve up last month's news in his works is irretrievably lost to reality. What such an objection actually reveals, of course, is the lamentably short view of so much recent book criticism, its failure to recognize a fact which even the hastiest survey of the literary past would make evident. The fact to which one refers is the preference on the part of all the more notable members of that past, from the Greek tragic poets to such more recent figures as Goethe and Flaubert, for expressing their sense of the present, or what they believed to be most essential in their present, against a more or less remote background of time. The use of a mythical or distantly historical framework for the communication of profound and universal themes has only in our time been considered an escape from what Mann in another work refers to as "the cynical aspersions of the present." When Sophocles gave vent to his feelings about filial ingratitude in the guise of blind Oedipus at Colonus, when Shakespeare raged against mankind through the lips of Timon of Athens, when Racine made Bérénice and Mithridate the spokesmen of his seventeenth-century morality, it is not recorded that their contemporaries found anything unusual or suspect in the convention. Indeed, it would seem, from the examples of the past, that it is the mark of the great writer always to project the deepest experience of his own time in terms of some earlier period in human history. And it gives perhaps further strength to their claims to greatness that both Joyce and Mann, at about the same time and in the full maturity of their powers, have returned to the mythical in their fiction.

Even more than its predecessor does *Young Joseph* reveal the appropriateness of the particular myth which Mann has chosen for his trilogy. For here as elsewhere he is concerned with solving the mystery of the recurrent and often indistinguishable processes of life and death; and Joseph, as is clear from the beautiful early chapter in the grove of Adonis, is to be identified with all those half-human, half-divine creatures in every religion who rehearse in their careers the whole cycle of birth, death, and regeneration. It is this sense of the rôle that he has to play which induces in Joseph, according to Mann's elaboration of his character, that peculiar arrogance of spirit which in turn forces the brothers to be the unconscious agents of his destiny. When the brothers throw him into the well and later haggle over his prostrate body with the Midianites, they are not so much acting as letting things "happen." The ritual has occurred before and it will occur again, but it must be carried out to the letter. Despite their envy and rage and final brutality, the brothers are good, simple folk; and Mann has delineated each of them, especially the soft and indecisive Reuben, with such fairness of understanding that it is hard not to share their resentment against the vain, brilliant, spoiled son of Rachel, the true wife. But Joseph is the man of imagination, the dreamer of dreams, the shaper of future races and religions. He is "the bearer of the blessing." And if one understands this often repeated phrase aright it amounts to saying that in him is embodied the whole moral and spiritual heritage of mankind, the principle of true human progress, the triumph over the material in every time and place; "for the life of mankind cometh to an end several times, and each time cometh the grave and the rebirth, and many times must he be, until at length he finally is."

Besides dispelling more completely the notion that Mann is indulging in some crudely romantic escape into the past, this second volume is in its more strictly creative presentation of character and background superior to the first. Except for a few pages relating Joseph's education at the hands of Eliezer, there are none of those prolonged excursions into the abstract which halted the narrative progress in the earlier book. Instead there are some of the most memorable dramatic passages in the whole range of Mann's work: the conversation between Joseph and little Benjamin in the myrtle grove, the wheedling of Rachel's bridal veil from the doting Jacob, the savage attack of the brothers at the end. And the book is written in a prose which comes through in Mrs. Lowe-Porter's translation as the exquisite culmination of one of the great self-conscious literary styles of our age.

Thomas Mann: Myth and Reason

[*1938*]

Like nearly all the more important writers of his generation, Thomas Mann has turned finally to the frank and open exploitation of the myth. The tendency that has taken him to it very generally is that which took Yeats, Joyce, Valéry, and others— the inveterate tendency of the literary imagination to deal with whole patterns of experience.

More particularly, it has been the late nineteenth-century movement of protest against the devastating incursion of the scientific temper into the realm of literature and the arts. But Mann has come to the myth, not in the manner of the heirs of French Symbolism, who reconstructed it gradually out of the tattered remnants and fragments still floating along the mainstream of literary tradition, but only after the most conscious and deliberate threshing-out of all the problems involved in giving adequate expression to our cultural predicament. His masters were Dostoievski, Ibsen, Tolstoy, and Wagner; and like those hard-working titans of the "great and suffering nineteenth century," he has never been able to separate the problems of art from the problems of the historical mind. He has been at least as much influenced by philosophers like Schopenhauer and Nietzsche, by psychologists like Freud and Jung, as by any particular practitioners in the literary tradition itself. If he has turned to an application of the "mythical-psychological" method described in his essay on Wagner, therefore, it is the result of a decision supported by reason and judgment, of a necessity imposed by his special view of the extremely responsible rôle that must be played by the artist at any time.

By some of his admirers, however, this decision has been greeted with an ill-concealed lack of enthusiasm, a certain vague sense of apprehension and discomfort. And indeed the contemporary mind is sufficiently negative even to the sound of the word myth, which has become synonymous with the idea of organized falsehood. Some of the worst tendencies in every department of modern life and thought derive their impetus and authority from one or another of the old myths of the past surviving into the present. We live in an age whose atmosphere has become so charged with the sulphurous fumes of conflicting mythologies that reason has less and less air in which to respire. And for Mann, who has been, above all, the spokesman of a more "enlightened" humanity, to invite us back into the dark and tortuous regions of Hebrew myth cannot but seem to some people a kind of spiritual and intellectual backsliding.

But the purpose of this essay is to suggest that, rather than being inconsistent with his long devotion to the cause of reason, Mann's turning to the myth in his new work represents a synthesis between reason and experience that is full of the highest possibilities for our time. Moreover, it is to point out that the processes involved in this synthesis have been implicit in his work almost from the beginning. For even the most casual reading of his earlier novels and tales must reveal to what extent the images and symbols underlying or appearing alongside the analytical and discursive exposition are capable of being ordered according to the immemorial pattern of the myth. It is as if we are confronted with two orders of meaning, with their corresponding structures —the logical and the symbolical—and as if the dialectic interplay between the two constitutes his work as a whole.

From the beginning, Mann discovered his hero in that lonely and neglected figure, that "marked man," that black sheep of modern bourgeois society to which he has referred as the artist type. In those carbolic little tales that he wrote around the age of twenty, the profound social ostracism of the type is frequently indicated through the device of physical deformity. Johannes Friedemann is humpbacked, Tobias Mindernickel's exterior "provoking to laughter," Christian Jacoby is colossally fat, and Praisegod Piepsam's face is a huge "funereal joke." Such is the fatality which in the case of every one of them leads to some terrible and overwhelming humiliation. Little Herr Friedemann is literally kicked back to reality by the beautiful woman to whom he makes love; poor Jacoby, in "Little Lizzy," forced to dress up in baby's clothes and sing a tune composed by his wife's lover, dies of mortification. As for Mindernickel and Piepsam, children jeer at them as they pass down the street. These stories reek of the sort of *fin de siècle* sadism and masochism that Mario Praz has treated in *The Romantic Agony*. For all their precocious urbanity and studied objectivity they are the products of an imagination which has not yet attained maturity, which is writing at the level of the abyss. Their characters are simply *Doppelgänger* for the young writer himself, who appears in less indirect guise in other and less interesting stories of the same period. In "Disillusionment" the narrator discovers in the unknown man of thirty whom he meets on the Piazza di San Marco a similar projection of what he will become a few years later. This stranger, who is also a prefiguration of the stranger whom Aschenbach is to encounter on his walk by the cemetery, confesses that his tormented yearning for a higher reality has led only to the conclusion that he is "alone, unhappy, and a little queer." Like the narrator in "The Dilettante" and the novelist Detlef in "The Hungry," he has had a disastrous love affair with a daughter of the bourgeoisie—the uniform pattern of frustration in all the stories. The "dilettante" comes to see himself as "a beggar, a poor wretch standing at a jeweler's window," and Detlef actually exchanges a glance of mutual understanding with a beggar outside an opera house.

Physical deformity, in Johannes Friedemann or in Christian Jacoby, was but the symbolical equivalent of that same deviation from the norm, of that same fatality of loneliness which separates the artist from the rest of the bourgeois world. The artist's excessive sensibility is a malformation that can only be hideous to the "children of light." Through such an oblique method of presentation the early Mann makes us realize, in a peculiarly compelling fashion, the intensity of his problem. It is a method comparable to that of the French impressionist and postimpressionist painters, who, as Meyer Shapiro has suggested, were in the habit of representing themselves as bullfighters, jockeys, acrobats, or dancers—all cynical or wistful servants of a public from which they are forever separated as by some impassable barrier. Later on, in the wandering street singer of "Death in Venice" and in the sinister hypnotist of "Mario and the Magician," Mann, too, gives us examples of the artist as a despised and secretly despising entertainer.

From the malformed to the diseased, from the ugly duckling to the pathological case, is not such a great transition, and exactly this is accomplished in *Buddenbrooks*. But now for the first time it is hinted that deformity and disease are to be regarded not so much as deviations from a norm as potentialities inherent in any healthy body. Beginning as a rather straightforward chronicle novel in the Zola manner, tracing the vicissitudes of a more or less typical German middle-class family through the generations, this book seems to transform itself before our eyes, almost against its author's will, into another treatment of the theme that had occupied him in his very earliest stories. The great difference is that artist and bourgeois are no longer romantically pitted against each other as belonging to two eternally separate and absolute orders of existence, but the former is seen as an issue of the slow and inevitable deterioration of function of the latter. In other words, Mann turns to an etiology of the case whose symptoms he has either recorded analytically or demonstrated in his Gallery of Horrors. The health of the Buddenbrookses, their material and social well-being, with all that this had entailed of inner psychological stability for the individual members of the tribe, deteriorates in exact proportion to the development and refinement of their sensibility. Not until the third generation, it is true, do the evidences of this twofold process of growth and decay begin to show themselves in character and action. But it becomes distinct the moment that Gotthold, retracing the ancient pattern of Ishmael and Isaac, abandons his patrimony to his younger brother for the sake of a life of aimless romantic wandering. And their sister Antonie betrays all that dangerous restlessness of the spirit in its search for an adequate resting place that can only lead to disgrace and death. As for Thomas Buddenbrooks himself, the inheritor of the family "blessing" in every sense of the word, it must always be a question whether it was the reading of Schopenhauer in the summer house or the defection of his heart that brought about his too early death, together with the utter destruction of the business. He has already reinforced the foreign virus in the Buddenbrooks blood stream through his marriage with the dark, exotic, and music-loving Gerda. And through Gerda the whole malady that is creeping in upon the Buddenbrookses takes on a more definite form in its identification with art. Despite his father's foreboding protestations, little Hanno cannot help but acquire that mastery of the piano which will enable him to improvise a swan song for his race. The unconscious generations have labored only to bring forth this sick child, this incipient artist of the keyboard, this precocious scoffer, whose death is made an irrefutable rejection of everything for which they had stood. For Buddenbrooks is not only a study in the genesis of the bourgeois artist type; it is also a definitive evaluation of bourgeois society as a whole. Nothing in modern literature gives us a more concentrated image of that society's will-to-death than little Hanno's refusal, at the height of his fever, to hear "the clear, fresh, mocking summons" of life. "But if he shudders when he hears life's voice, if the memory of that vanished scene and the sound of that lusty summons make him shake his head, make him put out his hand to ward it off as he flies forward in the way of escape that has opened to him—then it is clear that the patient will die."

Love, disease, and death—these themes are already clearly identified with the notion of art in Mann's first long book. Far from being a Balzacian parabola of monomaniac passions, or a Zolaesque diagram of socio-economic forces, *Buddenbrooks* traces the downward-moving spiral process by which beauty is produced only at the cost of all the "normal" values, by which the powers of light and darkness are kept in a sterile equilibrium, and which achieves its only possible termination in death. As an artist the young Mann is able to transcend the last of these conclusions through the act of the imagination by which he makes the separate processes of the conflict his material and their interplay his form. Art is still able to rise above death. It is able to rise above death, with which it is nevertheless inextricably bound up, through the intellect that has been able to perceive such relationships in the first place. Through the intellect the artist can still enjoy that sensation of an active and ever changing reality that rises from the recognition of the anomaly of his own rôle. Such a motive power is summed up in the complaint of Tonio Kröger a few years later, "I stand between two worlds. I am at home in neither and I suffer in consequence. You artists call me a bourgeois, and the bourgeois try to arrest me."

For there must be an inescapable ambiguity in a writer who will neither go the whole road to the graveyard of the artist *pur sang* nor treat the bourgeois with the proper degree of respect. Tonio Kröger is a little Hanno who has enough conviction of the paradox of his existence to make it also the sufficient reason for his existence. With all that longing for "the bliss of the commonplace" that had characterized the first desperate examples of the type, he is able to carry on through the sheer momentum of the conflict. Here again "the blond and the blue-eyed" are on the side of the bourgeois, the pathetic and the grotesque on the side of the artist, but the activity of intellect necessary to play the one against the other is able to generate a sufficient self-perpetuating warmth. And is there not also the hope of some far-off resolution in the letter which Tonio writes to his authentically Bohemian friend, especially in the reference to "those shadows of human figures who beckon me to weave spells to redeem: tragic and laughable figures, and some that are both together?" The desire to redeem is one with the desire to love, and in the possibility of love lies Tonio's own sole promise of redemption.

Of love there is indeed very little in "Tristan," the other important story of the same period, in which Mann appears to have relieved himself once and for all of the contempt and disgust that he had come to feel toward the unregenerate artist type. Hysteria takes the place of resolution. The ridicule heaped on the vain, pompous, and altogether egoistic novelist hero, who has taken up residence in a sanatorium for the sake of its esthetic atmosphere, is as unequivocal as the mirthful squeals with which the bourgeois infant in the perambulator greets the sight of his face. But in "Death in Venice," published in 1911, which deals with a quite different specimen of the artist type, Mann makes his first important step toward a complete resolution of his problem.

At the moment at which this story appeared, the so-called "musicalization" of literature had already proceeded to such a point that Julien Benda, a few years later, was forced to direct against it his famous attack in *Belphégor*. More and more writers were taking Verlaine's dictum, *De la musique avant toute chose*, quite literally, and the movement was dissipating in the diffuse "tone-poems" of Verhaeren and the crepuscular fluidities of the Maeterlinckian drama. Any amount of vague and undefinable feeling was being purveyed in the name of Music. But the direction that this movement had taken was not at all what Schopenhauer, Nietzsche, and Wagner had intended in their exaltation of music above all the other arts. For Schopenhauer the patterns of music corresponded to the irreducible yearnings of the human will in its effort to express itself in nature, and in this sense of being freest from any specific contentual experience music was to be regarded as the purest of art forms. But music had its own content in sound, and the mistake of the Symbolists had been to confuse its merely quantitative medium with the more complex medium of words. In appropriating the Wagnerian leitmotif, for example, the Symbolists were not introducing a new literary device, as they thought, but simply returning to those archetypal patterns from which later study has shown both literature and music derive their common origin. What is the leitmotif but the musical equivalent of a symbol, or a symbol but the verbal equivalent of a leitmotif? It is not quite true, as Benda argued, that the difference between the two arts is one of intellectual consciousness, for literature insofar as it is literature and not something else is no more capable of exact logical transcription than is music. The meaning in both is something implicit in the whole pattern into which the separate motifs or patterns are made to fall. If the Wagnerian influence on nineteenth-century writing was so baneful in its effects as Mann himself has shown, it was because Wagner never managed to accomplish such a pattern in his own music dramas; they dissolved in the same romantic *Sehnsucht* out of which they were born. But in his strict adherence to the mythical subject he enables us not only to measure the extent of his failure but to recognize the imponderable nature of the relationship between music and literature. "Death in Venice" has been submitted to more than one analysis in terms of musical themes and motifs. And there is no reason why it should not also be submitted to a similar analysis in terms of color or smell. But all separate modes of analysis are included or subsumed in that more general type of analysis that we must bring to the proper understanding of the myth.

For what emerges through the highly civilized modern tone and hushed rhetoric of this remarkable story but the fundamental pattern of the ancient initiation rite? Freud had already written of the adolescent crisis in terms of the heroic struggle of the individual for self-survival; and Jung, following Lévy-Bruhl and Durkheim, had explained the manner in which this is institutionalized in the primitive *rites de passage*. The novelist in Mann's story is someone who has come to his initiation too late, and the rite must be played out on the silent plane of the consciousness. For many years, nature in Aschenbach had been "kept quiet," like the cholera plague later on in Venice, lest it disturb the even flow of his reputation, the steady accumulation of honors, the adoption of his books as texts in the schools. Too early in life had he publicly renounced "all sympathy with the abyss," and devoted himself to the responsibilities of his position. Not until he has reached the age of fifty does the sight of a coarse and vaguely foreign-looking face during a walk by a cemetery stir up in him the desire for travel and relaxation. But this is enough to start him on his "journey by water" (which young Joseph is to reenact in the monkey land of Egypt) to the forbidden land, to the city that is the meeting place between the East and the West, to the classic Venice of the North German imagination. At once it becomes evident that he could never have forsworn the abyss, because he has never known it, or he would not be so shocked and disgusted by his observations on the way. And no sooner is he in Venice than he feels himself completely at the mercy of the rather sinister, animal-like gondolier who rows him to his hotel without waiting to be paid. The man was without a license, it appears, and this is the first distinct note of the illicit. It is the illicit, however, that strikes him full in the face next day when he sees the boy Tadzio for the first time in the hotel waiting-room. Then begins his long season of anguish and humiliation in the underworld of his own unsuspected impulses and desires, which become subtly identified with the sights and the sounds and especially the smells of the corrupt city. For nature takes revenge on Aschenbach by asserting herself through one of her most anti-social manifestations; he becomes the victim, in Freudian terms, of an infantile regression. But homosexuality, which Freud explains as a type of psychological narcissism, is also emblematic of the immaturity of an artist whose images have never been more than the reflexes of his own unchecked idealism. As the earlier denizens of the abyss had been subject to the hallucinations of the sensibility, so that we never know whether the stranger in "Disillusionment" or the beautiful lady in "The Wardrobe" were real persons or mere dreams, the noble Aschenbach is the victim of the mind's own tendency to project images of its unappeasable love of perfection. Both tendencies are fatal to mature creation; both lead to a reprehensible sterility. (It is to this aspect of the homosexual passion that Mann directs his attention in his curious discussion of the subject in Count Keyserling's *Book of Marriage*.) So the aging novelist is made to pursue through the labyrinthine streets of Venice what is really only the sterile projection of his mind in its effort to create form out of its own substance, to breed beauty and spirit out of the mere ideas of these things. Tadzio is compacted half of material reality, half of a tired and wordy Platonism. For Aschenbach he is the materialization of that ideal perfection of form which he had cultivated all his life, so that he is the image of Narcissus in the pool. And the tantalizing smile that Tadzio returns him several times throughout the story is also the Narcissus smile of recognition. As an object of desire, however, he can only be frustrating, absurd, impossible, the mere dream of him as such leading his worshipper straight into the depths of the abyss.

Through the suffering and humiliation of the pit, the initiate in the rites not only learns the horrors involved in the full experience of living, but also acquires the grace and strength that will enable him to endure them. He sloughs off the old arrogant, childish self that had made the world seem like a mirror of his own emotions and emerges as a mature and responsible member of the tribe. A real dialectic process occurs by which the old individual self is reborn on the higher plane of the moral and social. And so Aschenbach, that tardy initiate, already sickening from the poisoned berries that he has eaten to allay his thirst, is made to go for a last time to the beach to catch a glimpse of Tadzio. An abandoned camera on a tripod records the scene: Tadzio, playing with some of his friends, is suddenly downed, his face pressed into the sand, and when he is freed he walks sullenly away. At that instant occurs a profound transformation in Aschenbach's vision of him: he is no longer an object of desire, but an object of contemplation. In the first place, his little exhibition of outraged pride has made him a human being. Now that Aschenbach himself has tasted this emotion to the full he is no longer able to confuse reality with the reflections of his own overdeveloped esthetic sensibility. Tadzio is no less beautiful in his eyes, but now the beauty "flashes off" the organism as a whole, as from the bird in Hopkins' sonnet, and it is impossible to distinguish between the physical and the spiritual in the perfect harmony of their functioning. The recognition that the boy's superior physical charms have been intimately bound up with a superior moral nature enables Aschenbach to discover in him a completed symbol of his own predicament. The tussle between Tadzio and the boy of "coarser nature" on the beach is the allegorical correspondence of the terrible struggle that he has just been through in his private abyss. Morally, Tadzio supplies a living and breathing example of that working alliance between matter and spirit, feeling and reason, "knowledge of the abyss" and intoxication with form which the artist must effect if he is to preserve his own identity. And, finally, there is the analogical meaning of the tale. Like Tadzio, "tracing figures in the wet sand with one toe," Aschenbach must transcend his experience in a period of renewed artistic creativeness: "It seemed to him the pale and lovely Summoner out there smiled at him and beckoned; as though, with the hand he lifted from his hip, he pointed outward as he hovered on before into an immensity of richest expectation."

Such a reading is not unlike the procedure adopted by those students of the Grail legends who are forced to penetrate beneath the layers of social presuppositions implicit in their tone and narrative method to the underlying pattern described by the symbols. It enables us to realize to what extent Mann identified the artist with the hero even in his earliest work, to what extent he made the problem of the artist the problem of society, and how this problem was to be solved only by a clear-minded approach to the myth. Aschenbach suffers in private all the agony involved in performing the rôle of scapegoat for a schizophrenic society; his initiation has come too late for his own regeneration; but his creator is to take us well into that distance indicated by "the pale and lovely Summoner."

In *The Magic Mountain* the hero is not an artist but an engineer, that is to say, a representative of one of the most characteristic and therefore most honored of the bourgeois professions. And he is even, by his own admission, a rather mediocre specimen of his class. But Hans Castorp is "a delicate child of life" for all of that. By implication the virus that had attacked Hanno Buddenbrooks, Aschenbach, and all the other members of that allergic crew has now spread by contagion into every rank and department of the society: the whole bourgeois world is ready for the sanitorium. In selecting such a commonplace figure for the center of his novel, therefore, Mann is not so much deserting the artist type of his early works as assimilating him into a more complete vision of the moral and psychological crisis which Western European man had reached in the years preceding the last Great War. In the person of Hans Castorp a whole culture makes the tragic journey upward to the high and lonely place where salvation is to be attained only after the most harrowing trials of the body and the spirit.

The structure of *The Magic Mountain*, it is true, is much complicated by the ambivalent character of its dominating symbol. Everything depends on whether the mountain is taken as a point of culmination or as a separate object in space. On the one hand, it may be equated with the spiral, the ladder, or any other of the traditional symbols of inspiration or attainment, in which case Hans Castorp's story becomes a parable capable of interpretation on all three planes of meaning. Allegorically, his ascent of the mountain corresponds to the arduous quest for certitude through the mind of a world conditioned to an absolute individualism in religion, politics, commerce, and all the other branches of life and thought. The particular nature and content of each of these categories are made amply explicit throughout the narrative. Morally, it provides an example of what Mann believes to be the proper mode of salvation—not surrender to one or another of the voices crying from the abyss but a still more vigorous application of the conscious mind to the problems of experience. (The arena of conflict is the brisk and sunlit mountain top of the mind, as it had been the lush jungle of the sensibility in "Death in Venice.") And, anagogically, it leads us back to the world of concrete living experience, to the world of men in action, where all the conclusions or resolutions of the mind must finally be brought to test.

But such a reading relates the work exclusively to that rather simple type of folk myth in which the hero is not required to pass beyond the boundaries that separate the human from the divine, the terrestrial from the supernatural. And there is actually the hilarious suggestion that the mountain sanitorium represents an *absolute* separation from the rest of the earthly planet. The mountain is a "magic" one, peopled with all sorts of elves and trolls, who play at their special variety of dice for Hans Castorp's soul. It is the old evil abstract world of the Northern imagination: the macabre hangs about it from beginning to end. But Mann has also been influenced by the brighter Mediterranean tradition, and we hardly need his hint that the work is epic in form to distinguish in its more important characters modern parallels for Apollo, Dionysus, Aphrodite, and the other incumbents of the Hellenic heaven. The sanitorium is above all a kind of Mount Olympus, an international theocracy of invalids and cranks, who personify all the attitudes and points of view current in the Europe of the period. It is as if we are brought to a much later stage of literary development than was represented by the primitive ritual-drama of "Death in Venice." We are at that more civilized and more irreverent stage in which not only is the culture hero made to cut a ridiculous figure among the gods but the gods themselves are deprived of their dignity as the projected idealizations of the race. In brief, Hans Castorp is a "strayed bourgeois" among the malingering Immortals of the bourgeois epoch.

For convenience the Olympian contestants for Hans Castorp's soul may be divided into the two groups of the Apollonian and the Dionysian—a classification that with a little effort can be made to fit each of the innumerable, more abstract formulations of the dialectic conflict between reason and feeling which is the subject of the work. It enables us, for example, to bring under a single aegis two such apparently irreconcilable characters as Naphta and Settembrini. For to what does the bitter struggle between these two self-avowed exponents of reason correspond but to the tension that must always exist in the Apollonian between the form of reason and its medium or expression, between logic and rhetoric? In Settembrini, the representative of the Renaissance tradition of liberal bourgeois democracy, reason expresses itself in a language overwhelming to the young civilian from the lowlands. As champion of science, progress, and the glory of the individual, the heir of the Garibaldian *risorgimento* stands for values that cannot but be sympathetic to Hans Castorp; but they are rendered suspect by the diseased medium through which they are defended: rhetoric is made to seem like an elephantiasis of the intellect, in which words are swollen too large for their meaning. The humanist exalts above all else the art of letters, by which man was first able to engrave his word symbols on stone, but it is necessary to point out to him that its tutelary gods, Thoth and Hermes Trismegistus, became in time transformed into soul guides in the land of the dead. So also does every one of Settembrini's most positive conceptions become transformed into its opposite, dissolve into pure nothingness, in the hard light of its historical application: the beneficent and liberating aspect of science is cancelled out by the infernal uses to which it has been put in the modern world; progress is another name for the deathward-moving direction of the romantic will; and the rights of the individual are translatable as the right of one class of individuals to exploit another and less fortunate class. If Settembrini on his mountain top does not suspect that he is living a hundred years too late it is because of the natural coloration with which language supplies the mind in its contacts with experience. But to Hans at the end he must appear for what he is—a windbag, an organ-grinder, a Philistine "forever playing on his penny-pipe of reason."

Yet his bombastic humanism, which is after all the reflection of a certain geniality of soul, is never so offensive as the "analphabetic barbarism" purveyed by the other distortion of the Apollonian—the little Jewish Jesuit, Naphta. Even in his name the latter gives off a suggestion of the suffocating odor left by his volatile and inflammable mixture of scholasticism and Marxism. For it is no true dialectical reconciliation between reason and nature that he achieves in his famous "synthesis" of the two doctrines: it is once again reason breeding on itself, seeking its proofs in its own already elaborated structures of dogma, without bothering to check either of these with an ever changing world of reality. It is another example of the terrible incest of the spirit. And from such a sterile union nothing can be born but the vague "Terror" that Naphta envisages for the future. (For readers living in that future, of course, the terror has long since lost its character of vagueness.) As the hyperbolic effusions of Settembrini had seemed like a burlesque of language, the traditional medium of reason, Naphta's cobwebby arguments are like a macabre parody of logic, its form. They are like those "uncanny, anti-organic, life-denying" patterns which Hans is to discover in the snowflakes later on and which will represent for him the very marrow of death. It is this genuine sclerosis of the intellect that makes Naphta, in the last analysis, a more dangerous character than his opponent. After all Settembrini clings to what he calls love to the very last; his humanism is not incapable of a corrected and re-ordered statement; his most fundamental defect is that he is hopelessly out-of-date.

In the duel between them Mann symbolizes the exasperating dilemma of the whole bourgeois intellectual world. This may be stated historically as a death struggle between the exhausted tradition of liberal bourgeois humanism and a re-emergent mysticism or supernaturalism. Politically, it is to be more sharply defined as between democracy and one or another form of totalitarianism. (By a brilliant stroke of economy Mann manages to telescope two of the prevalent forms of the latter—ultra-montane Catholicism and Soviet communism—in a single person; he was unable, as early as 1925, to foresee the rise of Fascism.) But ultimately there proves to be no difference between these counterpositions when their exponents are brought face to face with each other on the field of action. Neither liberal humanism nor authoritarian terrorism is able to engage the complete will of the individual: Naphta shoots himself in impotent rage, and Settembrini goes on making speeches. Neither reason nor spirit makes a successful accommodation to the realm of matter. All that we are made to understand is that Settembrini, despite his fatuous pose of martyrdom, is still in possession of some of the right values. But there is a tragicomic dissolution of the conflict rather than a real resolution; and the realm of matter bursts in upon the inhabitants of the Magic Mountain to put both reason and spirit to flight.

Before this scene Hans Castorp himself, however, has achieved something like a resolution within the less public sphere of his own thoughts and feelings. But to understand what this has involved it is necessary to turn from the mock-epical to the mythical aspects of the work, from the Apollonian to the Dionysian elements of its hero's experience.

Unlike Aschenbach, Hans has apparently crossed the Freudian border line at adolescence and has no trouble in rediscovering his schoolfellow Pribislav Hippe's features in the thoroughly feminine countenance of Clavdia Chauchat. Dark, brooding, and of an exotic origin, the latter represents a final accentuation of the type already encountered in the mothers of little Hanno and Tonio Kröger. At the same time she has much of the sadistic callousness of those Amazonian women who tormented Mann's earlier artist heroes. Perhaps the lady from the "good" Russian table, with the dirty fingernails and the habit of slamming doors, is best regarded as a modern avatar of Ishtar, Isis, or any other one of those old fertility goddesses who combined in themselves the two rôles of mother and mistress. In her mother-aspect Clavdia can afford to show a certain amount of tender sympathy for the *joli petit bourgeois*, whose conception of making love is to deliver pedantic speeches in questionable French. For Hans can express his deepest needs only through a medium which permits the same sense of irresponsibility that belongs to the dream. Only in the unreal atmosphere of the "Dance of Death" can he bring himself to speak of the desires of the body, employ the intimate *tu*, and seek at least a substitute satisfaction through the vicarious instrument of language. (Something like this last would seem to be the meaning of the playful insistence on the pencil symbol.) This is altogether consistent with the attitude toward love earlier in the book, in which Hans's infatuation is registered with clinical accuracy on the mounting thermometer of his fever. And it is also consistent, of course, with that general identification of sex with disease and death, with the assembled powers of darkness, that has been a feature of Mann's writing from the beginning. But what is particularly significant here is that it is not the special artist type but a rather commonplace product of the culture who has been incapacitated for any direct and spontaneous emotional expression. It is bourgeois man as a species that the little earth goddess from Daghestan rejects when she puts the carnival hat on Hans Castorp's head. As mistress she must descend to the lowlands and seek out a more adequate lover.

Presented almost entirely through symbols, a remarkable composograph of Falstaff, old man Karamazov, and Zarathustra, Mynheer Peeperkorn is not only one of Mann's greatest triumphs of pure creation but one of the few real *mana*-characters in modern fiction. As the two lobes of the Apollonian brain had competed with each other in their own sterile realm, this living embodiment of the Dionysian is pitted against nature itself—as in the famous scene by the waterfall. Even his extreme verbal incoherence attests to the dynamic fluidity of a personality that is "the organ through which God consecrates his marriage with roused and intoxicated life." What Peeperkorn stands for historically, of course, is the other side of the liberal bourgeois medal —the movement of diffuse, inarticulate, and self-consuming romanticism that was the revenge of feeling on its much-vaunted and socially more respectable worship of reason in science. And he is made to serve as an awful example of the consequences of attempting to make of the romantic attitude a satisfactory attitude toward life. For the man to whom feeling is such a sacred duty that a failure in feeling amounts to nothing less than blasphemy must suffer the ignominy of his own impotence. If Naphta must turn a revolver against the head that had fabricated so much confusion, Peeperkorn must inject into his veins one of the worst poisons of that same earth whose "classic gifts" he has made his sole criteria of value. (By an ingenious piece of poetic justice the hypodermic syringe, as scientifically described, proves to be identical in mechanism with the phallus.) In the pact that Hans and Clavdia seal with their lips during his "Gethsemane," the cult of life and feeling becomes one with the cult of death: their loyalty is to the terrible image of death-in-life on the hospital bed. In the end Peeperkorn does not quite escape tragedy, for he cannot escape self-consciousness, that is to say, the human. "They saw the head sink sideways, the broken bitterness of the lips, they saw the man of sorrows in his guise." All his show of exuberant vitality had been but a pose, a disguise, something suspect from the beginning, and therefore a futile attempt at denying the human problem.

The same betrayal of the essentially deathward tendency of the romantic attitude is included in Clavdia's rebuke to Hans that he exists for self-enrichment rather than self-forgetfulness. No more than in the heady region of the Apollonian does Hans find solace in the feverish morasses of the Dionysian: the two cancel each other out in the altogether empty equation of death. But during his walk in the snowstorm he has his waking vision, dreams "the Mediterranean dream-poem of humanity," in which they are once again restored to their proper relationship to each other and in a much more comprehensible fashion than in the celebrated Nietzschean synthesis.

In this episode the whole pattern of the work is contained in microcosm: the process by which Hans stumbles blindly over the mountain peaks and hollows parallels minutely its antitheses, its self-contradictions, and its circular development. The blank and unstable precipitations of the atmosphere floating everywhere around him correspond to his own now quite completed sense of the terrifying metaphysical identity of all things. The immediate problem is literally one of life or death; but before this problem of the will can be solved the mind must restore its distinction between these processes which have become so hopelessly interfused. Significantly, it is only by shifting from leg to leg that he is able to generate enough warmth to maintain that "form through change of substance" which the Hofrat had offered him as the definition of organic life. But the snowflakes, condensing into their too strict geometric designs, also help through their challenge to the living principle, force him to maunder on, sense or no sense, as from a bourgeois sense of duty. In the last analysis, it is not logic but the secret and unpredictable triumph of the life instinct over the death instinct that leads to his vision of the dancing youths and maidens, of the ceremonial beauty of the family groups in the market place, and finally of the two old witches dismembering a child in the temple. It is a terrible and a beautiful dream. But for Hans it constitutes a total vision of "the human being, the delicate child of life, man, his state and standing in the universe." And in his acceptance of it he resolves in a flash all the warring contradictions of the conscious mind: "The recklessness of death is in life, it would not be life without it—and in the center is the position of the *Homo Dei*, between recklessness and reason, as his state is between mystic community and windy individualism." Since it is man alone who can perceive these counterpositions, since they exist only by virtue of the freedom of his mind, he is master over them, more "aristocratic" than either life or death. More aristocratic than death—"that is the freedom of his mind. More aristocratic than life, too aristocratic for life, and that is the piety in his heart." For this mastery the proper name is not reason but love; only through love come "form and civilization, friendly, enlightened, beautiful human intercourse—always in silent recognition of the blood-sacrifice."

And the form of *The Magic Mountain* itself finally emerges as just such a humane and loving rehearsal on the plane of the esthetic of the struggle between the intellectual and the emotional, the abstract and the concrete, the epical and the mythical, as is traced out in Hans's experience on the mountain. It is, in Mann's own words, a "dialectic novel." This is to say that it is a work which can hardly be expected to meet with the whole-hearted approval of those who believe either that art should be the precise reflection of an organic culture, as in Greek tragedy or the medieval romance, or that it should provide a consistent correspondence to some systematized body of intellectual dogma, as in Lucretius or Dante. To the first the answer must be that, in the absence of an organic cultural situation, Mann, like the other ambitious writers of his generation, had no choice but to base his structure on the tension that must always exist during the period of transition between one culture and the next. Where Pound, Joyce, Eliot, and the other heirs of the Symbolist tradition solve the problem through a formal juxtaposition of the symbols of past and present which renders any explicit comment unnecessary, Mann dissolves the modern world itself into its contradictions and makes of the dynamic interplay between them at once the structure and the meaning of his work. As for the second objection, Mann's intelligence and imaginative insight prevented in him from the first any belief that it is possible for the artist to work out a body of absolute doctrine that has not already been thoroughly absorbed into the concrete active experience of the race. For the particular type of esthetic solution that he offers we must turn for a precedent to such works of the past as also belong to a transitional period between two cultural epochs, to such writers as Chaucer and Cervantes, for example, whose tone, style, and mixture of literary genres reflect the same precariously maintained equilibrium. These comparisons must never be pressed too far, of course, but they help us realize that final evaluation of a work of literature is inseparable from evaluation of the culture of which it is an expression.

In the Joseph cycle Mann reverses his procedure and throws the symbolical pattern of the myth in the forefront of his work. The progress is from the personal myth of the individual, fulfilling itself secretly beneath the social and intellectual encrustations of the bourgeois consciousness, to the *social* myth, that is, the objectified projection of the highest experience of the race on the plane of the imagination. Now the concern is not so much with the unique predicament of the modern world as with human

history, not so much with European man as with man himself—
"his state and standing in the universe." The work is an exhaustive formal application of the ideas of time adumbrated in
The Magic Mountain. For time in this series is at once novelty
and repetition, change and permanence, progress and retrogression. The "bottomless pit of time" invoked in the prologue is
shown to reveal its own dialectic pattern when viewed with a
sufficient perspective. So also in attempting to explain the motivation of an individual at any given moment of time it is not always
possible to distinguish between happening and doing, between
the imperative reenactment of some established form of conduct
and the present deed. When the brothers throw Joseph into the
well, for example, we are told that "it had come about, indeed,
through them, but they had not done it, it had simply happened
to them."

For Mann, in search of an appropriate myth from the past to
illustrate such a reading of history, nothing could be more perfect
than the story of the Hebrew Joseph. Nomadic in their habits,
belonging as much to the West as to the East, and through their
religion serving as a bridge between the two, the Jews take on a
more universal character than that of any other race. (For the
same reason Joyce makes Leopold Bloom his complete symbol
of "normal" humanity.) Moreover, the long, unbroken continuity
of their legend and history makes possible the clearest demonstration of the ideas of time and causality that are being developed in the work. As for the particular choice of Joseph, we may
observe, in the first place, that as a hero he is still safely within
the confines of the human. He belongs to a late, mature, and
rather precociously refined stage of primitive religion when not
only has the separation between the chthonic hero-demon and
the sky god already occurred, but the latter has taken on the
highest spiritual attributes of the race. This is the very first note
struck in the book: Joseph is rebuked by his father for slipping
back into the old worship of the moon, which is bound up in the
less advanced cults with the worship of the earth and the dead.
And if so much is immediately made of the passing on of the

"blessing"—from Abraham to Isaac, from Isaac to Jacob—it is to emphasize that we are still in the realm where progress is possible —the realm of the human. For what is the "pact" with God, of which we are told so much, but the pact that man makes with that part of himself which he has projected into the Deity and which later theology will erect into an absolute system of dogma? In other words, Joseph belongs to the stage at which man is still occupied in "making" his God. As the half-crazed Cardan said of himself, he is *in extremitate humanae substantiae condition-isque*, but not yet among the immortals.

Although Joseph remains a man, he is a *superior* man. And this leads to the consideration that must have been the most profound source of Mann's attraction toward him. For what is he but the ancient prototype of that modern individual whose marked superiority both of experience and insight has incurred the hostility of all right-thinking people, forced as he is into the lonely pit of humiliation, and driven into a bitter exile? Joseph will be many things before we are through with him—slave-gardener, overseer, diplomat, and prophet—but he is first and foremost "the man of words." To his exceptional gift of language he owes, in the first place, his inheritance of the "blessing" over the heads of his older brothers. To the same gift he owes the fateful interest in him taken by the Maonite merchant who leads him into Egypt, by the overseer Montkaw in the house of Potiphar, and by the impressionable Potiphar himself. And through his ability to give beautiful and prophetic expression to his dreams he will undoubtedly attract the attention of Pharaoh and earn his deliverance from the pit a second time. In Joseph the suffering artist of the early tales will undergo a purgation by which all that knowledge of the abyss, all that sympathy with disease and death, becomes translated on the higher plane of moral and social responsibility.

In our very first glimpse of him, Joseph betrays what we have seen as the inherent narcissism of the type. Moreover, this time it is a narcissism of the body as well as of the mind or spirit, for as a mythical character Joseph can be as beautiful as he is wise—

the union of Tadzio and Aschenbach in a single person. Again physical beauty is the outward and visible sign of a superior moral and spiritual nature. As the child of Rachel and Jacob, he is the fruit of the marriage between beauty and spirit. But it is his too casual and unreflecting assumption of the rôle, the naive conviction that everyone must love him as he loves himself, the inevitable arrogance of the wearer of the ketonet that leads to his brutal treatment at the hands of the brothers. Like Aschenbach, he must pay for his sensuous relaxation into his own image—the moon; like Tadzio, he must be pushed into the earth by his more coarse-grained fellows. Before his descent into the well Joseph is hardly a person; he is no longer a child but not yet a man; he has no status in his social group. He exists only in the light of his infantile appreciation of himself, as the moon that he worships was supposed to mirror the light of the earth. But after his three days in the well, in darkness and surrounded by his own filth, he learns the classic lesson of humility. Through the chastisement of the self through the body, the spiritual through the physical, Joseph attains to his "second birth," which, as the first has been simply into the realm of sterile and self-contained matter, is into the realm of a more active moral and social consciousness.

Without this initial moral experience Joseph would never have been able to acquire the knowledge and self-discipline necessary for the performance of his rôle. Without his successful working-out of the personal problem he would not even have been able to take his place by the side of his fellows, much less lead them to a higher destiny. The point is important, because it is evident that Mann does not intend us to understand that everyone in the social group is submitted to such a rigorous test of endurance. The common run of humanity, the ordinary members of the tribe, the social mass, as represented here by the brothers, are never disturbed by considerations of the relationships between God and man, the spirit and the flesh, the old and the new. Only through the intensely personal ordeal of "the marked man" among them, to recall Tonio Kröger's phrase, do they ever rise above the level of the soil which they spend their lives tilling.

And it has already been suggested what unpopular figure in the modern civilized world Mann has in mind for the possible fulfillment of this rôle today. Only the artist, in a culture given over to the false and sentimental optimism of a unilinear view of progress, has anything like a sense of the responsibilities involved in being a complete human being. The artist, through his preoccupation with the esthetic integrity of his work, has been forced into a recognition of the fundamentally dialectic nature of the processes at work in reality, of the never altogether resolved conflict between form and matter. He alone has appreciated the interrelationship between the old and the new, conservatism and radicalism, time and history. And he alone has attained to the knowledge that even the most temporary equilibrium between these processes is a matter of the most intense individual discipline.

In *Joseph in Egypt* Mann exposes his hero to the full spectacle of a great civilization in decay so that he may come to recognize that the same struggle between the old and the new from which he has just emerged in his own experience is also to be traced out in history. Indeed, the whole pattern of his adventures in the "monkey-land" of Egypt may be related to the Freudian description of the relations of the individual ego to the world. As in all the classic myths (Oedipus, Theseus, Beowulf), the hero recovers from some nearly fatal experience in infancy or youth to appear in triumph in some foreign land. In Freudian terms, this corresponds to the new equilibrium that has been set up in the individual psychology; and the foreignness of the material setting emphasizes the transition from the narrow world of the self to the wider world of complex social relations. It is also, in Joseph's case, into a more "advanced" world that he moves, insofar as the cosmopolitan civilization of Egypt represents a higher level of social and economic development than the pastoral life of his fathers. But it is the meaning of these two volumes that in another sense the corrupt and decadent customs of this new land betoken a much lower stage of *human* development, so that

Joseph's journey into Egypt is a descent in the most literal sense of the word.

This ambiguous progress is also indicated through Joseph's transference of the object of ego-identification from the noble and high-minded Jacob to the practical and matter-of-fact merchant, and from the merchant to the ailing overseer Montkaw, who may also be taken as a kind of entrepreneur. The process of substitute-finding reaches its end in the high priest Potiphar, before whom Joseph is finally made to have such feelings as Hans Castorp experienced before Peeperkorn. For Potiphar, the functionary without any function, the soldier who wears but cannot use the sword, the husband as pure social form, is the human zero who symbolizes the complete cancellation of experience that is evident in every phase of Egyptian life and thought. As the child of incest he is the past breeding on the past; and his emasculation stands for the empty formalism of the state religion. For Joseph such a figure cannot stand as the center of a new equilibrium of psychological forces, as the Freudian analysis demands; he represents the pathetic and reprehensible attempt to preserve an already established equilibrium of the past. This is made very clear in the conversation between the incestuous brother-sister pair that Joseph overhears in the closed garden.

As happens when the individual cannot discover an adequate object for self-identification in the outside world he makes the fruitless attempt to lose himself in his own superego. Here the tragic consequences of such an attempt are brought out in the climactic episode of Joseph's affair with Potiphar's wife. Mut-en-emet, with her smoldering and angry passion, is in the direct line of Gerda Buddenbrooks, Clavdia Chauchat, and all those other feminine denizens of the abyss. But unlike Hans Castorp, who dissolved in an agony of self-abasement before the feet of his mother-mistress, Joseph exposes himself to Mut's company merely to test his own powers of endurance. The voluptuous chords of the *Liebestod* give way to a sterner music. Love is not to be accepted in terms of another and even more speedy descent into the pit. In the terrible and magnificent scene in which the unfortunate woman, after conjuring up the whole monotonous ritual of delight, threatens him with mutilation, Joseph is calm enough to remind her: "Yet behold, my friend, how madness reduces you for a time below the level of the human! For its advantage and special property it is to think beyond the moment and consider what comes after."

Joseph's second fall is the result of the still insufficiently purged arrogance of his spirit that is implicit in this speech. It is, as a matter of fact, the arrogance of the superego in playing with a situation that is more dangerous than it is willing to admit. For the didactic tone that he adopts toward the erring Mut, as is made clear through the symbolism of the two dwarfs, is really the indirect expression of the first stirrings in him of his own sexual nature. The whole purpose of his Egyptian experience has been to submit his new-found manhood to the contingencies of a particular and concrete social situation, to bring the spirit into contact with matter. But the spirit too proves to have its own kind of arrogance, to overestimate its strength in a world of unexpected subterfuges and betrayals. Those long dialogues between Joseph and Mut are more than a little reminiscent of the medieval debates between the soul and the body; and their mournful termination is a reminder that the soul cannot be too wary of its opponent.

Joseph is made to pay for his failure to discover a symbol that will enable him to give force and direction to his life. But in the final volumes we may expect that he will emerge from the Egyptian prison house with that full knowledge and control of his world which will make him a true "nourisher" of his people. He will discover his generating and organizing symbol in the *idea* of the moral and spiritual tradition of his race.

In the purposely ambiguous title that Mann has chosen for his hero we may discover the answer to the question that must have occurred all through this discussion. Are we to understand that in taking Joseph as his arch symbol of the responsible artist type Mann intends that the modern artist also should be an active political leader—the shepherd of his tribe in the *literal* sense of the word? To say that such is the implication is of course to throw the door wide open to that description of the artist's role as propagandist of one or another social doctrine, to that confusion between creation and action which is enjoying such a vogue at the moment. But it is also to betray a rather profound misconception of the nature of the myth, in which everything is possible because everything exists in the pure realm of the imagination. As beauty may be united with wisdom, so also may the *Homo Dei* and the man of action reveal themselves to us in a single person. To mistake the pure world of myth for the world of contemporary reality is to mistake the potential for the actual. In the Joseph story the superior man becomes the "nourisher" of his race in both senses of the word, the literal and the symbolical, but it is only in the symbolical that he can become so today. It is in the sense of an example, a model, a guide to "a free and enlightened humanity" that the suffering artist of the early Mann stories achieves his epiphany in Joseph.

Is such a conception of art and the artist likely to sound too mystical for modern ears? The answer must be that it becomes mystical only if we fail to distinguish between myth as a process, as a formal pattern undergoing continuous modification and change of content, and myth as a fixed and immutable conformation of experience. In the heroic myth Mann has attempted to provide a final solution to the problem of tradition and progress —the problem that had been argued to the death by Naphta and Settembrini in *The Magic Mountain*. Perhaps the solution may be stated in terms of the old distinction between form and content: while the archetypal form of experience remains constant and invariable, its content undergoes profound differentiation from age to age, from culture to culture. Although there is no progress in the form, which is to be defined as the perpetually recurrent pattern of birth and rebirth, there is a kind of progress in the context of historical conditions in terms of which the heroic individual must work out his salvation. For the unilinear and altogether mechanical view of progress of the nineteenth century, Mann substitutes a description that has much more in common with that of Hegel and Marx. But it must immediately be added that in the important function that he assigns to tradition he is to be sharply distinguished both from the master of German idealism and the father of economic determinism.

The great difference between these three sharers in the same general mode of thinking is to be looked for in the ground on which the dialectic process of history is made to occur. By ground is meant of course field of reality, and about the nature of reality there must always be considerable disagreement between philosopher and poet. For Hegelian idealism the field of reality was first and last the rational intellect, in which the Divine Idea was able in the course of the ages to progress by dialectic stages to its supreme culmination in the Prussian state. Such a description had the excellent advantage of reconciling eighteenth-century subjectivism with the emergent optimism of the nineteenth; for in the history of philosophy also it is possible to trace out a dialectic interplay between the new and the old. So also Marx, while recognizing the appropriateness of the triadic method for a revolutionary theory of political economy, was forced to redefine the ground of Hegelian metaphysics in terms more in keeping with the scientific materialism of his time. But, contrary to the often quoted statement of Engels, Marx did not actually turn Hegel "upside down"; he merely substituted a metaphysics of matter for a metaphysics of mind; and between a philosophic materialism and a philosophic idealism there is not nearly such an important choice as many people have believed. The whole dialectic process of history is still made to occur on the ground of the rational intellect. For the nineteenth-century scientific world-view, as has been often enough pointed out by this time, was an abstract intellectual construction. However valuable it may have been as a stimulus to practical science within its own circumscribed limits, it can lay no more claims to being a description of absolute reality than the idealist *Weltanschauung*. To Mann must be credited the abundantly fertile suggestion that only in the myth do we get the dialectic process working itself out on the *whole* ground of human reality. In the myth the interplay is between reason and nature, between the constructions of the mind and the immediate presentation of experience at any given moment of history, between the principle of form and the principle of life. The myth is the concrete and dynamic image of the human microcosm as a whole, of which the movements of the mind and the feelings are to be taken as the defining processes. It is in this sense, as Mann has recently declared, that art supplies us with "the pattern of the human." It is in Goethe's phrase, "the scale of humanity," on which all of its moral, social, and political aspirations must finally be weighed. And it is our only Absolute; "for it is pure quality; it stand for the unsatisfied, the unsatiable demand."

Postscript *

[1956]

In Mann's earlier uses of myth (as in *The Magic Mountain*, where Castorp was a bourgeois folk hero, the mountain an Olympian Heaven) the effort was to understand the present through the perspective of ancient myths. The Joseph series is an interpretation of ancient myth through the perspectives of the modern consciousness with its vast apparatus of science, anthropology, comparative religion, archaeology, analytic psychology. *Joseph* is among other things a kind of encyclopedia of all our current knowledge in these fields. Thus *Joseph* comprises a glossary or commentary on a work of the imagination. For myths come out of the unconscious processes of mankind. The symbols on which they are based have more meanings or layers of meaning than the conscious mind can ever grasp.

This is to say that *Joseph and His Brethren* does not represent the application of the pattern of ancient myth to modern materials as in Joyce's *Ulysses*, or Eliot's *Waste Land*, or any number of other modern works, or in Mann's earlier works. Nor is it the

* From a lecture at The New School for Social Research. Previously unpublished.

straightforward recital of an ancient myth. Rather is it the extended commentary upon and analysis of a particular myth of the past by a highly informed, sophisticated, and ironic modern mind.

For this reason it is difficult to classify the work in ordinary literary terms. Is it a work of art, that is, of the imagination? Or is it more like a combination of a German Ph.D. thesis and a discourse on history?—a work largely of scholarly research and critical interpretation? Or lastly is it an attempt to reconcile the imagination and the analytical intelligence? These are the questions with which the Joseph series, like so many other modern books, confronts us. It is, very generally, the question of the relationship between symbolic presentation and analytical discourse in the novel. And, as far as Mann is concerned, upon the answer to it depends any final evaluation of his work from an artistic point of view. How successfully does he reconcile the symbolical and the analytical in later works, such as the *Joseph* and *Dr. Faustus*? There is considerable difference of opinion about this; and there is perhaps more widespread disagreement about his claims as an artist than about those of any writer of comparable reputation in this century.

To state the difference between what we have called the symbolical and the analytical modes of presentation in the novel:

The symbol in literature and the arts is always something concrete: a situation, an object or set of objects, or even a person. And its forcefulness depends upon the amount of meaningful human feeling with which it is charged. Since the symbol is a concrete particular, plus the feelings or attitudes it invokes in us, it is compound. It is also infinitely variable, because human attitudes and feelings differ from person to person, from age to age, from moment to moment, and associations with the objects, moreover, differ widely between one culture and another, one sex and another, one individual and another. In art and literature, that is, in early art and literature, symbols are arranged in patterns and presented directly, without any explanation or helpful comment on the part of the artist. They thus create a vivid impression of reality in all its directness of impact. For in life we perceive before we understand; ultimately we have to do the work of analysis and interpretation for ourselves. I have said that in art, symbols are presented in patterns, for a symbol can have meaning only in relation to other symbols. The original patterns of symbols in the history of the race we call myths.

The symbol, then, to catalogue certain of its attributes, is concrete, it is compound (the object plus the attitude); it is variable (meaning different things to different people and in different times); it is direct, partaking of the quality of reality itself. It can exist fully or significantly only in a context, which may be the myth or a work of literature or of the other arts.

Of analysis it is not necessary to say that it is the process by which the logical mind breaks down the symbol. If the impulse behind the symbolical or the imaginative is above all integrative, that of the analytical is dissociative. Analysis is, therefore, by its very nature, hostile to the work of art as it has traditionally existed, that is, as a pattern of symbols.

Yet we know that the whole history of Western literature since *Hamlet*, which is a play about analysis, has been a history of the steady and triumphant encroachment of the analytical spirit upon the domain of the imaginative. And in this process the novel has assumed the rôle of being the most characteristic literary form of the last one hundred and fifty years. From Samuel Richardson to Proust the direct symbolical presentation of life in terms of people and events has often been subordinated to their analytical description. In Zola and his naturalistic descendants this analysis came to be less that of the complexities of human reality than of the socio-economic medium in which these existed. With psychoanalysis, it is true, there came a renewed interest in symbols, at least an admission of their existence. But the psychoanalytical novelist tended to use symbols like a scientist rather than an artist, as formulae having patent and immutable meanings. He was concerned not with creating symbols but with using symbols, whose meanings had been previously agreed upon, for the purpose of analysis.

However, Freud, in turning to myth and tragedy for illustrations of his formulae, was partly responsible for the increasing effort to restore the symbolical method in twentieth-century literature. As we have said, the treatment of myth by modern writers has varied profoundly: Joyce, Eliot, and Pound interpreting modern life from the perspective of ancient myth; Mann, at least ultimately, interpreting the myths of the past in the light of modern scientific knowledge.

But this is perhaps to put the matter too simply: Mann's purpose, however successful he has been in it, has been in these later books to reconcile the mythical with the analytical, the past with the present, to set the one against the other in a spirit of playful irony. Although Mann is a modern man, the product of nineteenth-century rationalism, he believes in the persistence of myth, both in our individual behavior and in our cultural forms; he believes that unconsciously man conforms to certain modes of responding and behaving from the past. Given a certain situation, he will behave as some legendary or historical figure in a similar situation. For example, there is the fundamental situation upon which the whole of the Joseph series is founded—fraternal rivalry, more particularly between an older brother who is coarse and unworthy, and a younger brother who is talented and morally superior.

For Mann's idea is that Isaac was not really deceived by his blindness into making Jacob, the second-born, "the bearer of the blessing," but chose the already Chosen. Mr. Harry Slochower, whose *Thomas Mann's Joseph Story* is a more complete analysis or summary of the book than I can hope to give here, calls this "mythical motivation" as opposed to "ethical or rational motivation." There are two observations to be made: Mann, unlike Jung, does not believe that our behavior is determined by any biological inheritance. The reasons for our behaving according to traditional forms are to be found in religious ritual, in myth, in oral tradition, and in literature and custom. Secondly, Mann, as a true son of the Enlightenment, believes that there is a real progress in moral and intellectual refinement from age to age, from generation to generation, from son to son. If there is repetition, it is repetition with a difference. Jacob is superior to his father Isaac, Joseph to Jacob, and so on, we may suppose, down through the ages (although who is superior to whom nowadays only Thomas Mann perhaps knows!). At any rate, in this way Mann reconciles his innate belief in nineteenth-century progress with his acquired interest in myth. The final chapter in the whole trilogy is "The Great Progress."

In *Joseph the Provider*, the poet-dreamer, the artist prototype, fulfills himself socially in both the literal and the symbolical sense. He conserves the source of the physical nourishment of the people by storing up grain against the years of no harvest. In the preface, Mann makes him a kind of ancient New Dealer. He is also the custodian of the highest spiritual values of his race. This is another instance of Mann's drawing a parallel between the physical and the spiritual, as, markedly, in *The Magic Mountain*.

What is the final meaning of the book? In the passage in which Joseph is engaged in one of his many dialogues with Iknahton, it is clear that he is the spokesman of Mann himself, as earlier Hans Castorp had been, the mediator between good and evil, the heights and the depths.

"For God is the whole," Joseph tells Pharaoh. It is clear that Joseph is a humanist: God is simply man taken in his combination of good and evil potentialities. He is not someone apart from man, to whom man is bound in piety and obedience. Pharaoh, on the other hand, is an absolutist: God is light, the sun, and men are a hopeless lot. He relates the cruelty of his own grandfather, who became a god. "Purify the godhead, and you purify me." To which Joseph responds that his grandfather, Abraham, was also strong, and had made a pact with God, who drove the robber kings from the East. "Did he take the field?" the Pharaoh shrewdly asks. How seriously are we to take the skillful sophistry of this passage? God exists only if he is on our side, we will give him homage if he will give us prosperity. This smacks more of Puritanism than of humanism. The pact is a business arrangement.

In the very last paragraph of the book, in the scene of Joseph's reconciliation with his brethren, there is to be noted the conception that the living are in a play, of which the rôles have been written. This suggests a kind of determinism, but once more Mann's optimism comes to the rescue: "Everything works for the best in the best of all possible worlds." If Joseph had not been cast in the well, there would have been no story, *i.e.*, no play.

I have not attempted a synopsis of the twelve-hundred-odd pages of this book, most of which consist of such speeches or dialogues as those just noted, of archaeological and historical information, often interesting in itself. The essential narrative is so familiar to readers as to provide little suspense. There remain a few scenes memorable for their poetic or dramatic quality. One might mention among these Joseph in the grove of Adonis, and his descent into the pit. As the work moves on to the final volume the method is more and more one of insistent, tiresome, and obvious parody. In *Doctor Faustus* the hero says: "all the methods and conventions of art today *are good for parody only*." While this may be true of Mann himself, it is not true of all modern writers. Not of Yeats, who mocks "mockers after that," nor of Joyce, a supreme parodist, whose work rests finally upon piety toward that humanity, all of whose vices and follies he has rendered for us.

In the Joseph series there are two examples of an irresponsible levity: the whole treatment of Potiphar's wife, whose passion for Joseph is made to appear a tremendous joke; and the characterization as an insipid prattler of Iknahton, composer of the great Hymn to the Sun and one of the purest spiritual figures of history. Not to fall into a complaint of the "lack of high seriousness," I question whether irony of this sort is a resolution of anything, or simply a state of feeling.

Of *Doctor Faustus* I have left very little space to say anything. And indeed there is nothing I can say that Mann himself does not say in the course of the work. Over and over again the nar-ator, a garrulous and mediocre German schoolmaster, apologizes to the reader for boring him so much. Briefly, it is the story of a talented young musician who makes a pact with the devil by which he will compose extraordinary music for twenty-four years, at the end of which time he must die. This is the substance of the action. The larger part of the work consists in highly technical descriptions of musical compositions, incomprehensible to any but experts in the field. The theme would seem to be that the great artist is always demoniac; and this demonism is somehow vaguely related to the demoniac influences at work in German political circles before the last war. This is an identification which I for one profoundly deplore; it gives aid and comfort to the enemy, the Philistines; and if there is such a thing as a fatherland of artists and if only this work of Mann's were to be considered, Mann should be sent out of that fatherland—in exile.

In a sense, everything in Mann is reducible to dialectical op-posites, from the bourgeois versus the artist of the earliest work, to the individual versus the social hero at the end of the Joseph cycle. Esthetically there is the contrast between the concrete narrative and the discursive, between creation and dissolution of the symbol. Style is the most intimate reflection of a writer's feeling toward life. The mood of Mann's style is the ironic. And the ironist is a mediator—a compromiser—and art and compro-mise are incompatible. There is some doubt at the end as to whether Mann's resolution is not simply a playing with words, a kind of irreverence toward humanity—at least in its emotional and instinctive manifestations; whether he does believe in the possibility of a redeemable and redeemed humanity.

If Mann's humanism is not as bombastic as that of Settem-brini, it is yet not tragic—but merely sentimental. He is not, per-haps, in the last analysis, *un homme sérieux*. It is as if the gods, who loaded him with so many gifts, denied him the most in-dispensable gift of all—the gift of faith.

IV TRAGEDY

Thoughts on Tragedy *

[1937–38]

Tragedy is something at once so simple and so difficult that its truths are in continual need of restatement in terms of the particular understanding of every age. If the tragic spirit is always with us, as I maintain, it is likely to be as a deeply assimilable attitude toward the world, so unconscious in its operation in thought and feeling as to become a whole mode of experiencing reality. To anyone who has completely absorbed this spirit the world is a tragic world, and to attempt to define this spirit is for him to provide a geography of the commonplace. Like the Oriental personage in a poem † by Wallace Stevens, he is himself the compass of that sea whose tide sweeps through his veins. And it is certainly true that there have been whole epochs of human culture when absorption of such intensity existed on a wide enough scale to make definition an altogether useless and unnecessary task: life was tragedy and tragedy life. But to members of later and perhaps less innocent epochs when we are confronted not with a single attitude but with many competing attitudes, no attitude can long remain undifferentiated by the mind without degenerating into something rather less than itself, and an uncritical devotion to the tragic view can be too easily confounded

* From drafts of a projected book. Previously unpublished.
† "Tea at the Palaz of Hoon."

with a temperamental idiosyncrasy, a conditioned state of mind, a mood. To be distinguished from mere gloom or irresponsible pessimism, it must be reconciled with everything that is most conscious in an age—its accumulated experience, its knowledge, its particular form of logic; and this means that it must restate what we have called its truths in an ever changing set of intellectual terms.

As for the difficulty of talking about tragedy, it is the same at any time when it becomes necessary to talk about it at all. It is impossible to say anything about it that is pertinent without at the same time saying something about every known department of human thought and expression. Aristotle, who came nearer to achieving an adequate statement than anyone is ever likely to again, merely succeeded in leaving us a batch of lecture notes that have caused two thousand years of confusion through their incapacity to be understood without word-by-word reference to the whole corpus of philosophy and science from which they derive their vocabulary. Medicine, ethics, physics, politics—all of course as these subject matters were grasped and formulated in his time —provide the language of the *Poetics*; and this is to take no account of the special technical vocabulary of verse and metre that also existed for his time. Tragedy was the name that he might have given to the province which he claimed as his own. For we may say that if every branch of learning must have its categories, in order to put some bounds to the realm of discourse, in the discussion of tragedy these branches of knowledge are themselves the categories: it is the realm of discourse which includes all the others—the realm of discourses.

This is not to say that we have in tragedy, in its developed form, a sort of handy compendium of the available knowledge of any time, a kind of Encyclopaedia of Universal Knowledge. If this were the case the difficulty of approaching it, although formidable enough, would be considerably less than it indeed is. Tragedy is a synthesis not only of what men think but of what they feel and how they act in the most important predicament with which they are confronted. The plane on which it addresses us, as a matter of fact, is not the plane of knowledge at all, nor any other plane but its own, which insofar as it subsumes all the others must be considered unique. In dealing with tragedy we are presented with a constellation of experience so profound, so comprehensive, and so final that we are taken, if not beyond the frontiers of the mind, at least to the farthest reaches of which it is capable—to that ever shifting point at which the most strenuous efforts of the rational must be merged with the press of experience.

Before such a task the mind, especially the modern mind, must falter; and so far as knowledge alone is concerned we need only compare the bulk and complexity of information which our science has made possible with what Aristotle had at his disposal to appreciate the increasing difficulty of talking about tragedy today. To describe the workings of the soul, Aristotle could take a crude metaphor from the undeveloped medical language of his time; but the process of "catharsis" has now become the separate subject matter of a whole science or pseudo science, with its conflicting schools, theories, descriptions, and mythologies. And all these hang over the modern mind with the weight and insistence of a duty. There is also the danger of attempting to dispose of the problems of tragedy exclusively through the attitude bred by the intellectual structure that has arisen out of all this information and theory—a type of error well illustrated by Dante in the derivation that he offers of the word in his epistle to Can Grande della Scala: "and therefore is it called from *tragus*, which is a goat, and *oda*, as it were a goat song, or noisome after the fashion of a goat." To the medieval Christian, committed to a belief in the ultimate resolution of human destinies in a supernatural realm, the earthly endings in the tragedies of Seneca (and those of Shakespeare if he had known them) could only have emitted a very bad smell. The absurdity of his interpretation was not so much the result of a defect of learning as of the disingenuous functioning of his system of thought. By the same kind of process we may not be saved, despite our superior knowledge of folklore and comparative religion, from committing a similar absurdity.

It is possible that we may be too well informed to catch the true smell of tragedy.

The only solution for the contemporary student of tragedy is to reduce his account to the simplest possible terms, keeping close at all times to the largest pattern of meaning which it describes in the mind. In this attempt he is immensely aided by the palpable simplicity of the pattern; he need only brood sufficiently long on its constituent parts to bring all the disparate movements, tendencies, and unformulated impulses of the modern world to an adequate reconciliation. He will also be aided by the fact that he is writing at a moment of history when all the current frameworks of interpretation, both actual and potential, are in a sufficient state of disrepair to permit of the most unimpeded vision. Moreover, there is increasing historical evidence that if our culture does not soon return to some apprehension of the nature and meaning of the tragic view of experience there will not be anyone left with even enough perception to mourn its demise.

For the contemporary man the world of tragedy is not so much remote as too near: the air has grown rank with the breath of heroes. Despite the multitude of disguises from emperor to clown which, like the god Dionysus, contemporary man has adopted to conceal his identity, we cannot fail to recognize the well-defined lineaments. Every man is hero of a drama in which unfortunately there are so many other heroes that it is not always possible to follow the action and never altogether the meaning. This is further complicated by the fact that some disguises are so cunning that the hero may be mistaken for the messenger or the slave: it is one of the idiosyncrasies of the modern hero to appear in rags or bear his viscera in his hands. And one will find him in the greatest assortment of places: the Chigi palace, Canterbury Cathedral, a revolutionary "cell," or the suburb of one of our large cities. Action enough there is in the drama, but conversation between heroes is bound to be a lagging affair. Instead of the rapid give-and-take of the Greek *stichomythia*, from which dialectical reasoning and hence all modern science is supposed to have arisen, we have only an unbroken soliloquy from beginning to end. Fortunately all the soliloquies are so much alike in substance and fit into each other so perfectly in form that it is quite simple to make out the general tenor. The difficulty rather is for contemporary man to stop talking long enough to hear what it is precisely that he is saying. It is the very great difficulty of occupying the stage and witnessing the spectacle at one and the same time.

This is to say that if the modern world is a tragic world, as the increasing accumulation of masonry about the heroes' feet makes more and more obvious, it does not necessarily follow that it is perceived as such by its host of suffering participants. For tragedy is not life but a pattern through which we may view life, a perspective on ourselves and the world. It is the result of a collaboration in which the rôle of spectator equals if it is not greater in importance than that of the players on the stage. In fact, it is quite impossible to use the word at all without constant reference to the spectator, who gives it its only value and meaning. And the difficulty is that the modern world has pretty successfully cleared the amphitheatre of all spectators. Even the so-called Olympian observer of the type produced in the last century with his "spectatorial view of the universe," proves upon closer examination, to be merely another actor strayed among the benches: he has mistaken his particular brand of hybris for a perspective. In such a situation, we might think that nothing short of an authentically supernatural view itself would be reliable, unless we recognize that tragedy, in its fully developed form, provides us with a means of vision for the correction of individual astigmatism by humility.

But tragedy has so far degenerated in meaning that it is perhaps not available to us unless we try to bring to it some of the same sort of perspective that it in turn may be claimed to supply to our whole view of ourselves and the world. On the lowest plane it has of course become a synonym for something sad, gloomy, painful, and generally unpleasant; and it is necessary to realize that in its completed meaning it is none of these things but actually their opposite. On the intellectual plane it has become confused with a certain fatalistic interpretation of history to the degree that it must suffer from whatever lack of clarity may be found in this interpretation. It is also necessary to excavate through the many layers of theoretical explanation that have accumulated around the term in the course of its own history as a literary form.

For Western man tragedy is likely to mean Greek tragedy; the norm is considered to have been established once and for all on an Athenian hillside some time in the fifth century; and the rules and regulations laid down once and for all by Aristotle some little time afterwards. All its subsequent manifestations, from Seneca to the Elizabethan age and the French seventeenth century, are capable of being treated in terms of the application or modification of this fundamental norm. While such an account has its conveniences, it is desirable, if we are approaching tragedy as a perspective rather than as a completed form, to reduce its meaning to something so simple and general that it is applicable at any time and in any place. As a matter of fact it is through the painstaking historical researches into the origins of Attic tragedy made in recent years that we are able to discover the remarkable simplicity and universality of the pattern that lies at its base. It is not that we are in any way able to improve on Aristotle but that we are able to give a little more content to his definitions than was possible in certain ages of the past. We have learned, for example, that if tragedy is "the imitation of an action" it is an imitation not "of men, but of life, of happiness," that is, the pattern of significant action that gives human life a certain order and meaning. And this pattern itself is embraced in the myth, or in that type of traditional story in which the experience of the race was supposed to be arranged in such a familiar and inevitable order that it never occurred to Aristotle to say very much about it. What the research of a scientific era has made possible is an analysis of the myth itself into its elements, a simplification to the extent that we can no longer fail to trace the identity of its pattern not only in Greek epic and drama but in all the great and comprehensive expressions of human experience everywhere in the world.

Tragedy begins with a metaphor: the life of man is a flower, a wave, a star. At least it is necessary to suppose that there must have been in the history of mankind a moment when the contemplative image was of such absolute purity that the image by itself was sufficient to generate feelings of wonderment and awe. For the first human being to whom the burden of a thousand lyrics occurred, the simple parallel would have to be recognized, brooded on, and related to every aspect of his experience before it could become expanded into an adequate pattern of significance for the whole of existence. What we must suppose is a moment when, through some accidental or miraculous relaxation of the will, the pressure of material necessities, the distractions of the senses, of the self, all dropped away at once, leaving in their place an openness of the whole being to whatever might shape itself out of memory and perception. This would be of course the mood of contemplation; but where in the type of person with whom we most associate the contemplative experience today, the mystic, the object is consciously or unconsciously determined in advance, we are here required to believe that the object is created by the experience. To the professional mystic of any period the object for the sake of which he cultivates abstinence, etc., already exists as the result of a whole religious and intellectual system; his problem is by an effort of will to follow a regimen which will enable him to become one with it. The kind of contemplation that could give rise to the particular metaphor in question is obviously more akin to that of the poet—the lyric poet of the purest type, in whom perception is not already directed and shaped by some anterior scheme of things, so that what we get is the Platonic copy of a copy, but on whom experience seems to leave its own authentic stamp and image. Moreover, there is not involved in this kind of contemplation any need for a resolution or moral: the moment is self-defined and self-sufficient. These belong rather to the next moment, which is the moment of reflection. We begin with the hypothesis of essentially lyrical intuition of the oneness of all life because perception must precede thought, because only out of some bold and overwhelming image of what reality is like can arise these vast structures of thought and action that are implicit in developed tragedy. Only out of some such unhampered original vision could have come the later, more concrete specification of

> The broken wall, the burning roof and tower
> And Agamemnon dead.*

For if tragedy begins with the simple metaphor, the contemplative mood, the lyrical outcry, it cannot long remain on this static plane. Through what we must call *brooding* on the parallel, the inherent dynamism is discovered by means of which man can, gradually, and by the most adroit contrivances of his mind, bring all the separate impulses of his nature into a living organic pattern. The recording of this process would constitute the history not only of tragedy but of religion, and not only of tragedy and religion but of all the philosophies that have been devised either to support religion or to substitute for it.

A metaphor may be considered static when the fusion that it represents answers to no other end than the satisfaction of the knowing mind suspended above all feeling and action. That life is a cycle of events following each other in time with an inexorable regularity, comparable to the passage of the seasons, and that nature exhibits in a million different forms an identical pattern of events—birth, growth, decay, and death—are facts that must have impressed themselves on human consciousness as soon as it had the power of detached observation and a sense of time. And that man was one of these forms of nature, subject to the same inexorable pattern, is a fact that must have impressed itself on him at about the same time. But a metaphorical identification of the two orders of reality, the external order of nature and the separate order of man that came into being through his very consciousness of belonging to a different order, could not have occurred until a much later date. For in the true metaphor what

---

* From "Leda and the Swan," in *The Variorum Edition of the Poems of W. B. Yeats*, New York, Macmillan, 1957, p. 441.

is accomplished is not a mere pointing out of likenesses between objects that are alike but between objects that are unlike in important respects in order to lead us to a realization of their identity in a higher order of reality. Between the observation that the life of man is like the passage of the seasons, the waxing and the waning of the moon, or the rising and ebbing of the tide and the metaphor with which we have begun, there must have lain a whole tract of time during which the mind had slowly to break down whatever barriers it had been led to erect between itself and nature. For in the metaphor human existence becomes one with all these processes; through the very consciousness that had at first experienced a sense of difference a sense of identity is attained. And in the light of all the consequences that this movement toward unity was to have, the creation of such a metaphor was the first great triumph of the human consciousness. Yet insofar as it was still only on the plane of contemplative knowledge, it cannot be said to comprise a full imaginative act.

Through brooding alone will the image yield up its meaning; and the last stage in the ubiquitous pattern will be seen always to contain within it the potentiality of a whole new cycle of existence. The rotting grain of winter will emerge in leaf and kernel in the spring, the old moon holds the new moon in her arms, the returning wave and so on. This is the language of poetry and unfortunately of a great deal of bad poetry; but we are dealing with a type of experience for whose description images rather than concepts are not only more convenient but more appropriate. It may or may not be an improvement to say that for the static metaphor, set in the imagination with the precision and immovability of an object of space, there is now the dynamic metaphor of an endless movement in time. In place of repetition, in the sense of the unrelated appearance of the same general sort of sequence, we now have rhythm, or the expectation of an integral relationship throughout a successive order of sequences. The metaphor may now be expanded to cover not only the particular flower, wave, or star but the whole of living nature, not only the individual man but the race of men. And in this transition from the original space metaphor to the time metaphor we take an immensely long step toward the understanding of what lies at the root of the tragic experience.

When life is seen as an endless movement in time rather than as a picture, as an "eternal occurrence" of the same reality rather than as so many separate and mechanically duplicated realities, the contemplative spectator must break his mood, if only for a moment, to evaluate his vision. Now what is perceived is hardly any longer distinguishable from the perceiver; not only the processes of his own body but the process of thinking itself become interfused with the whole process of existence. We may say that at this instant when the vision seemed to take all into itself, the dreamer along with the dream, the mind, by a kind of reflex action of its own being, was forced to assert itself in behalf of other interests. For we have to recognize the distinction, in a being gifted with consciousness, between the mind as an instrument capable at certain moments of transcending all interests other than that of knowing and the mind as the instrument by which we are accustomed to organize our interests, which include the results of our knowing. When the mind perceived itself as losing its own identity we can suppose that it was shocked, by what we may call a kind of metaphysical alarm, into a momentary lapse from the pure vision into its more habitual function of evaluation. It was inevitable that the vision should take on some of the feeling it would immediately generate in a conscious creature; and the moment we speak of feeling we are involved in questions of will or choice.

It might be objected that to the Oriental mind, comfortably inwound in the folds of Becoming, there may never have occurred such a moment of jolting recovery from the direction of the mind led by pure contemplation, such a resistance of the intellect to its own dissolution in the process. But this will be thought only if it is not recognized that the Oriental acceptance of this dissolution, its willing immersion in the flux, is itself the result of a choice. Of the Oriental type of mind, which is so much with us today, and of its profound opposition to the tragic mind, more will have to be said in a later place. But for the purposes of the present discussion all we need insist is that while mysticism of this general order may originally have been the fruit of a process of contemplation there must at some moment have been an interruption of the intellect and will when it was decided to continue the process as a programme. In brief, a renewed immersion in the vision is one of the possible expressions of the reaction made to the pattern that it has unfolded. To the Oriental mind the realm of human reality was such that it could be accepted only through becoming identified with a realm transcending suffering in which intellect and will are both forever at rest.

Between the two attitudes of a total acceptance or rejection there does not seem, in such a fundamental matter as this, to have been any gradient or compromise. The concept of acquiescence has been successfully reduced by students of ethics to something that is in the last analysis no more than a debilitated expression of one or the other of these central attitudes. To the conscious mind presented with a situation important enough to require choice, and here the situation is the most important of all situations, the failure to achieve an instantaneous judgment is a postponement or suspension of judgment that actually amounts to a refusal, with all its consequent effects on personality and action. It is impossible through mere acquiescence in any fact or pattern of facts to pass from the plane of understanding to that of the necessity of feeling and will; such a transition is imposed on man through the primary fact of consciousness, even though the feeling may turn out to be negative and the will to assert itself in a systematic regimen of self-annihilation. Nor should we be misled by the consideration that in earlier stages of culture choice does not seem to have presented itself at all, that most men even in advanced stages of culture are saved from the strain by the dominating bias of the prevalent system of beliefs. For what are these systems themselves but the architectural elaborations of some once momentously accomplished "leaning or listing of the will," and on what do they depend for their capacity to elicit belief but the continued adequacy of their choice to the general experience? They represent choice at second hand, perhaps, but still choice in the sense that their own health and well-being derives from the degree to which they in turn have been accepted. To insist too much on their determinist character, according to which we must suppose that men believe what they do because of some unconscious or automatic organization of their interests, is to ignore the remarkable fluidity that such "organizations" demonstrate in the course of history. The only constant through them all would seem to be the persistence of a vital need for altering beliefs to suit the necessities of one or the other of the two essentially irreconcilable views it is possible to take of existence.

Why the one view rather than the other should be taken, a question that will naturally occur, has never been satisfactorily answered by any of the branches of philosophy or science. In the first place, it has been impossible because these are themselves already implicitly committed to one or the other: all philosophy presents us with, on closer scrutiny, is either the laughing or the weeping face, and this is the reason that so much philosophy sounds exactly alike to the improperly attuned ear. For this reason philosophy, and science insofar as it is a philosophy, are more likely than not to build their structures without much direct attention to the question that is, of course, the most important question of all. That philosophical systems are "rationalizations" is itself one of the trite rationalizations by which a busy age relieves itself of the burden of careful sustained thought; and it is by no means the intention to suggest that all the works of the great philosophers are reducible to the functionings of heredity, temperament, glands, class interest, or any of the other handy instruments of motivation that are in the intellectual toolbox at the moment. For the lesser thinkers of every time this is no doubt a useful type of approach up to a point; but in dealing with philosophical thought at its best and most serious we are in a realm in which the range and variety of such motivating factors would be so numerous that any one of them would seem irrelevant. We are in a realm as a matter of fact in which the deepest and purest thought is merged with the deepest and purest feeling; and all that has been suggested is that since feeling, in order to be the spur and guide of thought, must have a unity of direction, we may look at the root of any large and consistent philosophy for some fundamental emotional attitude toward man and his world. The question "Is life worth living?" is not asked by most philosophies because its answer, in the affirmative, is assumed in the movement and order of their systems; and there must always be something suspect when the Weeping Philosopher, like Heraclitus or Schopenhauer, goes to such pains to prove the negative.

In the second place, it is not asked, because it is the type of question which philosophy, without transgressing its self-imposed bounds of reason and logic, is not at all prepared to raise. It is a question for the religious prophet, the mystic, the poet, and for the individual of every class insofar as his experience at times must approach that of these specialists. All that an honest and forthright philosophy can undertake is to give the order and cogency of an intellectual construction to what must originally be a movement not only of the intellect but of the whole being toward affirmation or negation.

This has not prevented science, as a technique rather than as a philosophy, from offering causal explanation as to why the one view rather than another has obtained in certain places and at certain times. It is natural enough that the economic materialist should establish a correlation between the general state of material well-being in a community and the dominant emotional attitudes. Theoretically, nothing seems more reasonable than that the guarantee of adequate food and shelter should promote an attitude of affirmation toward experience and its absence a corresponding attitude of negation. But students of primitive societies, in which proof for such a correlation would have to be discovered, throw some embarrassment into this logic by describing a state of affairs in which nothing of the sort seems apparent.

Before the whole question of that acceptance or rejection of the pattern of experience presented to the tragic vision, we are left, therefore, with that sense of intellectual helplessness and final humility expressed in Gerard Hopkins' memorable lines:

> Man lives that list, that leaning in the will
> No wisdom can forecast by gauge or guess,
> That selfless self of self, most strange, most still,
> Fast-furled and all foredrawn to No or Yes.*

All that the student of tragedy can attempt is an understanding of what seems to happen when a whole race devotes itself to giving expression to an emotion of complete and unequivocal affirmation. For once the dynamic metaphor is properly seized by the imagination, once it has been certified by the intellect and identified with the will, it must be realized in some appropriate mode of expression. It must be expressed in order to pass from the plane of pure contemplative knowledge to that of the senses, where it can be incorporated, in the literal sense of the word, in the very functioning of the human organism. And the appropriate mode of expression for such an intuition of the essential and imponderable oneness of all the processes of life must be language that is not of the tongue alone but of the whole body. Such a conclusion we might have reached even without the vast body of information that is now at our disposal in tracing the origins of tragedy.

Tragedy, in the sense of a formal expression, begins with the dance because in the dance, as a great contemporary poet has put it, "the leaf, the blossom, and the bole" are one. In the dance the metaphor with which we have been concerned becomes flesh, its separate terms discover their concrete analogue in the rhythmical movements of the body, and the body itself becomes a synecdoche of existence. In discussing the dance it is difficult not to be rhetorical, as nearly all writers on the subject demonstrate, because here the temptation to offer a translation rather than

---

* From "On the Portrait of Two Beautiful Young People," *Poems of Gerard Manley Hopkins*, New York and London, Oxford University Press, 1956.

analysis is even stronger than usual. What is being talked about is of course poetry, but poetry at a deeper and more elementary level, where the ordinary convenient distinctions of content and form can hardly be applied, so that translation into the more familiar medium seems enough. If, as R. R. Marett remarks, "men danced their philosophies before they wrote them, and probably also before they thought them," the road back that thought must travel is indeed an arduous one. But what is a difficulty need not be made into a mystery, unless of course one believes that the vision blossoming into expression in the dance has been achieved altogether outside the bounds of reason and judgment. It is possible to be unmysterious in approaching the dance if one recognizes in it a meaning which, although it may not have been arrived at through the thought of the philosophers, is still the result of a process of dealing with the materials of experience. Thought is a very large word, as recent researches into the thought processes of savages have made clear, and if one kind of thinking is involved in the making of the dance it is not impossible that by another kind of thinking one may be able to arrive at its meaning. The dance will then be understood as the incarnation in the human body itself of those patterns of movement which the mind had glimpsed as being common both to itself and the whole of nature.

> O chestnut tree, great rooted blossomer,
> Are you the leaf, the blossom, or the bole?
> O body swayed to music, O brightening glance,
> How can we know the dancer from the dance?

Modern investigation into the origins of tragedy as it is known to us in English, chiefly through the brilliant and painstaking studies of scholars like Jane Harrison, F. M. Cornford, and Gilbert Murray, might be described as the attempt to give historical content and meaning to a sentence that appears early in the *Poetics* of Aristotle: "Imitation, then, being thus natural to us, and, secondly, Melody and Rhythm being also natural . . . those persons in whom originally these propensities were the strongest were naturally led to rude and extemporaneous attempts, which, gradually improved, gave birth to Poetry."

While it is true that we cannot today use the word natural with the dogmatic freedom of the great Philosopher of Nature, nor refer to something as an instinct which experimental science is inclined to regard as an acquired habit, this description of the order in which tragedy was developed has hardly been improved on. All the facts gathered by students of primitive societies, of early religions, and of specific literary forms themselves merely serve to confirm the notion that imitation, if it is not exactly an instinct, is at least so widely disseminated a practice among mankind as to seem a universal habit. And what is imitated seems always some pattern of behavior possessing that property of rhythm which, since it seems to be widely present in the human organism itself, must also be considered universal. No matter to what refinements and complications of poetry or tragedy the pattern may later be submitted, in the end it is traceable to these "rude and extemporaneous" beginnings, to the simpler workings of the imitative habit.

Exactly what is meant by imitation itself, however, has caused a great deal of significant confusion in criticism ever since Aristotle first used the term mimesis, both among his immediate followers and those later in the Renaissance, who took it to signify the representation of the "typical" or "general" in human experience, and among the exponents of nineteenth-century realism and naturalism, to whom it was simply the photographic mirroring of the flow of phenomena. How far Aristotle was from meaning the first, with its free admission of an abstract, didactic allegory, and from the *tranche de vie* school, with its apotheosis of undifferentiated fact, is evident a little further on in the *Poetics* when he takes great pains to point out that the imitation in tragedy is of "an action that is serious, entire, and of a certain magnitude." "Because Tragedy," he says, "is an imitation, not of men, but of Action—of life, of happiness: for [happiness] or unhappiness consists in Action, and the very end [of life] is Action of a certain kind, not quality." If tragedy is an imitation of life it is of life already ordered into a pattern of significant action. This action (*praxis*) itself is implicit in some myth (*mythos*), already known, which it is the special function of the dramatic poet to reconstruct with a proper attention to plot, or the *synthesis* of its elements. Because all three of these terms refer roughly to the same thing, some sort of sequence of events, they have been indiscriminately handled by many translators; so that not only has the distinction between "action" in the philosophical sense and the traditional myth or story been blurred, but both have been lost in modern discussion of the permutations of plot, the formal aspect of tragedy. Of course the difficulty in determining what it is in tragedy that is being imitated has been, in most cases, the result of the translators' belonging to an age when even the notion of a traditional story had disappeared before the habit of inventing "original" stories or "plots." It is only then that we hear of literature as the *direct* imitation of life—as in the eighteenth century's "Art is nature to advantage drest" or in the nineteenth-century (Stendhalian) novel as "a mirror dawdling down a road." What the recent studies of social and religious origins have made indisputable is that when Aristotle speaks of imitation it is not imitation of life directly but of life given a pattern of meaning in the myth.

When we refer to a purpose or motive behind the dances with which men sought to celebrate rhythmically their participation in the rhythmical processes of nature, we depart a long way from our original pure contemplative image. We move from the sphere of an art that was an art of spontaneous and disinterested enjoyment (since it was based on nothing more than the desire to give expression through the body to the vision of the imagination) to an art that begins to take on a more and more utilitarian character. Why this transition occurred so promptly that it is perhaps impossible for students today to discover examples of a purely disinterested ritual is not hard to understand if we recognize that in a conscious being like man no vision can long remain in its original state of purity. If man is unique as an animal in possessing a consciousness capable at times of transcending spatiotemporal limitations, he is also an animal in the more common, in the practical sense.

Most of the dances of early peoples and primitive tribes described for us by the anthropologists are notably impure in the sense in which we have been using the word; they are imitations with a purpose; they illustrate the transition from the sense of simple identity to that of a special kind of sympathy between man and nature.

What has happened in fact is that the metaphor has been dissolved, the unity of the original vision has been destroyed, and instead of fusion we are presented with an antithesis between man and nature. Distrust and not enjoyment is the keynote of the impulse behind those dances which are aimed at forcing nature to conform to the pattern of man's will and necessity. Although they undoubtedly derived from forms which reflected the exuberant acceptance of the essential pattern of identity, what they now represent is a sly and artificial stressing of differences. We may call them sly because, though they pretend to be imitations for the sake of deceiving the powers or forces that rule the world, they are really based on a belief in the absoluteness of the difference that separates them from man. And they are artificial because what is cultivated in them is not so much an intensity of participation as an observance of rigorous rules, conventions, forms. For nature must be deceived even to the last slight movement of the finger or wrist.

The alienation of nature as forces which, though they are recognized as being identical with those operating in man's own life and physical welfare, are at the same time not only distinct from him but nearly always hostile, of course lies behind what we today understand by sympathetic magic. To turn for an irreducible definition to the authority whose name will most naturally be associated with the topic, we find in Frazer's *Golden Bough*: "magic is a spurious system of natural law as well as a fallacious guide of conduct; it is a false science as well as an abortive art." The essence of magic is to control something by the scrupulous performance of a rite, as is more than amply illustrated by the overwhelming collection of examples in this famous book; and as a technique of control there must already have been available the form of the imitative dance. But the function of imitation now becomes something much more than that natural pleasure which Aristotle was to ascribe to it; its function was to take over some of the power or virtue of the natural forces themselves, as the savage gathers strength to defeat his enemies by rehearsing the event in advance, or as the child becomes grown up by putting on its parent's clothes. Behind the ritual dances of the magical type lies the assumption that faithful performance of prescribed formulae can wrest from nature the very secret of her power.

So far is this from the attitude we shall discover underlying the true tragic spirit that magic is referred to only to contrast it with the other and fundamentally opposed response to the alienation of nature, religion. As Kenneth Burke has pointed out, religion involves social cooperation to the same degree as magic but with a different purpose: of propitiation rather than coercion. Moreover, for the arrogance that is at the root of the magic deception of nature, there is substituted humility, a bowing down of collective man before the recognition of an order that is not his order, which may be either friendly or hostile to his purpose, and which can be communicated with only on a plane of acceptance and love. How this transition from magic to religion was achieved, if the two are causally related and not alternative adjustments to necessity, is described by R. R. Marett in a lecture entitled "The Birth of Humility."

But it is also possible to discover an explanation for humility, which would make it the irreducible attribute of every stage of religion, in the process by which the natural forces gradually and with ever increasing distinctness take on shapes resembling those of man himself.

It is at this point that it has become customary to begin discussion of the historical relations between religious ritual and early tragic form. But the reason for beginning as far back as we did was to suggest that religion itself must have sprung from a vision which was like the tragic. Through religious ritual, tragedy found a means of making its form more developed than mere dance—a means of taking into account the moral, the social, and the spiritual order of man.

Nietzsche, in describing the form of Attic tragedy, is responsible for the conceit that the story or inner frame of action in that drama is a kind of imaginative projection of the chorus: tragedy is "a vision generated by a dance." Through the epidemic transport of the dance, with its annihilation of the ordinary bounds and limits of existence, the votaries of Dionysus entered a state of being in which they were able not only to behold themselves as satyrs, those purely "natural" creatures, but, as satyrs, to obtain a vision of the joys and sufferings of their god. "We have at last realized that the scene, together with the action, was fundamentally and originally thought of only as a vision, that the only reality is just the chorus, which of itself generates the vision and celebrates it with the entire symbolism of dancing, music, and speech." Although this is dangerously inaccurate in its confusion of what came to be two independent formal elements in the totally functioning Greek drama and is in any case unnecessarily mystical as an account of origins, it is a brilliant way of indicating the original unity of all the elements that make up that drama.

What makes the formal discussion of Greek drama so confusing is the fact that both the chorus and the action proper, distinct though they seem, are now known to have had a common origin in religious ritual. To say that it was common is to abandon the spontaneous-generation theory of Nietzsche for one that recognizes the late development of spoken narrative in every culture. For if the ritual dance was an imitative celebration of processes of nature that soon became embodied in anthropomorphic deities, as a soberer research has indicated, the epic itself may be shown to have originated out of the same impulse of expression. The difference between them is one of historical order. Instead of the spontaneous-generation theory advanced by Nietzsche, we may find an explanation for the later development of narrative myth in the fact that spoken language is a different medium of expression and developed considerably later. Nietzsche is probably nearer the truth when he refers to the *concretion* of the Dionysian vision in the particularized images and symbols of what he calls the Apollonian "dream-world" of the epic. As the fugitive and intangible forces of nature had been caught in the rhythms and postures of the dance, so we may suppose that in time these became condensed, through the pictorial imagination, into the much more definite figures of anthropomorphic deities. Through the instrument of language they were given, in the first place, a local habitation and a name, but they secured also more detailed biographies: the pattern was filled in, so to speak, with the concrete experience of the race. Indeed, we need only trace the process of ever more precise circumstantial definition in transmogrification of any historical fact or popular legend to realize how the religious myth must have developed once it discovered its basic pattern. Myth may be said to "spring" from the dance ritual, therefore, only in the sense that it is saying the same thing in a different and possibly more highly developed medium.

If these two types of expression are found side by side in Greek drama, it is in an interactive rather than the genetic relation suggested by Nietzsche. But to understand this relation, on which the whole formal unity of classic tragedy may be said to depend, it is necessary to examine some of the remarkable transformations which both the ritual dance and religious myth had undergone by the fifth century B.C.

If this discussion so far has seemed remote from tragedy as we know it, in which not gods but quite human heroes are the principal protagonists, it is because we are only now arriving at the point at which we must cross the line between the religious and the legendary or historical. This has been a hard-fought line indeed, along which those who believe in the historical existence of all the great figures of epic and drama are opposed to those who regard them as mere products of the racial imagination. The view here taken is one that has the advantage not only of being supported by the overwhelming evidence of recent scholarly research but of offering something like a reconciliation. It is the view that, while the historical actuality of most of these figures cannot be either proved or disproved, the pattern to which their action conforms is in every case identical with that underlying all the important religions of which we have any information. And if this religious pattern is the product of the imaginative experience, they are to that extent imaginary creations. This is not at all to deny the possibility of historical existence, as Lord Raglan seems to do in his study of the hero, in which he maintains that, because we have no documentary evidence for Moses, Theseus, King Arthur, and Robin Hood, they were therefore nonexistent. We can solve this problem only by the common-sense exercise of a very little imagination on our own part and recognize that men are in the habit of "filling in" already existent patterns of behavior with the particular contents of their experience, including their experience of the outstanding men who have appeared periodically in history. As religious myth has been shown to be the lending of concrete images of person-hood and specified action to a single archetypal pattern, so may the heroes of epic and drama be shown, with equal success or failure, to be the further derivatives of the same impulse.

As a matter of fact, Gilbert Murray has demonstrated beyond much doubt that the life cycles of all the heroes of Greek epic and drama correspond to a uniform pattern which is the pattern of the life of Dionysus. Prometheus, Oedipus, Agamemnon, Hippolytus, and the rest are all, as Nietzsche had anticipated in another of his remarkable insights, but the "masks" of Dionysus. Analyzing the Dionysus story (and this would be true for all its analogues, such as Adonis, Attis, and others) into its component elements, Murray shows that these may be classified as agon, pathos, peripeteia, messenger, and epiphany. Of the many illustrations of the manner in which this cycle recurs as heroic legend, we may cite Oedipus.

Why Greek tragedy dealt with legendary or historical avatars of the god rather than with the god himself is a complicated question, to which Murray gives the answer that to the pious Athenian even the mention of the death of Dionysus was something taboo, because it would have amounted to nothing less than the death of all nature. But to the fifth-century Athenian, with the whole world of Homeric culture behind him, it is hardly probable such temptation to return to primary sources ever occurred. What his drama represented was a synthesis of the highest expressions of his known culture, no matter to what final religious origins this might later be reduced by another age, with the still actively surviving fertility cult of Dionysus. And this contemplation of the god through the idealized heroes of the Homeric epic is in any case thoroughly consistent with the whole humanist temper of the Athenian mind.

It should now be evident that much of what seems arbitrary and dogmatic in Aristotle is really only an analytical description of the form as it had come to be shortly before his time. Tragedy is an imitation (*mimesis*) in the strict Greek sense of reproduction by physical gesture and movement; the word was associated especially with the dance. It is an imitation of an action that is "serious, entire, and of a certain magnitude," and all these attributes were, of course, inherent in the myth, in which this action was always contained. Seriousness is left undefined, probably because its meaning was self-evident, though in a later place Aristotle relieves us of the modern notion of tragedy as gloomy or depressing when he refers to poetry as "a more philosophical and a more serious thing than history," because poetry is chiefly concerned with general truth, history with particular. What is serious, therefore, would seem to be that which is universal and which comprehends the whole of experience; and nothing could be more comprehensive than the life stories of Prometheus, Oedipus, and the other mythological figures dealt with by the dramatists. So also for the notions of completeness and magnitude, which he defines only in esthetic terms; a complete action has "a beginning, a middle, and an end," corresponding to the primary rhythm of birth, death, and resurrection; and magnitude may be seen to refer to the momentousness of these processes taken separately and as a whole. We can also discover a better explanation than the snobbery which the feudal seventeenth century in France or the later bourgeois society derived from the doctrine that the characters of tragedy must be "our betters," as George Saintsbury translated the phrase. If Oedipus, Theseus, Agamemnon, and the others belonged to the best families it was not because of social snobbery on the part of the dramatists but because these families, being royal, were originally linked with the vital religious life of their communities. Most of them were actually worshipped as local deities. Of the connections between kingship and divinity recent anthropology has gathered so much evidence that we need no longer have any confusion on this point.

Whether Aristotle knew it or not, the action that was imitated was not any human action but myth. To discover what Aristotle meant by action itself would involve perhaps nothing less than a résumé of his whole philosophy; but the purpose here is only to indicate how his terms may be absorbed into the historical understanding of tragedy that we are likely to attempt today. It will be enough to recall only the baldest outline of his philosophy of being. As every species has its appropriate form, and as every form has its appropriate function, and this function is the fulfillment of its being, the particular form of man is shown to be defined by his reason. Through reason man sifts the evidences of his senses and determines what is the most appropriate course for him to follow in the fulfillment of his end—or happiness. Action follows being, according to the formula, and there is even the question whether there can be being without action.

Now the action in Attic tragedy may seem like a contradiction of this account; for surely the heroes, from Prometheus to Jason, are headed from the beginning not toward happiness but toward their own complete and utter destruction. The only answer to this objection that can be made is that for them, under the particular burden of guilt they bear, the course of action they follow is inevitable; they must fulfill themselves negatively, so to speak, for their particular end is destruction. But the best light can be thrown on the problem by some consideration of what has been the most fascinating of all the problems of the *Poetics*, the problem of the "tragic flaw," or *hamartia*.

This has caused so much bafflement because it has been singled out by the moralists of every age as referring to some *particular* vice in the hero's composition or some particular misdeed in his past. Thus, the fatal series of mishaps that overtook Oedipus was the consequence of his slaying of his father on a mountain pass; and this act was itself the result of an undue impetuousness in his nature. Agamemnon met his death because he had incurred the wrath of Clytemnestra for the sacrifice of their daughter at Aulis. In the study of Shakespeare in American schools this type of moral causation takes the form of assigning appropriate moral tags to each of the more important characters: Othello—jealousy, Lear—vanity, Hamlet—indecision, Macbeth—ambition and so on. But Aristotle makes a very sharp distinction when he describes the tragic character as someone "neither eminently virtuous or just, nor yet involved in misfortune by deliberate vice or villainy, but by some error of human frailty." The translation is Saintsbury's, and it is doubtful whether "frailty," with its sentimental Victorian associations, is as good as "flaw," or whether either is at once as graphic and as close to the Greek as the more contemporary "blind spot." In any case, Oedipus suffers not because he killed his father and not because he was headstrong but because of something even more deeply inherent.

Unfortunately, Aristotle offers no further light on the subject of *hamartia*; and it may even be suggested that in this failure there is reflected the difference between philosophy and poetry, between the abstract structure of moral idealism that his philosophy represents and the concrete reflection of experience that is tragedy. (This inability to transcend its own limitations might even be called the *hamartia* of philosophy.) For when we are actually experiencing a tragic action we are not aware of philosophical definitions of the proper end of man; we do not detach any of the characteristics or deeds of an Orestes, an Oedipus, or a Hamlet from our impression of him as a whole; his march from prosperity to misery or death seems something as inevitable as the passage of the seasons. For the time being we are swung along in the rhythm of an action that is inseparable from the rhythm of nature itself. It is only afterwards that the analytical mind, performing *its* appropriate function of discrimination, begins the process of splitting up into causes, motives, and other units of interpretation. But this mind can never bridge the gap between man as a natural organism fulfilling itself and the inevitably tragic culmination of that fulfillment. Philosophical (or causal) analysis of any kind must yield before the direct representation of reality. If Aristotle does not define *hamartia*, it is because it is not a unit of the moral composition of the hero but an aspect of his form as a whole. It is not a flaw in an otherwise beautifully shaped vessel (to take Goethe's metaphor for Hamlet) but an inner principle of dissolution within the vessel itself. It is the constant fact that runs through all the heroic stories, and this fact is of course the fact of individuality.

That the tragic flaw is not part of the whole but the whole itself will also be recognized if we consider that the varieties of special vices assigned to tragic characters—pride in Agamemnon, audacity in Prometheus, vanity in Lear—are all in the last analysis reducible to the same thing. All are but superficially different modes of that fundamental exaggeration or hypertrophy of the individual will to which the Greeks gave another name for the bewilderment of posterity—hybris. Although hybris is usually used only in a moral context—to define the impiety of man's attempt to transcend his own nature by arrogating powers that belong only to the gods—it is essentially indistinguishable from *hamartia*. It may seem a rather long distance from Prometheus, the most famous embodiment of hybris in this sense, to such a later character as Lear, but the essence of Lear's senile vanity is his arrogation (like Agamemnon's) of a homage that really belongs only to the gods. The essential guilt of the tragic hero is the burden of his own individual will which pushes him toward its fulfillment, in the Aristotelian sense, or what we today might call the exhaustion of its potentialities in action. And since to the tragic hero pushing on to his fulfillment this destructive principle is inseparable from the opposite principle of vital, expanding energy, it is no more perceivable by him than the blind spot in the mind's eye. If Aristotle does not define it for us, it is because it is not so much a category of nature as an aspect of nature as a whole. *Hamartia* reveals similar difficulties of definition when it reappears in Christian dogma under the name of Original Sin.

Tragic action is, then, a token or demonstration of man as nature, since the curve that it continually retraces is always the essential curve of nature. It is the consequence of his ever becoming a species, of his ever taking a form, of individuation. Nietzsche gives as his own reason for the adoption of so many different masks by Dionysus the highly ingenious metaphysical notion that the god, having once suffered dismemberment in his own person, did not again wish to assume the agonies of individuation. According to this conception, the hero would be someone whose professional function, so to speak, is to keep alive, in ever new guises, the scapegoat.

The final end of tragedy, which is to be sought in the spectator rather than in the chorus where Nietzsche seems to have located it and thus to have been led into romantic confusion, is to be seen, in the last analysis, as merely a more refined, developed, and elaborated attainment of that same reaffirmation of the fundamental vital force in the prototype, the first man who found an analogy between his own life and that of nature. The vision of the whole cyclic pattern of human life, contracted into a brief time span and achieved through an implied metaphor, has led not to a rejection of life but to a renewed acceptance of it. This has required the "detachment" of art, what Nietzsche called the Apollonian synthesis; and in this sense man has been saved from himself by his own art, and tragedy becomes the greatest of all arts from the standpoint of its profound serviceability to mankind.

Tragedy, through its derivations from religious ritual, which represents the socialization of experience and vision, gives a stronger sense of the bond that links man to man in their common bondage to the natural order, and man is thus restored to the communal life from which he is cut off in the purely personal vision. Tragedy is a communal art, not only in the sense that it requires the cooperation of a number of individuals, actors, chorus, musicians, and in the sense that there must be communication between players and audience, but also in the sense that finally the meaning of the action in drama is given perspective only through contrast between the destructive individual will of the hero and the collective values articulated by the chorus. This is to say that in the form of tragedy is involved a contrast between the individual and the social. The inner drama would be incomplete without the choral accompaniment; a fragment of human history without more significance than the account of a slaughtered animal. Finally, tragedy depends on the existence of a set of social values to give significant perspective to the recording of the individual will in action.

Antony and Cleopatra: The Poetic Vision

[*1960*]

In his private notes the great Coleridge, who was not often given to effusiveness, confessed that for him this was the most "wonderful" of the plays. He chose the word used by Enobarbus to describe Cleopatra when he tells Antony that not to have seen her would have been to have "left unseen a wonderful piece of work, which not to have been blessed withal would have discredited your travel." To discover some content for this much abused adjective will be the guiding effort of the following notes.

The tragedy of space. All modern commentators are in agreement that it is the most *spacious* of the dramas. The topographical backdrop is not a mere city like Verona, or a kingdom like Denmark, or a single empire like that of Rome or Venice, but the entire known world of classical antiquity. Caroline Spurgeon has carefully tabulated that the word "world" itself recurs some forty-two times, more than twice as often as in any other play. Nearly always it is in reference to Antony, as in the opening lines: "and you shall see in him/ The triple pillar of the world." After his defeat at sea, Scarus laments:

> The greater cantle of the world is lost
> With very ignorance, we have kissed away
> Kingdoms and provinces.
>
> Act III, Scene 10

There is the final summation by the noble Octavius:

> The death of Antony
> Is not a single doom; in the name lay
> A moiety of the world.
>
> Act V, Scene 1

But the immense scale of the action is perhaps most vividly brought home in the comic scene aboard Pompey's galley (Act II, Scene 7) in which the triumvirs Antony, Octavius, and Lepidus join hands in drunken dance to the song with the refrain:

> Cup us till the world go round,
> Cup us till the world go round.

It is nothing less than the whole Mediterranean world that is reeling dizzily before our eyes until Octavius calls a halt to the proceedings.

But even this is only the political world, with its poles at Rome and Alexandria; as the play expands we are to be carried upwards and beyond to the firmament on high:

> His face was as the heavens, and therein stuck
> A sun and moon, which kept their course, and lighted
> The little O, the earth.
>
> Act V, Scene 2

(Here very possibly the boy-actress who played Cleopatra gestured upwards to the "heavens" painted on the canopy over the Elizabethan stage and then to the circled pit of the theater.)

Both Antony and Cleopatra are like the stars; Cleopatra is addressed as the "Eastern star," and when Antony stabs himself "the star is fallen." In two of the most densely beautiful lines of all (with their improvisation on all the possible values of the sound of "r"), Cleopatra calls upon the great star to consume the earth around which it was supposed to revolve:

> O sun,
> Burn the great sphere thou mov'st in. Darkling stand
> The varying shore o' th' world.
>
> Act IV, Scene 15

At the end they pass beyond earth and heaven into the purest of the universal elements. Antony would fight "i' th' fire, or i' th' air," and when her time has come Cleopatra exclaims:

> I am fire and air; my other elements
> I give to baser life.
>
> Act V, Scene 2

The circumference of the soul. It is clear that all the vast imagery of physical space has its real significance in its symbolical relationship to the main theme of the play. As is usually the case in Shakespeare, the theme is adumbrated in the first scene, in the opening ten lines by Philo:

> Nay, but this dotage of our general's
> O'erflows the *measure:* those his goodly eyes,
> That o'er the files and musters of the war
> Have glowed like plated Mars, now *bend*, now *turn*,
> The office and devotion of their view
> Upon a tawny front. His captain's heart,
> Which in the scuffles of great fights hath *burst*
> The *buckles* on his breast, reneges all *temper*,
> And is become the *bellows* and the *fan*
> To cool a gipsy's lust.

All the words here put in italics refer to objects or movements having to do with the general law of measure. The same note is continued immediately afterwards by Antony and Cleopatra as they make their entrance:

> CLEOPATRA
> If it be love indeed, tell me how much.
> ANTONY
> There's beggary in the love that can be reckoned.
> CLEOPATRA
> I'll set a bourn how far to be beloved.
> ANTONY
> Then must thou needs find out new heaven, new earth.

If the struggle between East and West provides the external framework of the drama, the arena of the inner action is Antony's soul: the conflict between the centrifugal force of passion and the centripetal force of reason. According to the familiar cartography of the human soul inherited by Shakespeare's age through the Middle Ages from Aristotle, the proper balance between these two forces defined the circumference of the soul. So it is constantly in terms of the antipodes of East and West that the position of Antony's soul is charted at any given moment. In the first scene the needle seems stuck immovably in the East, as Antony declares:

> Let Rome in Tiber melt, and the wide arch
> Of the ranged empire fall. Here is my space.

But in the next scene it shifts abruptly westward, provoking Cleopatra's contemptuous, "A Roman thought hath struck him." Now Antony has come full circle to the decision:

> These strong Egyptian fetters I must break,
> Or lose myself in dotage.

Back in Rome by Caesar's side, he listens to the dubious counsel of the Soothsayer, who also employs the metaphor of space:

> O Antony, stay not by his side.
> Thy demon, that thy spirit which keeps thee, is
> Noble, courageous, high unmatchable,
> Where Caesar's is not. But near him, thy angel
> Becomes a fear, as being o'erpowered: therefore
> Make space enough between you.

This rapid, unpredictable, sometimes breathtaking oscillation back and forth between the two poles of Antony's soul supplies the most exciting psychological movement of the play. Indeed, as G. Wilson Knight and other recent commentators have pointed out, images of oscillation are elsewhere so prominent as to make this the dominating movement of the play, as, for example, in the description of the common people which

> Like to a vagabond flag upon the stream,
> Goes to, and back, lackeying the varying tide,
> To rot itself with motion.
>
> Act I, Scene 4

Or the beautiful simile that renders Octavia's speechlessness before the prospect of leaving her brother to depart with Antony:

> . . . the swan's down feather
> That stands upon the swell at the full of tide,
> And neither way inclines.

For Antony his "unnoble swerving" from his course is the source of his deepest suffering, and because this suffering is of a moral order it is what most surely qualifies him as a tragic hero in the classic sense. To measure the extent of his fall Shakespeare has very early built up, in Philo's opening lines and in Caesar's long account of Antony's exploits and deprivations (Act I, Scene 4), a picture of the original Antony. Now in losing his honor he loses his reputation, and in losing his reputation he loses himself, for honor is the center and circumference of his being, the self of selves.

> If I lose mine honour
> I lose myself. . . .
>
> Act III, Scene 4
>
> I have fled myself . . .
> I have lost command. . . .
>
> Act III, Scene 11

The most frightful thing about his passion is that it is a kind of blindness which keeps him from the knowledge of his true self. It is the excuse that he offers to Caesar:

> . . . when poisoned hours had me bound up
> From mine own knowledge.
>
> Act II, Scene 2

The whole formula, honor-knowledge-self-action, is perhaps most succinctly stated by his lieutenant Canidius:

> Had our general
> Been what he knew himself, it had gone well.
>   Act III, Scene 10

But all the deepest moral and metaphysical themes of the play condense in a single metaphor in the great cloud scene (Act IV, Scene 14), which is the philosophical center of the drama.

ANTONY
Eros, thou yet behold'st me?
  EROS
                    Ay noble lord.
  ANTONY
Sometime we see a cloud that's dragonish,
A vapour sometime, like a bear or lion,
A towered citadel, a pendant rock,
A forked mountain, or blue promontory
With trees upon't, that nod unto the world,
And mock our eyes with air. Thou hast seen these signs;
They are black vesper's pageants.
  EROS
                    Ay, my lord.
  ANTONY
That which is now a horse, even with a thought
The rack dislimns, and makes it indistinct
As water is in water.
  EROS
                    It does my lord.
  ANTONY
My good knave Eros, now thy captain is
Even such a body. Here I am Antony,
Yet cannot hold this visible shape, my knave.

Metaphysically, this is of course the problem of identity—the immemorial question which every human being must at one time or another demand of himself, "Who am I?"

Now at last Antony concludes that it is too late to recover that great property which was once Antony; it is his swan song as a man; his conflict, like everything else, dissolves into the elements. All the rest is rhetoric.

Antony and Cleopatra may thus be taken as Shakespeare's tragedy of the soul in space, of the soul struggling in a universe of illimitable space of which it is only a limited and self-limiting fragment.

Feliciter audax. To describe the language and style, Coleridge uses this Latin phrase, which he translates "happy valiancy," but which probably means something more like delightfully daring. Everyone, from Enobarbus to Cleopatra, seems engaged in stretching language to the utmost limits of communication. It is this straining to give expression to the inexpressible that glows through Enobarbus's now hackneyed barge speech (Act II, Scene 2). Even he has finally to admit:

> For her own person,
> It beggared all description.

There is more suspense in Cleopatra's own earlier attempt to find the exact word to designate to Antony the *absolute* nature of her desolation:

> Courteous lord, one word
> Sir, you and I must part, but that's not it.
> Sir, you and I have lov'd, but there's not it.
> That you know well: something it is I would.
> O, my oblivion is a very Antony,
> And I am all forgotten.
>
> > Act I, Scene 3

Again, after Antony's death, it is only through a series of negations that she can indicate the magnitude of her loss:

> The soldiers' pole is fall'n: young boys and girls
> Are level now with men; the odds is gone,
> And there is nothing left remarkable
> Beneath the visiting moon.
>
> > Act IV, Scene 15

Several of the most notable effects of style derive their potency not so much from the individual words of the statement as from its position in the text—superb instances of *contextual* poetry, as in Iras's classic requiem at the end:

> Finish good lady, the bright day is done,
> And we are for the dark.

When Antony returns unexpectedly from the battlefield (Act IV, Scene 8), Cleopatra overwhelms us with that "fine surprise" which Keats in his *Letters* says is the hallmark of the best poetry:

> O infinite virtue, com'st thou smiling from
> The world's great snare uncaught?

Much more frequent throughout of course are examples of the standard rhetorical figure, hyperbole: Antony will "outstare the lightning"; "we have kissed away/ Kingdoms and provinces"; "None our parts so poor,/ But was a race of heaven." And Cleopatra carries the device to its topmost in her eulogy:

> His legs bestrid the ocean, his reared arm
> Crested the world. His voice was propertied
> As all the tuned spheres, and that to friends;
> But when he meant to quail and shake the orb,
> He was as rattling thunder.
>
> Act V, Scene 2

It was probably in such a passage as this that Coleridge found that delightful boldness of style which caused him to regard this as the most wonderful of the plays. However, there will always be readers, not less momentarily swayed by the language, who find it as cloying a fare as all those other Egyptian feasts of food and passion. Hyperbole, it will be recalled, consists in carrying something too far. And here it is perhaps deliberately used by Shakespeare to point up the general theme of *excess* in the play. It is the way the characters speak because of the kind of people they are.

Limits of the histrionic. From their very first words, Antony and Cleopatra talk as if they are acting in a play—a play whose scene is grander even than earth or heaven. They possess what Francis Fergusson, in referring to the drama in general, has called the "histrionic sensibility." Not only did Shakespeare himself possess it to an eminent degree, but he liked to endow certain of his characters with the same sort of sensibility. Richard II, Hamlet, and Othello all belong to the type. T. S. Eliot long ago observed that Othello is always seeing himself "in a dramatic light." It is all part of Shakespeare's theatrical virtuosity, like the device of the play within a play, which would add dimension upon dimension to the structure of the drama.

There is no doubt that the audience to whom Antony and Cleopatra are playing is posterity:

> If from the field I shall return once more
> To kiss these lips, I will appear in blood.
> I, and my sword, will earn our chronicle.
>> Act III, Scene 13

>> My queen and Eros
> Have by their brave instruction got upon me
> A nobleness in record. But I will be
> A bridegroom in my death, and run into't
> As to a lover's bed.
>> Act IV, Scene 14

Enobarbus, who sees through everything, remarks:

> To follow with allegiance a fallen lord
> Does conquer him that did his master conquer,
> And earns a place i' th' story.

Cleopatra finally refuses Caesar's offer to save her because in Rome

>> Saucy lictors
> Will catch at us like strumpets, and scald rhymers
> Ballad us out o' tune. The quick comedians
> Extemporally will stage us, and present

> Our Alexandrian revels. Antony
> Shall be brought drunken forth, and I shall see
> Some squeaking Cleopatra boy my greatness
> I' th' posture of a whore.
>
> Act V, Scene 2

In their concern for their place in the chronicle, in the record, in song and story, they are troubled by the same anxiety that dominates Hamlet and Othello in their last moments. The important difference is that Antony and Cleopatra seem consciously to be adhering to their rôles throughout and that these rôles are of a divine order. Antony is like Jupiter, Mars, and Hercules, and he is implicitly identified with one or another of the Mediterranean fertility gods. Cleopatra is Venus, dressed up like Isis, and could be any moon or earth goddess. The truth is that in their drive to make their love infinite they cannot stop short of divinity. In the eyes of history their marriage must be a sacred marriage.

But to achieve this, to satisfy her "immortal longings," Cleopatra must put the asp to her breast; to become infinite like the gods she must cast off the finite trappings of humanity. "Husband, I come," she says, and the sacred marriage is consummated —in death.

The pity and the glory. The two extreme reactions to the play through the ages have been the moralistic and the romantic. Dryden, in his recasting it as *All for Love* in the mid-seventeenth century, steers an uneasy course between the two. Nothing certainly could be simpler than to reduce the whole action to yet another allegory of Reason and Passion, as some of these notes may seem to do, and indeed Shakespeare himself, principally through the choric character Enobarbus, could be made to lend support to such a reading. But, first of all, the frequent moral utterances are, as always in Shakespeare, relative only to the character speaking and at a particular moment of time. Secondly, there is nothing in Shakespeare's previous or later work that would suggest he could ever engage in simple moral allegorizing. Of the romantic view there is nothing to say except that it is the more popular one, and will persist as long as the identification of love with death exerts its powerful appeal upon the Western imagination. However, we have had in recent years an interesting view which purports to take us beyond both the romantic and narrowly moralistic into a realm which its chief exponent, G. Wilson Knight, calls "transcendental Humanism." To him it would seem that great passion, instead of leading to annihilation, as it is actually represented in the play, may serve as a stepping-stone to a "higher Unity." All the processes of "melting," "dissolving," "discandying" are not extinguishing, as assumed in this paper, but a *blending* in a transcendental order of being, the "new heaven, new earth" mentioned in the first scene, so that we receive a vision, in Mr. Knight's jubilant phrase, of "man transfigured by love's orient fire." Such a view probably rests on the intoxicating effects of Cleopatra's last speeches; these do approach the more than human in their grandeur, but their source is human, all too human. To call them humanistic in the lofty sense is like saying that man can raise himself by the bootstraps of his physical emotions. And so we are no further than what is the essence of the romantic view.

Vision it is, a complex vision of man in his baseness and nobility, his ugliness and beauty, his absurdity and magnificence. The vision is wonderful, for we cannot after all improve on Coleridge's choice of the shopworn adjective. The sober-minded Caesar is saying much the same thing in the closing lines:

> High events as these
> Strike those that make them; and their story is
> No less in pity than his glory which
> Brought them to be lamented.
> Act V, Scene 2

It is the combination of pity and glory, not the one or the other alone, with which we are left at the end of the spectacle, and for such an emotion we still have no better word than wonder.

Selected Bibliography

References listed represent William Troy's more important literary criticism, cited in chronological order.

"Crisis in the Novel," *The Figure in the Carpet: A Magazine of Prose*, no. 1 (October 1927), 11–15

"Gusto in Literature," *The Figure in the Carpet: A Magazine of Prose*, no. 4 (May 1928), 7–13

"The Position of Liam O'Flaherty," *Bookman*, LXIX, 1 (March 1929), 7–11. Revised for *The New Republic* as "Red Dusk in Ireland" (January 30, 1929), LVII, 306

"The Story of the Little Magazines," *Bookman*, LXX, 5, 6, Part I, "Revolt in the Desert" (January 1930), 476–481; Part II, "Making No Compromise with the Public Taste" (February 1930), 557–663

The Proof, by Yvor Winters—a review, *Bookman*, LXXII, 2 (October 30, 1930), 190

"James Joyce and his Ulysses," *The New York Times Book Review* (January 18, 1931), pp. 1 and 27

"Symbolism as a Generating Force in Contemporary Literature," *New York Times Book Review* (February 22, 1931), p. 2

"A Study of the Imagist Group of Poets," *New York Times Book Review* (April 19, 1931), p. 9

"Henry James and Young Writers" (reprinted in this book as "The Lesson of the Master"), *Bookman*, LXXIII, 4 (June 1931), 351–358; also in *Henry James: A Collection of Critical Essays*, ed. Leon Edel (Englewood Cliffs, N. J.: Prentice-Hall, Inc., 1963), pp. 79–91

Time Regained—a review (reprinted in this book as "Proust's Last Will and Testament"), *Symposium*, II, 3 (July 1931), 385–392

"Rimbaud: The Litteraturicide," *New York Times Book Review* (November 8, 1931), p. 9

"Virginia Woolf: The Poetic Method" and "Virginia Woolf: The Poetic Style" (revised, and reprinted in this book as part of "Virginia Woolf and the Novel of Sensibility"), *Symposium* III, 1 (January 1932), 53–63, and III, 2 (April 1932), 153–166. Revised version also in *Literary Opinion in America,* ed. Morton Dauwen Zabel (New York: Harper and Brothers, 1937; rev. ed., 1951), pp. 324–327

"The New Intellectual," *North American Review,* no. 233 (April 1932), 333–340

"A New Talent," *The Nation,* CXXXIV (April 27, 1932), 495–496

"Technique Is Not Enough," *The Nation,* CXXXV (December 14, 1932), 593–594

The Letters of D. H. Lawrence—a review (reprinted in this book as "D. H. Lawrence as Hero"), *Symposium,* IV, 1 (January 1933), 85–94

"Cummings's Non-land of Un-," *The Nation,* CXXXVI (April 12, 1933), 413. Also in ΕΣΤΙ: *eec: E. E. Cummings and the Critics,* ed. S. V. Baum (East Lansing, Mich.: Michigan State University Press, 1962), pp. 71–72

"Pathos Is Not Enough," *The Nation,* CXXXVII (July 12, 1933), 52–53

"A Note on Gertrude Stein," *The Nation,* CXXXVII (September 6, 1933), 274

"The Romantic Agony," *The Nation,* CXXXVII (October 11, 1933), 417–418

"Mr. Hemingway's Opium," *The Nation,* CXXXVII (November 15, 1933), 570

"Stephen Dedalus and James Joyce," *The Nation,* CXXXVIII (February 14, 1934), 187–188

"Studs Lonigan's World," *The Nation,* CXXXVIII (February 28, 1934), 252

"Making of a Masterpiece," *The Nation,* CXXXVIII (April 11, 1934), 421

"T. S. Eliot, Grand Inquisitor," *The Nation,* CXXXVIII (April 25, 1934), 478–479

"The Worm i' the Bud," *The Nation,* CXXXVIII (May 9, 1934), 539–540

"The James Credo," *The Nation,* CXXXVIII (June 13, 1934), 682

"Return to Tragedy" (reprinted in this book as part of "Three Novels by André Malraux"), *The Nation,* CXXXVIII (June 27, 1934), 735–736

"The Conversion of André Gide," *The Nation,* CXXXIX (October 17, 1934), 444–445

"Nada and Diamat," *The Nation,* CXL (January 9, 1935), 50

"The Canopy of Death" (reprinted in this book as part of "Three Novels by André Malraux"), *The Nation,* CXL (February 17, 1935), 254

"New Country," *The Nation,* CXL (March 13, 1935), 311–312

"And Tomorrow," *The Nation*, CXL (April 3, 1935), 393

"The Perfect Life" (reprinted in this book as part of "F. Scott Fitzgerald"), *The Nation*, CXL (April 17, 1935), 454–456

"Myth as Progress," *The Nation*, CXL (May 22, 1935), 606

"A Matter of Quality," *The Nation*, CXLI (October 30, 1935), 517–518

"The Critic's Job," *The Nation*, CXLI (December 4, 1935), 656

"In Search of Havelock Ellis," *The Nation*, CXL (December 11, 1935), 683–684

"On Being Contemporary," *The Nation*, CXLII (April 22, 1936), 511–512

"Tradition for Tradition's Sake," *The Nation*, CXLII (June 10, 1936), 747–748

"The Lesson of the Master," *The Nation*, CXLII (June 17, 1936), 780

"Soliloquy in the Dark" (reprinted in this book as part of "Three Novels by André Malraux"), *The Nation*, CXLII (June 24, 1936), 810–811

"The Poetry of Doom," *The Nation*, CXLIII (October 31, 1936), 524–525

"The Iron Maiden," *The Nation*, CXLIV (February 20, 1937), 216

"Revolution by Poetic Justice," *The Nation*, CXLIV (March 27, 1937), 354–356

The Years, by Virginia Woolf, a review (reprinted in this book as part of "Virginia Woolf and the Novel of Sensibility"), *The Nation*, CXL (April 24, 1937), 473–474

"Gloried from Within," *The Nation*, CXLIV (May 1, 1937), 511–512

"Roads to Tragedy," *The Nation*, CXLIV (June 12, 1937), 680–682

"The Symbolism of Zola," *Partisan Review*, IV, 1 (December 1937), 64–66

"The Lawrence Myth," *Partisan Review*, IV, 2 (January 1938), 3–13. Also in *The Partisan Reader*, ed. William Phillips and Philip Rahv (New York: The Dial Press, 1946), pp. 336–347

"Thomas Mann: Myth and Reason," *Partisan Review*, V, 1 (June 1938), 24–32, and 2 (July 1938), 51–64

"A Further Note on Myth" (reprinted in this book as "A Note on Myth"), *Partisan Review*, VI, 1 (Fall 1938), 95–100

"Notes on *Finnegans Wake*," *Partisan Review*, VI, 4 (Summer 1939), 97–110. Also in *James Joyce: Two Decades of Criticism*, ed. Seon Givens (New York: Vanguard Press, 1948; rev. ed., 1963), pp. 302–318; and in *Le Revue des lettres modernes*, ed. Joseph Prescott, VI, 49–51 (Winter 1959–1960), pp. 202–228

"On Rereading Balzac: The Artist as Scapegoat," *Kenyon Review*, II (Summer 1940), 333–344. Also in *The Critical Performance*, ed. Stanley Edgar Hyman (New York: Vintage Books, 1956), pp. 207–219

"Stendhal: In Quest of Henri Beyle," *Partisan Review*, IX, 1 (January—February 1942), 3–22

"The Altar of Henry James," *The New Republic*, CVIII (February 18, 1943), 228–230. Also in *The Question of Henry James*, ed. F. W

Dupee (New York: Henry Holt and Company, 1945), pp. 267–272

"Quintessence of Dust," *The New Republic*, CVIII (March 8, 1943), 324–325

"Selections: *Gaspard de la Nuit*," *Chimera*, no. 3 (Spring 1945), 29–42

"Postlude: Myth, Method, and the Future" (reprinted in this book as "Myth, Method, and the Future"), *Chimera*, no. 4 (Spring 1946), 81–83

"F. Scott Fitzgerald—The Authority of Failure," *Accent*, VI, 1 (Autumn 1946), 56–60. Also in *F. Scott Fitzgerald: The Man and His Work*, ed. Alfred Kazin (Cleveland: The World Publishing Company, 1951), pp. 187–193; *F. Scott Fitzgerald: A Collection of Critical Essays*, ed. Arthur Mizener (Englewood Cliffs, N. J.: Prentice-Hall, Inc., 1963), pp. 20–24; *Forms of Modern Fiction*, ed. William Van O'Connor (Minneapolis: University of Minnesota Press, 1948), pp. 80–86; *The Great Gatsby: A Study*, ed. Frederick J. Hoffman (New York: Charles Scribner's Sons, 1961), pp. 224–231; *Modern American Fiction: Essays in Criticism*, ed. A. Walton Litz (New York: Oxford University Press, 1963), pp. 132–137

"Paul Valéry and the Poetic Universe, *Quarterly Review of Literature*, III, 3 (1947), 232–239; also in *Modern Literary Criticism: An Anthology*, ed. Irving Howe (Boston: Beacon Press, 1958), pp. 79–91

"To So Little Space," *Partisan Review*, XIV, 4 (July—August 1947), 424–427

"The Passion and the Task," *Partisan Review*, XV, 3 (March 1948), 377–379

"The New Parnassianism and Recent Poetry," *Chimera*, no. 2 (Winter—Spring 1949), 3–16

"Poetry and the Non-Euclidian Predicament," *Poetry*, 74, 4 (July 1949), 234–236

"The Rebirth of Allegory," *Hudson Review*, no. 1 (Winter 1949), 587–589

"Virginia Woolf and the Novel of Sensibility" (reprinted in this book), *Perspectives USA*, no. 6 (Winter 1954), 55–76

"Antony and Cleopatra: The Poetic Vision," Introduction to *Antony and Cleopatra* (New York: Dell, 1961)

Index